163

*Everyday Mother Talk
to Toddlers*

Early Intervention

Everyday Mother Talk to Toddlers
Early Intervention

Frances Fuchs Schachter
Barnard Toddler Center
Barnard College
Columbia University
New York, New York

with
RUTH E. MARQUIS
ELLEN SHORE
CAROLE L. BUNDY
JUNE H. McNAIR

Foreword by
HERBERT ZIMILES
Research Division
Bank Street College of Education
New York, New York

ACADEMIC PRESS   *New York*   *San Francisco*   *London*   1979
A Subsidiary of Harcourt Brace Jovanovich, Publishers

ACADEMIC PRESS, INC.
111 Fifth Avenue, New York, New York 10003

United Kingdom Edition published by
ACADEMIC PRESS, INC. (LONDON) LTD.
24/28 Oval Road. London NW1   7DX

Library of Congress Cataloging in Publication Data

Schachter, Frances Fuchs ,
     Everyday mother talk to toddlers.

     (Educational psychology series)
     Bibliography: p.
     1. Domestic education--United States.
2. Children--Language. 3. Oral communication.
4. Speech acts (Linguistics) 5. Mother and child.
I. Title.
HQ774.5.S3   372.6   78-20049
ISBN 0-12-621360-7

PRINTED IN THE UNITED STATES OF AMERICA

79 80 81 82   9 8 7 6 5 4 3 2 1

Contents

Foreword

When Frances Fuchs Schachter began her program of research concerned with functional aspects of the language of young children and their caregivers a decade ago at Bank Street College, it was clear that she had identified an important research problem. A functional and communicative perspective to the study of children's language was long overdue. Her studies have helped to demonstrate the fruitfulness of such an approach.

What is noteworthy about Dr. Schachter's work is the degree to which it is guided by a sophisticated theoretical orientation to child development. Unlike many investigators who approach a problem in terms of its "methodological give," marching from one parametric study to another irrespective of their theoretical relevance, Schachter invests more heavily in shaping the method of study to fit a meaningful theoretical framework. She is less content to settle for an investigation that is methodologically safe but conceptually unclear. She digs longer and harder in formulating the observation categories that define the scope of her work. Because of their theoretical meaningfulness, her observation categories are themselves intrinsically valuable. Furthermore, they are more likely to lead to findings that are both relevant to the practitioner and replicable by other researchers.

This study of everyday communication between mothers and toddlers of diverse backgrounds will arouse great interest among early childhood educators and developmental researchers alike. The findings contribute articulation to child-centered programs for young children and their families. While some readers will doubtless interpret the findings as providing long sought-after prescriptive teaching behaviors, there is good reason to be wary of prescribing specific strategies of interpersonal interaction. Most child-centered educators interpret and respond to each situation in terms of its context; their mode of working is not compatible with prescriptive methods of teaching. As the author has helped to demonstrate, they are guided by the need to be responsive to the situation. Child-centered programs stand to benefit from any attempt to clarify the intricate processes entailed in this responsive style of interaction. Dr. Schachter's data on responsive strategies in caregiver communication help to elucidate these processes. While there is the risk that some may apply these responsive strategies in mechanical fashion, giving the appearance of responsivity without its substance, there is little doubt that Dr. Schachter's findings can serve to enhance the sensitivity of those who are committed to a responsive communication style.

Developmentalists will welcome this addition to our all too scanty literature on naturally occurring interaction between caregivers and their young children. Such painstaking ecological analysis is more often honored than adopted. Comparative developmentalists and sociolinguists will be especially interested in the author's distinction between talking *to* and talking *with* the child and the ways these communication patterns are related to ethnocognitive theory, on the one hand, and theories of early intervention, on the other. Developmental psycholinguists will be stimulated by the author's evidence for a distinctive communication style in talk to the language-learning toddler, a pattern of talking *for* the toddler. Dr. Schachter's study merits the attention of all those who believe that a child's developing mode of ordering and interacting with the world is influenced by the quality of early interactions with caregiving figures.

HERBERT ZIMILES

Preface

Since the inception of Head Start more than a decade ago, it has become increasingly clear that our most effective early intervention programs are those engaging parents as "teachers" of their own children. As programs of parent involvement in early education begin to proliferate—family-centered and home-based approaches—we need to consider carefully the kind of teacher model we want to promulgate for parents. Should we emphasize didactic techniques, adult-directed training in cognitive or linguistic skills, or should we advocate active learning in the child, exploration and self-discovery? And if the latter, what techniques or strategies can we recommend for parents? What are the kinds of caregiver communication strategies that foster active learning in the child?

Our task would be much easier if these fundamental educational issues were resolved as they apply to the teacher in the classroom. Unfortunately, this has not been the case. The controversy between didactic teaching and active learning is as old as early childhood education itself. Yet it is no nearer resolution today than before. Indeed, the more we learn about early development, the less we seem to know about the caregiver's role in fostering this development. Recent research, suggesting that the development of language and thought is largely an active process of experimentation and self-discovery, presents us with a challenging enigma. If children direct their own learning and development, what is there left for the caregiver to do? Apart from providing suitable materials for experimentation, does the caregiver stand idly by and watch the child's development unfold? Or are there certain kinds of caregiver–child interactions that might enhance this process of self-development?

More than ever before we need data on how learning and development take place in the everyday setting of the home. To provide these data, we undertook a microanalytic study of everyday communication between highly educated, economically advantaged, urban mothers and their toddlers and compared their interactions with those of inner-city mother–toddler dyads with no such advantages. We hoped that our advantaged mothers, operating under the most favorable day-to-day circumstances, could help us better understand how caregivers contribute to the education of young children.

Everyday Mother Talk to Toddlers is a report of our findings. Part I presents the rationale of our project, together with a description of the study sample and the everyday home setting where we collected the data. Part II describes a scoring system we have developed for everyday caregiver communication to young children, a method of classifying language as communication, as speech act. Part III reports the results of our study, comparing the everyday communication of advantaged mothers with that of mothers who function under trying circumstances at best. In Part IV, implications are derived for theory and practice in early intervention. The difference-deficit controversy is reconsidered, and we propose an alternative theory of cognitive–affective interaction based on our microanalysis of caregiver communication. Finally, on the basis of preliminary pilot work, we present a curriculum designed to illustrate how our findings might be applied to enhance communication awareness among caregivers.

The study was designed primarily to identify the kinds of early caregiver–child interactions that might enhance the educational potential of the child. As a secondary aim, we hoped to shed light on the environmental factors that contribute to language development in the toddler. Recent research in developmental psycholinguistics suggests that there are distinctive features in adult talk to toddlers that may facilitate language acquisition. Yet almost all of this work has focused on formal features of the adult's speech rather than on what is being communicated. The present microanalytic study of the ways mothers communicate to toddlers should serve to broaden our understanding of the unique characteristics of the verbal environment of the language-learning toddler. Accordingly, this book should be of interest to devel-

opmental psycholinguists and sociolinguists as well as students, profes-
sionals, and researchers in early childhood education, parent education,
or teacher training, and to psychologists (developmental, clinical, and
educational), psychiatrists, social workers, and pediatricians concerned
with the effects of early home experience on the child's later performance in school.

Acknowledgments

The William T. Grant Foundation provided the support for our project and for writing this book. We are deeply grateful to the foundation and for its generosity and flexibility.

We also wish to thank the dedicated people who contributed their considerable talents to our project: Diana Fosha, Sarah Stemp, and Nancy Brotman Jacobs for their help in developing the scoring system and assessing its reliability; Susan Campbell, Susan Chalfin, Sonia Ganger, Nancy Brotman Jacobs, and Yolanda E. Mancilla for data analysis; Delthea G. Até, Sharon D. Robeson, and Brenda A. Sullivan for their work in the pilot study of our caregiver communication curriculum; Howard B. Spivak and Stuart A. Vardon for statistical and computer consultation; Mary Thurston and Judith Field for editorial work; and Connie Budelis, Lorin Driggs, and Vilma R. Eaves for secretarial assistance.

A number of institutions collaborated in the project, and we would like to express our gratitude. Our base of operations was the Barnard College Toddler Center where we recruited many of our toddlers, developed our methods, and trained the research team. We thank all of the families at the center and its devoted staff, Patricia H. Shimm, Delthea G. Até, and the late Anne Quinn, for their generous cooperation. Previous work that formed the basis for this project was undertaken at the

Bank Street College Head Start Research and Evaluation Center. Herbert Zimiles of Bank Street consented to review this manuscript; his criticisms and suggestions were invaluable. Recent pilot work on the caregiver communication curriculum has been carried out in collaboration with the Pediatrics Department of Harlem Hospital, with the special help of Weiner Leblanc, Mohan Makasare, and Gene-Ann Polk.

We would also like to thank the Society for Research in Child Development for permission to quote freely from our 1974 monograph entitled *Everyday Preschool Interpersonal Speech Usage: Methodological, Developmental, and Sociolinguistic Studies* (co-authored by K. Kirshner, B. Klips, M. Friedricks, and K. Sanders); and Cambridge University Press for permission to quote freely from our 1976 article, "Everyday Caretaker Talk to Toddlers vs. Threes and Fours" (co-authored by D. Fosha, S. Stemp, N. Brotman, and S. Ganger), published in the *Journal of Child Language*.

Finally, I would like to thank my family, my husband David Schachter, and my children Jonathan and Leah Ann, for their continual encouragement and moral support.

Everyday Mother Talk to Toddlers

Early Intervention

PART I
Introduction

Chapter 1
To Talk to Children
in Productive Ways

This is a report on 24,192 speech acts of disadvantaged and advantaged mothers to their toddlers: a study of everyday talk in the naturalistic setting of the home. What is the speech act and why study it? Why focus on the verbal environment? Why in the home? Why the toddler? We intend to address each of these questions, but we would like to begin by presenting the overriding consideration in undertaking our study. In a review of research bearing on early intervention programs for the disadvantaged, Cazden, Baratz, Labov, and Palmer (1971) point out, "Surprising as it may seem, many adults need help in learning how to talk to children in productive ways [p. 167]." In order to make early intervention programs more effective, to enable all children to fulfill their educational potential, it seemed essential to try to identify these "productive ways." This was the central impetus for our study.

What Is the Speech Act and Why Study It?

The speech act (Searle, 1969) is a unit of interpersonal communication, a request, a report, a command, a refusal, just as a morpheme is a unit of language meaning and a phoneme is a unit of sound. The speech act refers to the interpersonal functions of speech (Halliday, 1970), the intentions, purposes or motives of the speaker, rather than to syntax or semantics; its social uses rather than its form or content. Since the revolutionary theories of Chomsky (1957), linguistics has focused narrowly on syntax and semantics, ignoring questions of speech usage. Recently a counterreaction to this formalism has emerged, and increasing attention is being directed to language as communication, to the speech act (Bates, 1976; Blank, Rose, & Berlin, 1978; Bruner, 1975; Dore, 1975; Ervin-Tripp & Mitchell-Kernan, 1977; Garvey, 1975).

Our own interest in the study of the speech act grew out of the fundamental controversy among early childhood educators as to what constitutes productive ways of communicating to young children. The controversy centers on two approaches to early intervention, the didactic or behavioristic approach—as represented by the language training program of Bereiter and Engelmann (1966) and the concept training program of Palmer (1972)—and Dewey's whole-child or child development approach—as represented by the Bank Street developmental-interaction program (Biber, 1977) and the Piagetian program of Kamii (1972). These two approaches present radically divergent views of the caregiver's role in fostering the child's development. Indeed, they diverge in the way they conceive the nature of development itself, in the way they formulate the problems of the disadvantaged child, and in their view of the contribution of early intervention programs and the role of language in such programs.

In didactic or behavioristic programs the teacher actively directs the child's learning in sequenced, structured lessons aimed primarily at developing specific linguistic or cognitive skills. It is assumed that development proceeds as a gradual, quantitative accretion of competence in a variety of specific and unrelated areas. Disadvantaged children are viewed as deficient in the accretion of linguistic and cognitive competence because their home environments do not provide sufficient training in these areas. Early intervention programs are designed to compensate for such environmental deprivation by providing specific lessons, practice, and drill. Regarding language, the primary focus is on training in syntax and semantics—in the correct grammar of Standard English, and in word or sentence meaning.

The whole-child or child developmental approach rejects this compartmentalized, teacher-directed method. Instead, it assumes that children actively propel their own development and that the acquisition of linguistic and cognitive competence occurs not in discrete lessons, but throughout the day in complex interaction with social and emotional factors, themselves extrinsic to questions of competence. Development is viewed, not as a quantitative accumulation of specific unrelated skills, but as a progression of qualitatively different stages, and these stages are assumed to be universal, characteristic of all children both disadvantaged and advantaged. Early intervention programs are justified not on the grounds of a need for training in deficit skills, but rather on the assumption that the environment of poverty is unlikely to offer the fertile soil required for optimum growth and development. Apart from the strains and burdens of poverty, there is the reality that economically disadvantaged families have generally suffered limited educational opportunities and have limited access to adequate child development information. Early intervention programs are designed to promote optimum development. With respect to the language component in these programs, viewing disadvantaged children or their dialect as deficient is judged to be simplistic at best and to undermine the child's self-esteem at worst. Instead of concentrating on the formal properties of language, the emphasis is on the quality of everyday caregiver–child communication and its contribution to the child's self-propelled development (Mattick, 1972; Minuchin & Biber, 1968). That is, the focus is on the everyday speech act, the natural flow of interpersonal communication, rather than on specific training in syntax or semantics.

Faced with these two radically different views of what constitutes productive ways of communicating to young children, what is the practitioner to do, whether teacher or parent? Two sources of evidence bear on this question: evidence from basic theory and research in child development, and evidence on the efficacy of our early intervention efforts to date. When we examine recent advances in basic theory and research in child development, the answer to this question seems to be unequivocal. It is the whole-child approach and not the didactic that finds support, with regard to both linguistic and cognitive development.

In linguistic research, Chomsky's theory has spawned a generation of developmental psycholinguistics (e.g., Bloom, 1970; Brown, 1973) who agree that toddlers learn language not by direct instruction from adults but through an active process of self-discovery. In this process, children creatively extract the underlying rules of grammar from the everyday flow of adult-child communication.

Similarly, in the field of cognition, Piaget's theory, which has gained widespread support from empirical research in the last two decades, rejects the didactic approach. Piaget presents a view of children as active explorers and inventors, constructing the organization of their own mind from the rich flow of everyday social and physical interaction (Piaget, 1970, 1973). In a Piagetian critique of the didactic approach, Kohlberg and Mayer (1972) warn that didactic programs tend to mimic rather than to stimulate development. Kamii, whom Piaget (1973) acknowledges as the valid interpreter of his theories as they apply to the education of young children,[1] sounds an even more ominous note. Kamii (1972; see also Kamii & DeVries, 1977) argues that the didactic approach threatens to stunt development, since children, as active learners, often need to generate the wrong solution before they go on to discover the correct one. The didactic approach tends to discourage such mistaken transitional solutions so necessary for growth. Kamii's warning is particularly alarming for very young children, since we run the grave risk of stunting development at its inception.

These advances in our knowledge of child development have not only undermined the didactic approach, they have also provided consistent support for the whole-child approach. Concerning language development, Cazden (1972a,b) has often pointed out that the home environment of children who are developing well resembles the environment in whole-child programs, rather than that in didactic programs. Regarding cognitive development, Flavell (1963) reminds us that Piaget is a self-avowed follower of Dewey's educational philosophy. Additionally Kamii (1970, 1972) repeatedly points out the striking resemblance between a Piagetian early childhood program and Dewey's whole-child approach. As Kamii (1970) puts it, "The two views seem to me to converge because Piaget provides a theoretical rationale for the traditional practices that have been defended merely on intuitive grounds [p. 37]."

Given this strong support from basic developmental research for the whole-child or Piagetian approach, one might expect that these programs have long since proven their superior efficacy in educational practice. In fact, this has not been the case. Citing Kohlberg and Mayer's key distinction between programs that stimulate development and those that mimic it, Cazden (1972b) vividly describes what is perhaps the major dilemma in our early intervention efforts to date: namely, while the whole-child programs are consistent with recent basic research, it is didactic programs—those that seemingly artificially force or mimic development—which have more often succeeded in demonstrating measurable gains, although the gains are likely to be short term and limited.[2] Cazden concludes: "Because . . . we want to stimulate development and not just mimic it, it is important to try to make 'natural,' less

---

[1]Piaget's acknowledgment is significant because, as he points out (1973), there are many programs called "Piagetian" that misapply his concepts. Also cited by Piaget (1973) as valid interpreters of his theory for education are Almy (1966) and Furth (1973).

[2]For comprehensive reviews of program evaluations see Smith (1973), Stearns (1971), Weisberg (1973), White, Day, Freeman, Hantman, and Messenger (1973), and Bronfenbrenner (1975).

didactic... environments more effective [p. 24; quotation marks in the original]."

To make "natural" environments more effective has been the goal of our research over the past decade, research begun in 1968 at the Head Start Research and Evaluation Center of the Bank Street College of Education and continued at the Barnard College Toddler Center from 1973 to the present. We took as our point of departure the disparity between science and application that apparently exists in whole-child Piagetian programs. Although consistent with basic research, such programs have yet to demonstrate their effectiveness when applied in early intervention.

Ordinarily, the gap between science and application is filled by a set of techniques or strategies designed to aid the practitioner in implementing scientific knowledge. For the caregiver role in didactic programs, these aids are available in abundance. Teacher–child interaction is highly structured in terms of specific didactic techniques—modeling new knowledge, eliciting repetitive practice and drill, providing confirming or corrective feedback—as well as specific content (the number system, the syntactic system, prescribed lists of basic concepts) (see Bartlett, 1972, for review of these programs). In contrast, the caregiver's role in whole-child Piagetian programs is relatively unstructured; techniques and strategies of teacher–child interaction remain relatively undefined.

This lack of definition may not be surprising in view of the fact that whole-child Piagetian programs focus on the actions of the child rather than on teacher–child interaction. It is the children who propel their own development as they explore, experiment, discover, and invent. Indeed, the caregiver's own actions are often viewed with suspicion as a possible interference in the child's self-regulated explorations (Biber, Shapiro, & Wickens, 1971; Kamii & DeVries, 1977; Piaget, 1970). Kamii (1972) highlights Piaget's relative neglect of the caregiver role by reminding us that the only pedagogical principle he has articulated concerns the importance of discussion and disagreement among peers. Similarly, Mayer (1971) points out that whole-child programs focus on child–child and child–material interactions; adult–child interactions are relatively neglected.

What of the caregiver's contribution to development? Apart from providing the materials for the child's self-exploration, what are the essential aspects of her[3] social role? How can we formulate the caregiver's role

---

[3]Because this is a report of a study of mothers, the feminine pronoun will be used in referring to caregivers. "He or she" will be used in referring to children.

in whole-child Piagetian programs in terms of strategies of interpersonal interaction that can be readily transmitted in parent-education or teacher-training programs?

Because whole-child Piagetian programs stress the quality of everyday communication between caregiver and child, rather than the teaching of specific lessons, it seemed to us that a microanalysis of the everyday speech act could be very useful. Yet, in marked contrast to the availability of impressive classification schemes for such aspects of care-giver and child language as syntax or semantics, there was no existing system for classifying the everyday speech acts of caregivers and children. Additionally no data were available indicating which everyday caregiver speech acts might foster the child's development. We set our-selves the task of providing this classification system and assembling this kind of data.

We planned our project in four phases. First, as it has been noted (White & Watts, 1973; and our own data bear this out), that a substantial proportion of the caregiver's interaction with very young children con-sists of responses to the child's initiatives, we began by developing a scoring scheme for the spontaneous communications of the child. It is called the *Functions of Interpersonal Spontaneous Preschool Speech* (FIS-P) (Schachter, Kirshner, Klips, Friedricks, & Sanders, 1974). Second, we developed a scoring scheme for both responsive and spontaneous com-munications of the caregiver, based on the FIS-P. It is called the *Interper-sonal Functions of Responsive and Spontaneous Speech of Caregivers* (FIS-C) (Schachter, Fosha, Stemp, Brotman, & Ganger, 1976). Third, in a study of teacher talk, we examined these caregiver speech acts in relation to the age of the child addressed, toddlers, and 3-, and 4-year-old children (Schachter *et al.*, 1976).

Finally, in the study reported in this volume, we have applied the caregiver classification scheme to the everyday speech acts of disadvan-taged and advantaged mothers in interaction with their toddlers. Such a microanalysis at the level of the speech act, ascertaining what caregivers of different backgrounds say when they interact with their young chil-dren in the naturalistic setting of the home, promised to provide specific suggestions regarding the kinds of verbal techniques or communication strategies that might be productive in enhancing the educational poten-tial of the child. The techniques identified would be useful in teacher training and parent education. Additionally, our study also promised to help resolve the fundamental controversy between the didactic and whole-child approach as to what constitutes productive ways of com-municating to young children.

Why Study the Verbal Environment?

With impressive consistency, broad-ranging observational studies of the early home environment of disadvantaged and advantaged children have found verbal stimulation to be a major factor distinguishing between the two environments, with higher levels for the advantaged. Wachs, Uzgiris, and Hunt (1971), using a comprehensive inventory, found verbal stimulation to be one of two major distinguishing factors at ages 15, 18, and 22 months. Similarly, Tulkin and Kagan (1972) found significantly greater verbal productivity among middle-class mothers interacting with their 10-month-olds, whereas they found few class differences on other dimensions, such as physical contact. In a comprehensive analysis of home interaction at the 3-year level, Schoggen and Schoggen (1976) also reported that receiving and giving messages through a verbal medium was one of the main factors yielding demonstrable social class differences.

In addition to these comparative studies of social class, comprehensive observational studies of early home influences on the young child's development have consistently found the verbal environment to be a key factor, regardless of social class. Clarke-Stewart (1973) found that the quantity of mother talk to 9–18-month-olds had a significant effect on the child's intellectual development—specifically on linguistic performance. Bradley and Caldwell (1976) found maternal verbal responsivity at age 2 to be significantly correlated with cognitive performance at age 4. White, Kaban, Shapiro, and Attanucci (1977) found that well-developing 1- and 2-year-olds had considerably more live talk directed toward them. They concluded, "Here, we believe, we have one of the key clues as to how to rear children well [p. 134]."

Finally, from the perspective of educational practice in early intervention programs, few areas have loomed as important as the verbal. The language of the child and of the caregiver has been the central concern in these programs (e.g., Cazden, 1972a). Any research that could shed light on productive ways of caregiver communication could make a direct contribution to practice.

Why Observe in the Home?

Comprehensive studies of home interaction have been useful in highlighting the importance of the verbal dimension in the early home environment, but they tell us little about which specific aspects of the verbal environment may foster child development. With minor exceptions, they report overall quantitative differences in the verbal environment, rather than specific qualitative ones. There have been a number of such qualitative studies of social-class differences in mother–child verbal interaction (Baldwin & Baldwin, 1973; Bee, Van Egeren, Streissguth, Nyman, & Leckie, 1969; Hess & Shipman, 1965; Olim, Hess, & Shipman, 1967; Snow, Arlman-Rupp, Hassing, Jobse, Joosten, & Vorster, 1976), but all these studies have been conducted in the laboratory rather than the natural setting of the home. Especially with regard to disadvantaged groups, it has often been noted (Baratz & Baratz, 1970; Labov, 1970; Sroufe, 1970; Tulkin, 1972) that data collected in the artificial setting of the laboratory may be of limited generalizability because lower-class subjects are likely to feel alienated and uncomfortable in these unfamiliar surroundings.

Apart from considerations of social class, the case for an ecologically valid developmental psychology has often been argued. Bronfenbrenner (1977) has most recently and vividly articulated this argument, characterizing contemporary developmental psychology as "the science of the strange behavior of children in strange situations with strange adults for the briefest possible periods of time [p. 513]." Belsky's (1977) evidence of striking discrepancies in mother–child interaction in the home as compared to the laboratory setting provides convincing empirical support for proponents of ecologically valid research.

Again, if we consider educational practice, we note that the most effective early intervention programs have been those that engage parents as teachers of their own children; home-based programs during the early years of life appear especially promising (Bronfenbrenner, 1975; Goodson & Hess, 1975; Honig, 1975; White, Day, Freeman, Hantman, & Messenger, 1973). Even in group programs, children with prior home-based experiences seem to benefit most (Bronfenbrenner, 1975). Yet a well-controlled study of one of our most promising home-based programs, Levenstein's Verbal Interaction Project, failed to replicate earlier positive findings (Madden, Levenstein, & Levenstein, 1976). If we are to fulfill the promise of these home-based programs, we obviously need more information on "productive ways" of mother–child interaction in the home.

Why Study the Toddler?

The finding of Golden, Birns, Bridger, and Moss (1971) that social-class differences in developmental assessments emerge between 18 and 36 months suggests that the toddler period may be critical for the verbal environment. Other investigators have found social-class differences even earlier, as early as 11 months (Wachs *et al.*, 1971), but the results below toddler age have been inconsistent (Bayley, 1965; Golden & Birns, 1968). By toddler age these inconsistencies disappear. Apart from these social-class comparisons, White and Watts (1973) claim that the critical years for the development of overall "competence" are prior to age 3.

There is another reason for studying the toddler: This is the age of first language acquisition. In fact, Golden *et al.* (1971) speculate that social-class differences in development begin at this age because environmental differences have a significant impact on the child's emerging verbal intelligence. Whether the environment plays a determining role in the acquisition of language and what role this might be, are issues receiving intensive attention in developmental psycholinguistic research (Newport, 1976; Phillips, 1973; Sachs, Brown, & Salerno, 1972; Snow, 1972; Snow & Ferguson, 1977). The typical strategy has been to compare baby talk (i.e., mother talk to the language-learning toddler) with mother talk to older children or adults, in an attempt to identify any distinctive features in baby talk that might assist language learning. Features that have already been identified, including shortened utterances, simplified grammar, self-repetitions, repetitions of the child, expansions, and questions, suggest that the early verbal environment may indeed play a role in language acquisition. Developmental psycholinguists are busily engaged in attempting to define this role.

Those of us interested in early intervention programs for the disadvantaged stand to benefit from the rapid developments and microlevel analyses in research on baby talk. Snow *et al.* (1976) have recently published data comparing formal features of baby talk in mothers of diverse social backgrounds. In the present study, we shall examine several of these features and compare our findings with those of Snow *et al.* Additionally, research on baby talk stands to benefit from a comprehensive examination of the speech acts addressed to toddlers. With rare exceptions (Gelman & Shatz, 1977; Gleason, 1977; Schachter *et al.*, 1976), previous studies in this field have been limited to an examination of formal features, although there is increasing interest in what the mother is saying (Snow & Ferguson, 1977). The present study provides this kind of data on how mothers communicate to their toddlers.

Finally, there is another compelling reason to study the toddler—an educational one. When we examine our early intervention efforts to date we find that programs in the first few years of life seem to be the most effective (Bronfenbrenner, 1975; Goodson & Hess, 1975). The data support White and Watts's (1973) claim that the years before 3 are critical for the development of competence or educability. It seems essential to learn more about the early home experiences that may affect these developments.

In his delightful, unbuttoned introduction to his book on language acquisition, Roger Brown (1973) points out that we need consciousness raising with regard to grammar, since we tend to take it for granted. The evidence presented here strongly indicates that, if we are to design more effective early intervention programs, we will need consciousness raising with regard to the everyday speech acts of caregivers to toddlers. Our study is intended to generate this heightened awareness of how we talk to very young children.

Chapter 2
Sample: Mothers, Toddlers, and the Home Setting

There were 30 mother–toddler dyads in the study sample, 10 in each of three groups: black disadvantaged, black advantaged, and white advantaged. We studied poverty in the black community primarily because of our inner-city location, but also for another important reason. Although black poverty has been the focus of early intervention research, to date there are almost no data on highly educated black groups.[1] Instead, either the black disadvantaged have been compared with the white advantaged or both black and white disadvantaged have been compared with white advantaged. This persistent confounding of black ethnicity with poverty not only makes it impossible to separate the independent contributions of race and poverty, but, more important, tends to perpetuate racial stereotypes, especially since white advantaged samples have generally been drawn from highly educated university-based populations. The Barnard College Toddler Center, a university-based play group located at Columbia University in New York City, presented an opportunity to put these racial stereotypes to rest, since it

[1] In research on mother–child interaction, only Hess (1969; Hess & Shipman, 1965; Olim, Hess, & Shipman, 1967) seems to provide data on a highly educated sample of black families, a group described as professional.

provided ready access to a sample of black and white mothers from the same highly educated population.

We added a white advantaged sample because we were interested in social class not merely as a status variable. What we wanted to get at were the environmental processes that may underlie the persistent correlation between poverty and the high risk of developing school problems. Both groups of advantaged toddlers, black and white, would be considered at low risk developmentally, while the black disadvantaged group would be classified as high risk. We, thus, planned to focus on those specific aspects of the verbal environment where the two low-risk advantaged groups did not differ significantly from each other, but where both differed significantly from the high-risk black disadvantaged group.

Advantage was defined in terms of years of maternal education because we felt that this aspect of social class status had the greatest impact on the child, by virtue of the association between maternal education and access to adequate child development information. Maternal education was also the preferred criterion because half our disadvantaged group was either fatherless or on welfare.[2] In any case, the other social class indices, when available, correlated highly with mother education. Table 2.1 presents the data on these indices for all three groups. It can be seen that the average level of education for the black disadvantaged mothers was somewhat below the level of high school graduation, whereas that for advantaged mothers was a year of graduate school. There was no significant difference between advantaged groups, and a highly significant difference between both advantaged and the disadvantaged group.

For fathers, data were available for all 20 advantaged toddlers and 5 disadvantaged. Table 2.1 shows that educational differences among fathers were similar to those for mothers, although fathers in all groups were somewhat better educated than mothers. The average black disadvantaged father was a high school graduate, whereas advantaged fathers averaged 2 years of graduate school. Again there was no significant difference between advantaged groups, but there was a highly significant difference between advantaged and disadvantaged groups. The fathers' occupational status was professional or executive for all advantaged fathers and, where data was available, laborer for all disadvantaged fathers. Overall, there was a marked disparity in social class

---

[2]The lack of access to fathers in the disadvantaged group made it impossible to include data on father–child interaction in the study.

TABLE 2.1
Social Class Characteristics of Sample

Characteristics	Groups		
	Disadvantaged	Advantaged	
	Black	Black	White
Maternal education			
Mean	11.75	17.05	17.70
SD	1.40	1.26	1.64
Paternal education[a]			
Mean	12.60	17.75	18.70
SD	.82	2.53	1.57
Paternal occupation[a]			
Professional—Executive		10	10
Skilled Laborer	1		
Unskilled Laborer	3		
Unemployed	1		

[a] Data unavailable for five disadvantaged black fathers.

status between advantaged and disadvantaged groups and no significant differences between black and white advantaged groups.

Contacting the Sample

Advantaged mother–toddler dyads were contacted mainly through the Barnard College Toddler Center, a play group sponsored by the psychology department as an adjunct to teaching and research. Toddlers attend two mornings a week during the academic year for a total of 24 weeks, and mothers grant permission for naturalistic observational research before enrolling them in the program. All but two of the advantaged dyads, one black and one white, came from the center. Because the number of toddlers at the center was small—24 in all—and the number of variables for matching groups was large (see pp. 16–18); it took 2 years to come within reach of completing our sample. To avoid further delay, we located our final two dyads by enlisting the cooperation of friends.

The disadvantaged mother–toddler dyads were contacted mainly through a black undergraduate at Barnard. With the help of her relatives, who lived in low-income housing projects and had young children of their own, we contacted 7 of the 10 subjects. The disadvantaged mothers were paid for their participation. In addition, our student contact made two preliminary visits in order to help make the mothers more comfortable, simulating the role of the observer and familiarizing them with observation procedures. It was felt that as advantaged mothers were accustomed to student observers at the toddler center and were generally familiar with research procedures, preliminary visits would be unnecessary.

For the remaining three dyads of the disadvantaged group, two were contacted at the street corner of 125th Street and Broadway in Harlem by a black teacher from the Barnard College Toddler Center, and one attended the center. There were preliminary visits for the two who did not come from the center.

It is important to note that at no time during the 2 years of data collection were any of the mothers aware of the existence of our scoring scheme for caregiver speech acts, the FIS-C. Knowledge of the FIS-C scores themselves was withheld from the teachers at the toddler center as well. In addition, none of the mothers, either advantaged or disadvantaged, were exposed to any parent education program during the study period.

Altogether, conditions were especially auspicious for making the mothers feel at ease during the home observation. Almost all advantaged mothers felt themselves identified with the college and the observers by virtue of their children's attendance in the play group. Almost all disadvantaged mothers were contacted in an informal manner by our student whose relatives knew them personally.

Characteristics of Mothers

Apart from social class indices, Table 2.2 summarizes the descriptive characteristics of the mothers, including employment status, number of children, mean age, and national background. Mothers were selected so that groups would be matched for maternal employment and number of children. Table 2.2 shows that all but three in each group worked as housewives and that the groups, with the exception of one black advantaged three-child family, were evenly divided into one- and two-child families. It was not possible, however, to match the groups for maternal age. Advantaged mothers were significantly older than the disadvantaged, with no differences in the advantaged means. This age differential is undoubtedly a by-product of the extended education of advan-

TABLE 2.2
Description of Mothers

Characteristics	Groups		
	Disadvantaged	Advantaged	
	Black	Black	White
Maternal employment			
At home: Housewife	7	7	7
Outside: Full-time	2	2	2
Outside: Irregular[a]	1	1	1
Number of children			
1	5	5	5
2	5	4	5
3		1	
Age			
Mean	25.50	32.70	32.70
SD	4.12	5.40	5.29
National background			
Afro-American	9	8	
Afro-West Indian	1	2	
Northern European			5
Jewish			5

[a] Either part-time or occasional full-time.

taged mothers, so that age and education are invariably confounded. As has been widely reported (e.g., Rubin, 1976), disadvantaged mothers marry and bear children at a younger age, often sharply curtailing further education.

National background was a matter of concern within both black and white samples. Our previous research on poverty in New York City (Schachter *et al.*, 1974) revealed that West Indians were often overrepresented among educated black mothers. To avoid confounding socioeducational status and national background, the black groups were matched on the latter variable. As shown in Table 2.2, almost all of the black mothers in each group were Afro-Americans. National background was also controlled in the white sample to ensure heterogeneity. Half of the sample was North European and the other half was Jewish. It can be seen in Table 2.2 that all three groups were well matched for maternal employment and number of children; that the two advantaged groups were matched for age of mother; and that nationality was controlled where it seemed appropriate.

TABLE 2.3
Description of Toddlers

	Groups		
	Disadvantaged	Advantaged	
Characteristics	Black	Black	White
Age			
Mean	28.05	27.90	28.00
SD	4.56	4.31	4.23
Sex			
Boy	5	5	5
Girl	5	5	5
Birth order			
First-born	6	6	6
Second-born	4	3	4
Third-born		1	
Cognitive performance			
MA > CA	3	9[a]	10
CA > MA	7		

[a] One advantaged black toddler moved out of town before testing.

Characteristics of Toddlers

Table 2.3 summarizes the descriptive characteristics of the three groups of toddlers including mean age, sex, birth order, and level of performance on cognitive tasks. Toddler groups were matched for age and sex by selecting one boy and one girl at ages 22, 25, 28, 31, and 34 months (± 1 month). Groups were also matched for birth order; each included six first-born and four later-born toddlers. With the exception of one third-born black advantaged girl, all later-borns were second children.

Performance on cognitive tasks was assessed by Stanford–Binet tests, supplemented by Catell Infant Scales where necessary. Children contacted through the Barnard College Toddler Center, were tested in the familiar setting of the center with their mother or teacher present if the child so desired.[3] Children contacted through other sources, including almost all the black disadvantaged toddlers, were tested in the familiar

[3]Children at the Barnard College Toddler Center were tested at the beginning of the school year to eliminate possible effects of the toddler program.

setting of the home with their mothers present. To maximize rapport between tester and child for black disadvantaged subjects, testing was administered by the same black student who had visited the home earlier for preliminary observations. Test results are reported in terms of whether the child's mental age (MA) exceeded chronological age (CA), because longitudinal research indicates that test scores at toddler-age are unreliable unless they are expressed in terms of broad distinctions (Elkind, 1972). Table 2.3 shows that MA was higher than CA for all 19 advantaged toddlers tested (one moved from New York shortly after the home observation before being tested), while CA was higher than MA for 7 of the 10 disadvantaged toddlers. These findings are consistent with previous reports indicating that poor children perform less well on cognitive tasks by the time they reach toddler-age (Golden *et al.*, 1971; Wachs *et al.*, 1971).

Characteristics of the Home Setting

Mothers and toddlers were observed during their everyday activity in the home. Mothers cooked, cleaned, read newspapers, worked at their desks, knitted, or interacted with their toddlers. Toddlers played alone or interacted with their mothers. We urged the mothers to act as naturally as possible and to ignore the observer as much as they could. Since it was obvious that we were recording mother–child communication, and since we wanted the mothers to be as relaxed as possible, we provided them with the following rationale: We explained that we were trying to understand how the miracle of language learning occurs, that no one quite knows how it happens and with such impressive speed during this stage of their child's life. To help understand it, we needed to study children in their natural setting and to record everything the child says and hears. This, we explained, was why it was so important for the mother to act as naturally as possible.

Because we were interested in the effects of socioeducational status on the quality of mother–child communication, it was necessary to control for gross situational factors that might affect such communication. These gross situational factors included: First, *time of day*: All observations were conducted in the morning after breakfast and dressing. Second, *other people present*: We observed only with mother and child present. On the whole, mothers were able to arrange this and we offered babysitter help if needed. Occasionally, other people were present in the home, but they removed themselves to an area of the home where the mother and child were not interacting. If others entered the area of observation, recording was interrupted until they removed themselves again. Speaking on the phone was not precluded in order to preserve naturalness. Third, *television*: Observations were conducted with the television set off. If the child was accustomed to watching "Sesame Street" regularly, observation was postponed until the program was over. Radios and records were not precluded because their impact on conversation was insignificant in comparison to that of television, and because we wanted to preserve a natural atmosphere.

In addition to controlling for these gross situational factors, we studied the extent to which the mother's talk was concerned with feeding, dressing, and toileting to see if these important situational factors varied among the three groups. Although the observers arrived after breakfast and morning dressing, a considerable proportion of mother talk was concerned with these activities, a mean of 6.3% for feeding (including drinking), 3.0% for dressing, and 2.9% for toileting. However, there were no significant differences in this regard among the three groups.

It can be seen that most of the major aspects of the situational context were quite comparable for all three groups of mother–toddler dyads. Differences in the everyday verbal environment could therefore be attributed mainly to between-group differences in maternal education levels and access to adequate child development information.

Part II

A Scoring System for Everyday Caregiver Speech Acts

Chapter 3

Instrument Development, Units, and Recording Procedures

To study the everyday speech acts of mothers from diverse backgrounds, we applied our classification scheme for the interpersonal functions of caregiver speech, the FIS-C. This chapter will describe the development of the FIS-C, define the scoreable units, and present the recording procedures. Chapter 4 presents the scoring scheme and, in Chapter 5, reliability assessment and methods of data analysis are described. Additionally, a more detailed description of the FIS-C, a Supplementary Scoring Manual, is provided in Appendix A.

Developing the FIS-C

Perhaps the most fascinating feature of the speech act is that the same string of words, with the same syntax, can express a variety of speech acts or interpersonal functions depending on the total context in which it is uttered. To take an example from Searle (1969), the philosopher of language who coined the term "speech act," the utterance *It's really quite late* when spoken by a wife at a party can be an objection if someone has just remarked on how early it is; it can be a desire request if spoken to her husband ('Let's go home'); or a warning ('You'll feel rotten in the morning if we don't go home'). To give an example from our own data on caregiver talk to young children, an adult remark *It sure is noisy* might be a confirmation to a child who has just reported on the noise; it might be an admonition to some noisy children; or it might merely be a report on a low-flying jet.

It can be seen that a wide variety of extralinguistic and paralinguistic factors, mainly those concerning social and emotional aspects of communication, play a key role in assessing the interpersonal functions of an utterance. Among these factors are the relations between the speaker and the listener, the effects on speaker and listener, the place of the utterance in the sequence of discourse, gestures, facial expression, and intonation. The complex manner in which the speech act depends on the total interpersonal context commands the attention of contemporary linguists.

To the social scientist constructing a classification scheme for scoring and measuring speech acts, the dependence of the speech act on such a wide range of interpersonal factors presents a serious challenge. How can one take all of these factors into account? Our approach in constructing the FIS-C was to rely on the intuitions and empathy of the observer, and also to draw upon the relevant literature. We referred to literature on general developmental theory, motivational theory, the nonlinguistic research on categories for caregiver–child social interaction (Caldwell, 1968; Schoggen, 1963, White & Watts, 1973), the noncaregiver research on categories for the communication functions of speech (Ervin-Tripp, 1964; Searle, 1969; Soskin & John, 1963; Jakobson, 1960; Skinner, 1957; Piaget, 1926), and the research on speech of disadvantaged mothers (Bee *et al.*, 1969; Bernstein, 1962, 1965, 1970; Hess & Shipman, 1965).

Essentially, we adopted the method of latent content analysis, widely used in psychology (e.g., Dollard & Auld, 1959; Ervin-Tripp, 1964, 1972). We assumed, as did Ervin-Tripp (1972), that what the linguists call "topic" refers to manifest content, while what they call "interpersonal function" refers to latent content—the often masked, often neutralized intentions of the speaker. In assessing speaker intentions, although adequate definitions should be provided, we are inclined to agree with our clinical colleagues (Dollard & Auld, 1959) that ultimately the analysis relies on the empathy of the observer. The category system was developed by a child-clinical psychologist and should always be applied by empathic observers, experienced with young children.

We originally devleoped the FIS-C scoring scheme on the basis of empirical observations of teacher talk to toddlers, 3- and 4-year-olds during free play in group-care settings (Schachter *et al.*, 1976). The original version of the FIS-C needed very little modification when applied in the present study of mother talk to toddlers in the home. There were almost no revisions necessitated by the change in caregiver or setting. Most modifications resulted from attempts to define scores more precisely in order to increase scorer agreement or reliability, as the psychologist would put it, to clarify contrast rules, as the linguist would put it.

Modifications were suggested by the following factors: Observation time was twice as long for the mothers as for the teachers. The augmented speech sample called attention to distinctions that were overlooked when they occurred rarely. In addition, we introduced computerization of the scoring system in the study of mothers. Computer techniques could be applied to generate new scores based on the ratio of one score to another. Research in related areas also suggested a few revisions. Studies of discourse, especially that of Garvey (1975), and of speech acts, especially that of Dore (1975), were helpful here. Finally, a few scores were added or omitted and a few were redefined based on a preliminary reliability study designed to identify scorer discrepancies. In describing our classification scheme, we will report on the FIS-C as currently in use, as it was applied in this study.

Scoreable Units and Terminology

Speech Act

The caregiver speech act is the basic unit of the FIS-C. The speech act is defined using the usual criteria of a single intonation contour preceded and followed by a pause (see Dore, 1977; Gelman & Shatz, 1977). Subordinate clauses (e.g., *'cause it's wet*), introductory words or phrases (e.g., *Yes, No, Look, Oh, name of child*) and terminal tag words (e.g., *Right, Okay, See? Huh?*) are combined with the main clause when the intonation is judged to be a single contour. On the other hand, these same clauses, words, or phrases are scored as a separate unit when pauses and intonation indicate a separate utterance contour.

Although the scoreable unit is the speech act, the score assigned to each speech act depends on the place of the unit in the sequence of discourse. For example, the utterance *What are you doing?* followed by *Stop it* is scored as part of a sequence of commands—a "preparation" for the directive, as Garvey (1975) calls it. On the other hand, *What are you doing?* followed by *Dancing?* is scored as eliciting a report. Similarly, the utterance *It's wet* following the utterance *Don't* is scored as part of a sequence of commands, an explanation justifying the command—an "adjunct" of the directive (Garvey, 1975). On the other hand, *It's wet* spoken while the caregiver is teaching the difference between "wet" and "dry" is scored as part of a sequence of teaching talk. (See Appendix A for additional instructions on scoring in relation to the sequence of discourse.)

The term "speech act" is not as familiar to the nonlinguist as "statement" or "utterance." For readability and variety, we have used these three terms interchangeably, although each has specific connotations among linguists.[1] It should also be noted that Searle's term "speech act" has generally replaced Austin's (1962) original term "illocutionary act" in the current psycholinguistic literature. In 1969, Searle described three components of the speech act: (a) the "illocutionary act"—denoting interpersonal function or communication intent; (b) the "propositional act"—denoting meaning or semantics; and (c) the "utterance act"—denoting form or syntax. The term "speech act" is now generally used to mean "illocutionary act" (see Ervin-Tripp & Mitchell-Kernan, 1977; Bruner, 1975). Similarly, the term "communication function" is rapidly replacing Halliday's (1970) term "interpersonal function" in research on the speech act (Ervin-Tripp & Mitchell-Kernan, 1977; Rodgon, Jankowski, & Alenskas, 1977). In this volume we use "communication function" more often than "interpersonal function."

Other Scoreable Units

Although the speech act was the main focus of the present study, we were also concerned with the mother's nonverbal communications and with the child's verbal and nonverbal communications. The mother's nonverbal communications would indicate whether some mothers compensated for verbal activity by using nonverbal communication in its place. The child's communications were of interest because we planned to study the extent to which group differences in mother speech could be accounted for by group differences in the communication initiatives of their children.

To examine these issues, we attempted to classify the mother's nonverbal communications using the category scheme we had developed to classify her speech acts, the FIS-C. Similarly, we attempted to classify the child's nonverbal communications, using the category scheme previously developed for classifying the speech acts of young children, the

[1]Technically, "statement" is used to refer to declarative assertions; "utterance" in discussing syntax and semantics; and "speech act" in discussing interpersonal function.

Note that it is not clear whether words read from a book or sung in a song are viewed as speech acts. We do not score them. On the other hand, comments and questions about the contents of a book or song, often including the words, are clearly scoreable speech acts. The latter were far more frequent in our speech sample than was conventional reading or singing, which was rare.

FIS-P (Schachter *et al.*, 1974). In both cases, we found that the same category system could be applied to verbal and nonverbal communications. For example, if the caregiver seized a fragile object from the child's hand, the gesture would be scored as a single communication serving the same function as the single speech act *No, no.* Similarly, if the child babbled and pointed inquiringly to some sudden noise, the nonverbal communication would be scored as a single communication serving the same function as the speech act *What's that?* In this way, we found that we were able to score verbal and nonverbal communications of caregiver and child.

NONVERBAL COMMUNICATIONS OF THE CAREGIVER

In the present study, only 1% of the mother's communications were found to be nonverbal. Since previous research suggested that the early verbal environment of disadvantaged children played a key role in later development, we decided to limit our report to the mother's speech acts—provided that these few nonverbal communications had no effect on the findings based on speech acts alone. We proceeded to analyze the results, both including and excluding these nonverbal communications, and found that the results for all FIS-C scores were the same whether or not these nonverbal communications were included in the analysis. Apparently, nonverbal communication did not serve to compensate for a lack of verbal communication. In fact, nonverbal communication was simply too rare to compensate for anything. On this basis and in view of our persistent interest in the early verbal environment of the disadvantaged child, we have limited the present report to the mother's speech acts alone.

CHILD COMMUNICATIONS

While nonverbal communication appears to be rare among caregivers of toddlers, it is common among toddlers. In the present sample, 8.9% of the toddlers' communications were nonverbal, and 4.5% of the mothers' speech consisted of responses to these communications.

In segmenting the child's communications, whether verbal or nonverbal, we take into account the widely reported observation that sequences of toddler discourse often consist of repetitions, false starts, and reformulations (e.g., *Mommy, paint. Look, Mommy, paint* [points to spill].) At times the caregiver responds to these sequences as if they were functionally single units (e.g., *I'll get the mop.*). At other times, she segments the sequence into two or more units (e.g., Child: *Mommy, paint.* Caregiver: *Paint?* Child: *Look, Mommy, paint* [points to spill]. Caregiver: *I'll get the mop.*). In this way, the caregiver provides the scorer with her own intuitions about how to segment the child's sequence. Rather than relying on the intuitions of the unfamiliar scorer, we adopt the perspective of the familiar caregiver in segmenting the child's communication. Thus in the first example, the child's sequence would be scored as one unit, whereas in the second example it would be scored as two units.

Finally, the observer also notes when the caregiver seems to ignore a child's communication unit and when no response is needed. Most spontaneous communication units toddlers address to their mothers, as well as all queries addressed to her, seem to demand a response. On the other hand, the child's responsive communications can serve to terminate a conversation so that a response is not necessarily required.

Procedures for Recording

A number of factors contributed to the decision to rely mainly on what Soskin and John (1963) call "eyewitness observers" for manually recording their own data and scoring it. Classifying the interpersonal functions of early caregiver talk is so dependent on a variety of subtle and complex context cues, many of them visual (e.g., gestures, body movements), that only videotape used in conjunction with a zoom lens could substitute adequately for eyewitness observation. In addition, mobile equipment would be necessary to record the rapidly changing pace and location of everyday caregiver–child activity. We concluded that empathic observers could adapt to change and movement more quickly than they could adjust mobile equipment. Under ideal circumstances, mobile videotape could be used in addition to eyewitness observation. However, the rooms of the New York City apartments where we conducted observations could not comfortably accommodate mother, child, and two observers. When two eyewitness recorder–scorers were required for the reliability study the crowding produced was awkward and unnatural. Most important, manual recording was undertaken because it was possible to obtain reliable results (see Chapter 5). No doubt the abbreviated utterances of early caregiver–child speech contributed to obtaining reliability, probably unattainable with manual recording of adult–adult discourse or of caregiver talk to older children. Altogether, the single eyewitness recorder–scorer seemed to be the best solution to the problem of processing the complex array of contextual and visual cues we were dealing with.

We considered supplementing the manual recording of the eyewitness observer with lightweight mobile audiotape equipment that the observer could carry. Our only reservation to this idea was that disadvantaged and advantaged mothers might react differently to being taped. It seemed likely that advantaged mothers would be more familiar with taping equipment and therefore more comfortable during its use.[2] We adopted a compromise between auditory taping of the entire sample and no taping at all by using audiotaping for half of the subjects in each group—matching taped and nontaped subjects for toddler age and sex. When audiotaping, a lightweight Sony-55 cassette recorder was carried in a knapsack on the back of the observer-scorer, and a small microphone was held in the hand that supported the clipboard. Attached to the clipboard were note pad and stopwatch.

The scoring scheme was applied to 48, 3-minute intervals of mother–child discourse with 24 intervals or 72 minutes on each of two mornings. Observers recorded a running account of all verbal and nonverbal communications of mother and child, noting the context and tone of the communications. Because of the rigorous demands of recording, scoring was delayed until after the recording period. The two morning sessions were scheduled at the mother's convenience during the month when the child reached the age required to match the groups. The average interval between the two sessions was 11.6 days.

The 3-minute observation interval was used to allow the observer to rest between arduous intervals of recording, whenever necessary. Mother–toddler dyads were observed on two mornings to evaluate the consistency of our scoring categories. As will be reported in Chapter 5, the results were sufficiently consistent to justify combining the data of both sessions.

To maximize intelligibility, recorders were instructed to move as close as was possible to the area of mother–toddler interaction, to avoid eye-to-eye contact, and to adopt a benign expression. Very few of the mother's speech acts proved to be inaudible: (a) possibly because only mother and child were being observed; or (b) because mothers talk to toddlers in short sentences; or (c) because the observers were too busy recording intelligible speech acts. It has been generally noted that talk to toddlers is highly intelligible (Newport, Gleitman, & Gleitman, 1977), perhaps because the caregiver adjusts to the toddler's limited language comprehension.

When mother and child were in different rooms, recorders located themselves somewhere between the two to discourage communication with the observer. Under these conditions, observers were generally

---

[2]Our final impression was that both advantaged and disadvantaged mothers were less comfortable with tape-recording than they were with manual recording, but that they reacted to the discomfort differently. Advantaged mothers seemed to talk somewhat more with taping; disadvantaged mothers seemed to talk somewhat less.

ignored by the children, a reaction widely reported in the preschool literature. On the other hand, mothers knew that they were under observation and could see that we were recording communication. However, they were not aware of the categories of speech that were under study, as noted earlier. Although the advantaged mothers were accustomed to student observers at the toddler center, and the disadvantaged mothers were given two preobservation visits to familiarize them with the procedures, it is impossible to determine the degree to which the observers influenced the results. When either the child or the mother addressed the observer, recording was discontinued, to be resumed as soon as possible.

Recorder–scorers and mothers were matched for ethnicity to help put the mothers at ease. The recorder–scorer was black for the black mothers and white for the white mothers. The black recorder–scorer was a psychology major at Barnard College and the white recorder–scorer was a young former nursery school teacher. Both were selected on the basis of empathy and experience with young children and their mothers.

The black observer played an additional role of importance in the development of the scoring scheme. We had originally constructed the scheme on the basis of a sample of teachers who all spoke Standard English, although they varied in ethnicity (black, white, and Puerto Rican). We had not yet applied the scoring scheme to caregivers who spoke only Black English. Our black observer, who was familiar with Black English, was assigned the task of alerting us to any new scores required or any existing scores needing modification for use with Black English. As it turned out, no changes in the scoring scheme were needed. This finding is not surprising since classifying speech on the basis of communication function is largely independent of how the utterance is structured. As we pointed out at the beginning of this chapter, the same words with the same syntax can express a variety of communication functions depending on the total context. Similarly, recent sociolinguistic research has demonstrated that the same communication functions are expressed in various languages using diverse syntactic devices (Ervin-Tripp & Mitchell-Kernan, 1977; Gumperz & Hymes, 1972).

What are these functions in caregiver talk to young children? The following chapter describes our system for classifying the communication functions of everyday caregiver speech.

Chapter 4
Scoring Procedures

The last decade has witnessed a radical change in the way we view early caregiver–child interaction. As Michael Rutter pointed out in his address to the Society for Research in Child Development in 1977, we have traditionally been concerned with what caregivers do **to** children. Research demonstrating that much of the caregiver's interaction occurs in response to the child has challenged this traditional view (Stern, 1977; White & Watts, 1973). Researchers are increasingly concerned with how caregivers interact responsively **with** children rather than with what they do **to** children (Schaffer, 1977).

In classifying caregiver speech acts, it seemed essential to develop a vocabulary to describe how caregivers talk responsively **with** children as well as how they talk **to** children. This distinction formed the basis for selecting our FIS-C scores. Scores were identified that are typical of both the caregiver's responsive and spontaneous talk. "Responsive talk" is defined as talk that is instigated by the child's verbal or nonverbal communication to the caregiver. The definition disregards whether the caregiver's verbal reaction is "responsive" in the sense of sensitive or perceptive, noting only whether it is instigated by a prior child communication to the caregiver. "Spontaneous talk" is defined as talk instigated by the caregiver without the stimulus of a prior communication of the child. A speech act is considered spontaneous if it follows a child communication to the self (Piaget's "monologue," 1926) or if it is instigated by some action of the child (e.g., child messes, runs, falls) other than a communication to the caregiver.

The FIS-C scoring scheme covers all caregiver speech acts, both responsive and spontaneous. There are four sets of scores as follows:

1. Total-talk scores denoting the total number of caregiver speech acts
2. Communication-function category scores, subcategories, and subscores denoting the interpersonal functions of caregiver speech
3. Routine scores denoting such stock phrases and interjections as *What? God bless you; Hi*
4. Appended scores for formal discourse features denoting self-repetitions, repetitions of the child, questions,and justifying explanations

Each set of scores is described in the following pages, with examples provided as needed. Since the scoring scheme is comprehensive, covering every kind of speech act no matter how rare, it was necessary to exclude from statistical analysis scores that occurred too rarely to generate reliable results. Only those scores that exceeded a mean of 1% frequency in the speech of two of the three groups of mothers under study were included in the present analysis.[1] In the following description of the scores, a plus sign (+) denotes that the score exceeded the 1% criterion.

Total-Talk Scores

TOTAL TALK[+]. Total number of caregiver speech acts both responsive and spontaneous.

TOTAL RESPONSIVE TALK[+]. Total number of responsive caregiver speech acts.

TOTAL Ch:S → C:R RESPONSIVE TALK[+]. Total number of caregiver responses (C:R) to spontaneous communications of the child (Ch:S).
TOTAL Ch:R → C:R RESPONSIVE TALK[+]. Total number of caregiver responses to responsive communications of the child (Ch:R).
TOTAL SPONTANEOUS TALK[+]. Total number of spontaneous caregiver speech acts.

---

[1]We intended to include in the analysis any score where one group exceeded a mean of 2% even though the mean of the other two groups was less than 1%, but there were no such scores.

Communication-Function Category Scores, Subcategories, and Subscores

The list of scores for the communication functions of caregiver speech acts comprises 10 categories, 21 subcategories, and 10 subscores of adequate frequency. The 10 categories cover the major interpersonal functions of caregiver speech, both responsive and spontaneous. They include the following:

- I. RESPONDS TO CHILD EXPRESSIVE COMMUNICATION (Child: *Ow!* Caregiver: *Gee, that hurt.*)
- II. RESPONDS TO CHILD DESIRE COMMUNICATION (Child: *Chocolate cookie.* Caregiver: *You want a chocolate cookie?*)
- III. RESPONDS TO CHILD EGO-ENHANCING COMMUNICATION (Child: *I did it!* Caregiver: *Great!*)
- IV. RESPONDS TO CHILD COLLABORATIVE COMMUNICATION (Child: *Here's some ice-cream* [pretends]. Caregiver: *Um, delicious* [pretends].)
- V. RESPONDS TO CHILD REPORT (Child: *I got bubbles.* Caregiver: *You sure do.*)
- VI. RESPONDS TO CHILD LEARNING COMMUNICATION (Child: *What's that?* Caregiver: *It's a bead.*)
- VII. CONTROLS, RESTRICTS–COMMANDS (*Don't throw it on the floor, honey.*)
- VIII. TEACHES, PROVIDES KNOWLEDGE (*Your pants are red.*)
- IX. REPORTS ON CHILD (*You made a picture.*)
- X. REPORTS ON SELF, OTHERS, THINGS (*I hafta make up my bed.*)

Within each category, subcategories denote the major ways of expressing the communication function. For example, subcategories for the category CONTROLS (VII) include DO'S, DON'TS, and REFUSALS. Subscores were introduced for two of the categories, CONTROLS and TEACHES, in order to study stylistic variations in control talk (e.g., DON'TS with explanations versus DON'TS with threats) and content variations in teaching talk (e.g., teaches about the physical world versus the social world). These variations in style and content have received considerable attention in the literature on caregiver talk, both sociolinguistic (Bernstein, 1970; Hess, 1969) and educational (Cazden, 1972a).

Deriving the Categories

DERIVING FIS-C CATEGORIES I–VI

Categories I–VI and their subcategories represent our attempt to develop a vocabulary describing the responsive speech acts of caregivers.

Since it seemed reasonable to assume that the caregiver's responsive speech could be defined in relation to the kinds of child communications evoking it, we began by developing a category scheme for the spontaneous speech acts of young children, the FIS-P (Schachter *et al.*, 1974). These FIS-P categories include the following:

    I. EXPRESSIVE COMMUNICATION (*Ouch!*)
    II. DESIRE COMMUNICATION (*I need red.*)
    III. POSSESSION RIGHTS COMMUNICATION (*That's mine.*)
    IV. EGO-ENHANCING COMMUNICATION (*Look at my big house.*)
    V. SELF-REFERRING, SELF-INCLUDING COMMUNICATION (*Me too.*)
    VI. JOINING COMMUNICATION (*You're my friend.*)
    VII. COLLABORATIVE COMMUNICATION (*The garage goes there.*)
    VIII. REPORTS ON SELF, OTHERS, THINGS (*I run.*)
    IX. LEARNING COMMUNICATION (*What's that?*)
    X. CALLS WHEN OUT OF SIGHT (*Mommy.*).[2]

Using these FIS-P categories for the child's spontaneous communications, we proceeded to examine samples of caregiver speech evoked by each of these categories (i.e., Ch:S → C:R responses). We found that each child category evoked a typical set of caregiver responses. For instance, in response to a report by the child (*I'm making a cake.*), the caregiver might provide a confirmation of the report (*Okay.*) or she might ask the child to elaborate further on the report (*A birthday cake?*). Each of these typical caregiver responses forms the basis of a responsive FIS-C subcategory, and the set of subcategories that occur in response to each kind of FIS-P category form the basis of each responsive FIS-C category. For example, the set of subcategories that typically occur in response to the child's reports constitute the FIS-C category RESPONDS TO CHILD REPORT and the set of subcategories in response to the child's desire requests constitutes the FIS-C category RESPONDS TO CHILD DESIRE COMMUNICATION. Six of these caregiver categories reached adequate frequency in the present sample of mother speech; they are designated FIS-C Categories I–VI as shown on page 33. The remaining FIS-C cate-

---

[2]This is a new FIS-P child category that does not appear in the published version of the FIS-P (Schachter *et al.*, 1974) which is based on child discourse in the classroom. At school, with child and teacher always within viewing range, it is possible to interpret the communication function of the child's call (*Teacher. Pat.*) as a desire request or a report, etc., in which case the latter score is assigned. In the multiroom setting of the home, neither the caregiver nor the observer could interpret the child's calls from another room because context cues were missing. It was therefore necessary to add this new FIS-P category, CALLS WHEN OUT OF SIGHT. A similar category appears in Dore's (1975) classification scheme for child speech.

gories similarly derived occur rarely in caregiver speech and are listed in Appendix A.

Although the set of FIS-C categories was derived from samples of caregiver Ch:S → C:R responses, they also apply to caregiver Ch:R → C:R responses. For instance, a caregiver might elicit a report (*What you making?*), and the child might respond with a report (*Pancakes.*). The caregiver might then respond by confirming the elicited report, just as she confirms a spontaneous report by the child. The same caregiver subcategory score, denoting confirmation of a report, is applied to the caregiver's Ch:R → C:R response as is applied to her Ch:S → C:R response.

In addition, the subcategory scores of Categories I through VI occasionally apply to spontaneous speech acts of the caregiver. For instance, although the majority of ego-enhancing responses (*That's very good.*) occur in the caregiver's responsive speech, a considerable proportion occur in her spontaneous speech. In view of these variations, the percentage of responsive and spontaneous speech acts that were classified in each category of mother speech will be reported in the next chapter. For the present, it is sufficient to note that the vast majority (95.1%) of mother speech acts in Categories I–VI were responsive. On this basis, we will hereafter refer to these categories as "predominately responsive."

DERIVING FIS-C CATEGORIES VII–X

FIS-C Categories VII–X represent our attempt to classify the caregiver's spontaneous speech acts. Here it was rarely necessary to develop new vocabulary. The English language has many verbs denoting how we talk **to** others (Searle, 1969). We had only to see which of these verbs apply in caregiver talk to young children. The categories were empirically derived from samples of the caregiver's spontaneous speech. Four of these categories, those designated VII–X, reached adequate frequency in our sample of mother talk; a fifth such category with low frequency is described in Appendix A.

Subcategory distinctions were suggested by the empirical data in conjunction with the relevant caregiver and linguistic literature. For example, the frequently noted distinction between positive and negative commands (e.g., White & Watts, 1973) is reflected in the control talk subcategories DO's versus DON'TS. Similarly, the often discussed distinction between modeling new knowledge and eliciting practice of already acquired knowledge (e.g., Bartlett, 1972) is reflected in the teaching talk subcategories PRESENTS KNOWLEDGE versus ELICITS KNOWLEDGE. There was one exception to this procedure for selecting subcategories. The subcategory REFUSALS was classified in the control talk category, although it appears mainly in the caregiver's responsive speech (usually in response to desire requests). This is because REFUSALS, like DON'TS, function to control and restrict the child.

In addition to these procedures, the set of child FIS-P categories was included in the list of FIS-C categories for the caregiver's spontaneous speech because of the possibility that caregivers and young children might use speech to communicate similar intentions. Only one of these FIS-P categories, REPORTS ON SELF, OTHERS, THINGS (FIS-C Category X; FIS-P Category VIII) reached the 1% frequency criteria in our mother data. This suggests that mothers and toddlers use speech in very different ways. For examples of those FIS-P categories that occur rarely in caregiver speech, see Appendix A.

Although FIS-C Categories VII–X were derived primarily from samples of spontaneous caregiver talk, they occasionally apply to the caregiver's responsive speech. Apart from REFUSALS, which are virtually all responsive, other subcategories of Categories VII–X may also occur responsively. For instance, the caregiver might say *don't* in response to a child's report of some forbidden action, or she might teach in response to a desire request. The percentage of spontaneous and responsive speech acts classified in each of these FIS-C categories in the present sample of mother talk is reported in Chapter 5. Except for REFUSALS, the vast majority (77.9%) of mother speech acts in FIS-C Categories VII–X were spontaneous. Consequently, we shall refer to these categories as "predominately spontaneous."

The following list describes the six predominately responsive FIS-C categories (I–VI) and the four predominately spontaneous categories (VII–X) of adequate frequency, together with their subcategories and subscores. Note that speech acts are classified in whichever category best describes their function, whether the form is declarative, interrogative, or imperative. For example, the interrogative *Should we clean that up?* and the imperative *Clean that up!* are both scored CONTROLS. Similarly, the declarative *Looks like you made a house* and the interrogative *Did you make a house?* are both scored REPORTS ON CHILD.

Predominately Responsive Categories

CATEGORY I: RESPONDS TO CHILD EXPRESSIVE COMMUNICATION+

A child simply abreacts an emotion, a positive expression of joy (*Goodie!*), a negative expression of distress (*Boo-hoo* [cries].), or a mixed emotion (*Yikes!*). The following subcategories of caregiver responses were noted:

EXPLICATES EXPRESSIVE. The caregiver explicates the child's expressive communication at the same time that she asks the child if her interpretation is correct. As Brown (1973; 1977) points out, these kinds of speech acts serve as communication checks—the caregiver is asking, " 'Is this what you mean by what you just said?' [1977, p. 13]." Accordingly, explications almost always take the interrogative form. They occur in response to toddler's nonverbal communications (Child: [cries]. Caregiver: *You bumped your head?*) as well as to their verbal communications. As a response to verbal communications, the explication may be an exact repetition of the child's word(s) (Child: *Thumb.*   Caregiver: *Thumb?*), an altered repetition or an expansion (Child: *Hit nose.* Caregiver: *You hit your nose?*), or a new string of words (Child: *Ouch!* Caregiver: *You hurt yourself?*).

CONFIRMS EXPRESSIVE. The caregiver confirms the truth value of the expressive communication. Confirmations usually follow the expressions of positive rather than negative feelings (*It is delicious! Yummy!*).

ACCOMMODATES: COMFORTS DISTRESS[+]. The caregiver attempts to alleviate negative feelings that have been expressed. These attempts are usually accompanied by comforting actions (*I'll kiss it* [kisses]. *Mommy get a Band-Aid* [gets it].).

SEEKS FURTHER ELABORATION OF EXPRESSIVE. The caregiver asks for elaboration or expansion of the child's expressive communication. These requests are usually in interrogative form (*Where does it hurt? Which one?* [asks about injured finger]).

Note that these kinds of subcategory distinctions, explications, confirmations, accommodations, and requests for further elaboration, appear in a number of the other predominately responsive Categories II–VI. Typical examples will be presented for each of these categories.

CATEGORY II: RESPONDS TO CHILD DESIRE COMMUNICATION[+]

The child requests goods or services (*More cookie. Fix it.*). Caregiver responsive subcategories include:

EXPLICATES DESIRE[+]. (*More cookie? Another one? You want some more?*)

DISINHIBITS DESIRE. The caregiver encourages the child when the child seems to be asking for permission or support to pursue some desire (*Go ahead. You can have some.*).

ACCOMMODATES: FULFILLS DESIRE[+]. The caregiver fulfills the desire with words usually accompanied by actions to bring the desired object to the child, or to provide the desired service (*Here. I'll get it. Yeah, some more bananas* [gives].).

SEEKS FURTHER ELABORATION OF DESIRE. (*The white one or the green one? Which one?*)

ASSISTS CHILD TO FULFILL OWN DESIRE[+]. The caregiver points out whereby or how the child can self-fulfill the desire (*It's over there. Open the door.*).

CATEGORY III: RESPONDS TO CHILD EGO-ENHANCING COMMUNICATION+

The child boasts, displaying prowess (*I did it!*), or uneasily admits defeat (*That's hard.*). Caregiver responsive subcategories include:

EXPLICATES EGO-ENHANCING COMMUNICATION. (*You did it? A big house?*)

EGO-BOOSTS[+]. The caregiver affirms the child's boast or display of prowess (*That's terrific! What a big boy!*).

PROVIDES EXCUSE FOR EGO BLOW. The caregiver offers a reassuring reason for the child's failure (*That was too heavy. That's too hard.*).

CATEGORY IV: RESPONDS TO CHILD COLLABORATIVE COMMUNICATION+

The child initiates one of four kinds of collaboration, and the caregiver responds to each in the following subcategories:

ENGAGES IN COLLABORATIVE DISCOURSE. The caregiver participates in role-differentiated child project, game, or discussion initiated by child (Child: *I'll play the drum.*   Caregiver: *I'll play the xylophone.*).

ENGAGES IN COLLABORATIVE DRAMATIC PLAY[+]. The child play-acts and communicates in a fantasy role, usually altering intonation; the caregiver responds in role usually altering intonation of her voice also. All speech acts produced while enacting fantasy roles are scored in this subcategory, no matter what their function within the fantasy itself (e.g., greeting, command) (Child [on toy phone]: *Hello, Mommy.*   Caregiver: *Hello, honey, this is Mommy* [both using high pitch].).

ENGAGES IN COLLABORATIVE CHANTING. The child communication is followed by caregiver repetition or complementary communication in a playful sing–song tone (Child: *Away we go.*   Caregiver: *Away we go.*   or Child: *Up.*   Caregiver: *Down.*).

RESPONDS GRATEFULLY TO COLLABORATIVE GIVING. The child gives something to the caregiver and the latter expresses gratitude (*For me? Thank you.*).

EXPLICATES COLLABORATIVE. In addition to these four responses, the caregiver may explicate the child's collaborative communications. (*This hand?* [playing doctor] *Over here?*).

CATEGORY V: RESPONDS TO CHILD REPORT+

The child reports on self, describing actions, states, attributes, possessions, productions, fantasies, etc. (*I helping.*); on others (*Baby cry.*); or things (*Police car.*). Caregiver responsive subcategories include:

EXPLICATES REPORT+. (*Are you helping me? You put it on your finger?*)

CONFIRMS REPORT+. Caregiver confirms truth value of report (*Yes, the truck fell down. Right.*).

ACCOMMODATES: GIVES REPORT. The child seeks information, usually about the location of a person or the possessor of an object, and the caregiver supplies the information requested (Child: *Where Daddy?* Caregiver: *Daddy bye-bye.* or Child: *That Susy?* Caregiver: *Yes, it's your sister's.*).

SEEKS FURTHER ELABORATION OF REPORT. (*What are you going to write? Which book are you reading?*)

CORRECTS REPORT. The caregiver negates the truth value of the report, corrects misinformation (Child: *Gramma coming.* Caregiver: *No, Gramma sick.* or Child: *That's Daddy's?* Caregiver: *No, it's Godfrey's.*).

CATEGORY VI: RESPONDS TO CHILD LEARNING COMMUNICATION+

The child seeks to acquire new words, skills, or knowledge, usually by asking a question (*What's this?*); or the child practices recently acquired words, skill, or knowledge (*Cement truck, Mommy.*). Asking about words and practicing words or word-labeling are a common form of learning communication among toddlers. Caregiver responsive subcategories include:

EXPLICATES LEARNING. (*That? A cement truck?*)

CONFIRMS LEARNING+. The caregiver confirms accuracy of recently acquired learning (*Yes, it's a cement truck. Good.*).

ACCOMMODATES: SUPPLIES LEARNING[+]. The caregiver supplies new learning (*It's green. That's sherbet.*).

CORRECTS LEARNING[+]. The caregiver corrects an inaccuracy or error in learning (*No, it's a giraffe. It gotta go on that foot.*).

COMBINED SUBCATEGORY SCORES

We have noted that several types of subcategories appear in a number of the predominately responsive categories. The list includes explicates, confirms, accommodates, seeks further elaboration, and corrects. These five ways of responding to the child's communications suggested the following combined subcategory scores:

ALL EXPLICATIONS[+] including those in Categories I–VI.
ALL CONFIRMATIONS[+] including those in Categories I, V, and VI.
ALL ACCOMMODATIONS[+] including those in Categories I, II, and VI.
ALL REQUESTS FOR FURTHER ELABORATION including those in Categories I, II, and V.
ALL CORRECTIONS[+] including those in Categories V and VI.

Predominately Spontaneous Categories

CATEGORY VII: CONTROLS, RESTRICTS—COMMANDS[+]

The data indicated three major kinds of control talk: (*a*) positive commands or suggestions, called DO'S; (*b*) prohibitions or admonitions, called DON'TS; and (*c*) refusals of the child's demands for accommodations, called REFUSALS. All three kinds of control talk often occur in masked or neutralized form. For example, they may bear a surface resemblance to desire requests (*I'd like some quiet.*) or reports (*It's getting messy.*). Sometimes only the justification or explanation of the restriction appears (*You'll hurt yourself. Look at your pants* [getting dirty].). In all cases, these speech acts are scored on the basis of their restricting and controlling function, disregarding their form. The three major kinds of control talk form the basis of the following three subcategories:

DO'S[+]. This subcategory covers positive suggestions and directions for play activities or actions of the child; orders to perform conventional actions (e.g., toileting, putting toys away, washing hands); and directions in the course of helping the caregiver with chores (*How about this book? Wanna clean up? Now, turn that on.*).

DON'TS[+]. The Caregiver intervenes to prohibit or prevent an action of the child (*That's a no-no. That's dangerous, remember? What you doing?* [harsh intonation]).

REFUSALS[+]. As noted earlier REFUSALS generally occur in conjunction with a desire request of the child. However, they can also occur in response to other child communications, such as expressive or learning communications (*That doesn't hurt* [in response to a cry]. *I'm too busy* [in response to a learning question]. *You just had one* [in response to a desire request].).

In addition to these three subcategory scores, there are subscores showing the proportion of DO'S, DON'TS, and REFUSALS that are modified in some way. There is an extensive literature on social-class difference in maternal control strategies (e.g., Bernstein, 1970; Hess, 1969), but no data on how or if these differences are reflected in everyday mother talk to toddlers. These subscores were designed to provide these data. It should be noted that many restrictions and commands are unmodified (*No! Stop it! Watch out! Be careful! Hold it!*). Others are modified as follows:

Modified by appealing to norms:

(*a*) PHYSICAL NORMS, appeals to principles of physics (*It's going to fall* [to prevent child from dropping an object].)

(*b*) SOCIAL NORMS[+], appeals to social conventions (*Look at your pants* [dirty].)

(*c*) SELF-NORMS[+], appeals to biological norms (*No, you'll bump your head.*)

Modified by providing

(*d*) SUBSTITUTE GRATIFICATION[+], substitutes, alternatives, distractions, or fantasy channelization (*Where's your radio?* [when child tinkers with stereo])

(*e*) POSTPONED GRATIFICATION (*When your brother comes home.*)

(*f*) MOMENTARY POSTPONEMENT (*Wait a minute. Just a second.*)

(*g*) PARTIAL GRATIFICATION (*That's too much* [takes some away].)

Modified by

(*h*) APPEALS TO PRIDE (*Don't be a baby.*)

(*i*) APPEALS TO REWARDS (*We'll get some ice-cream in the park.*)

(*j*) APPEALS TO THREATS OR PUNISHMENT (*No* [threatening gesture].)

(*k*) APPEALS TO PLAYFUL THREATS, teasing (*The devil's gonna get you.*)

Modified by

(*l*) ACKNOWLEDGING SUBMISSION to the command (*That's good. Thank you.*)

Modified, for REFUSALS, by

(*m*) SUGGESTING ANOTHER PERSON who may not refuse (*Ask Daddy.*)

(*n*) URGING CHILD TO GRATIFY HIMSELF (*You get it.*)

Modified by appealing to

(o) ANY NORMATIVE EXPLANATION[+] including (a), (b), or (c).

Finally, one additional subscore (p)[+] was added based on the appended score JUSTIFYING EXPLANATIONS (see list on page 46) when it was found that almost all such explanations occurred in relation to the control talk in this category. The subscore JUSTIFYING EXPLANATIONS consists mainly of the kinds of normative explanations covered by subscore (o) mentioned earlier. Hess (1969; Olim, Hess, & Shipman, 1967) calls these kinds of explanations "cognitive–rational." There is, however, another kind of explanation that Hess calls "personal–subjective," appealing to the personal feelings or preferences of the speaker rather than to societal rules or conventions. For example, the mother might refuse the child because she is too tired, or because she wants to finish her coffee. Both kinds of explanations are scored JUSTIFYING EXPLANATIONS.

CATEGORY VIII: TEACHES, PROVIDES KNOWLEDGE+

The data indicated that caregivers impart knowledge or teach in three main ways, by presenting new information (*That's an apricot.*), by eliciting previously learned material from the child (*What do you call that?*), and by eliciting imitations of their own words or phrases (*Say, "sock."*). These three ways of teaching formed the basis for three subcategories. There was a fourth subcategory concerned with teaching words, a frequent occurrence in talk to toddlers.

PRESENTS KNOWLEDGE[+]. (*The triangle goes in there. See the tongue?*)

ELICITS KNOWLEDGE[+]. These speech acts are usually interrogatives (*What color is this? What did the baby bear say? Make a circle.*).

ELICITS IMITATIONS OF OWN WORDS. (*Say "mug." Say "shoe."*)

WORD TEACHING[+]. This subcategory combines word teaching in the subcategory PRESENTS KNOWLEDGE with word teaching in the subcategory ELICITS IMITATIONS OF OWN WORDS. Word teaching in the subcategory ELICITS KNOWLEDGE was not included because it was often difficult to determine whether the caregiver was eliciting words or testing the child's memory or understanding of a concept as in *What color is that?*.

In addition to these subcategory scores, there are subscores denoting the proportion of teaching in a variety of content areas as follows:

(a) PHYSICAL NORMS[+] (*I blow it to cool it.*)
(b) SOCIAL NORMS (*We need our smock when we paint* [putting smock on].)
(c) SELF-NORMS (*We wash our hands when we eat* [washing child's hands].)

(d) PHYSICAL WORLD[+] (*See the snowflakes.*)

(e) SOCIAL WORLD[+] (*The mailman brings us letters.*)

(f) FINE MOTOR (*The beads go this way.*)

(g) GROSS MOTOR (*This way* [demonstrates hopping].)

(h) LETTERS AND NUMBERS[+] (*Make an A. One, two, three, four, five little piggies.*)

(i) ANY NORMATIVE EXPLANATION[+] including (a), (b), or (c).

Note that there are normative explanations for both the control talk of Category VII and the teaching talk of Category VIII. When a normative explanation is used in control talk, it justifies the restriction or command. In teaching, however, the normative explanation is simply the content of what is being taught, some rule, convention, or principle.

CATEGORY IX: REPORTS ON CHILD[+]

The caregiver describes the child's actions, states, attributes, possessions, products, etc. Subcategories are based on whether the caregiver uses an interrogative format eliciting a report from the child, or a declarative format presenting a description of the child. Subcategories are also based on whether the report refers to a specific child action, state, attribute, etc. (*What are you painting?*), or refers to the child in general terms (*What you doing?*). There are four subcategories:

PRESENTS REPORT-SPECIFIC[+]. (*Oh, you found Teddy. You look happy today.*)

PRESENTS REPORT-GENERAL. (*There you are. Here's Gemeer.*)

ELICITS REPORT-SPECIFIC[+]. In eliciting a report from the child, the caregiver may ask a "yes–no question" that provides a full description of the child and elicits only a *yes* or *No* response from the child (*You making a necklace? Did you comb your hair?*). Alternatively, she may ask a "wh-question" that elicits the appropriate description from the child (*What's that you're making? What did you do to your hair?*).

ELICITS REPORT-GENERAL. (*Where are you? What's Jimmy doing?*)

CATEGORY X: REPORTS ON SELF, OTHERS, THINGS

The caregiver reports on actions, states, attributes, possessions, etc. of herself; of others excluding the child being addressed; and of inanimate objects. Categories are distinguished on the basis of whether the report is on the self, others, or things.

REPORTS ON SELF[+]. (*I'm freezing. Gonna close the window.*)

REPORTS ON OTHERS. (*That baby is always crying* [neighbor]. *Benjy's coming home soon.*)

REPORTS ON THINGS [+]. (*It's raining. What's that funny noise?* [outdoors])

Routine Scores

Routine scores cover the following speech acts:

WHAT?[+] This score occurs when the caregiver is indicating that she cannot hear what the child is saying (*What did you say? Huh? What?*), or that she does not know what the child means (*What do you mean? Huh? What?*). Although the caregiver usually uses the word *what* or *huh*, the score is also applied to statements that are functional equivalents (*Say it again. I can't understand you.*).

GOD BLESS YOU.
NEVER MIND.
YOU'RE WELCOME.
HI OR OTHER GREETINGS. (*Hello. Hiya.*)

The list of routines also covers the following scores, which occur rarely and that do not seem to fit into any of the main categories for the communication–functions of speech:

OFFERS FOOD AT UNSCHEDULED TIME. This speech act is rare in our data only because we conducted observations after breakfast in the home setting and during free play in the preschool setting. When the child asks for food at an unscheduled time and the caregiver provides it, her response is scored ACCOMMODATES: FULFILLS DESIRE rather than this routine score. The latter applies only to spontaneous offers of food. The score covers offers of drink, medicine, and vitamins (*Want a cookie? How about some juice? Come get your vitamins.*).

I DON'T KNOW. This speech act is rare because caregivers usually know the answers to the questions of young children.

ACQUIESCES TO OR EXPLICATES CHILD NEGATION. The child negates either a command of the caregiver (*No. No wipe.*) or a teaching statement (*No, it's blue.*). The caregiver may acquiesce to the negation (*Oh? Okay, it's blue.*) or explicate the child's negation (*You don't feel like? No?*). These responses are rare because the caregiver generally does not verbally acquiesce to the young child's negation. Instead, she often makes repeated efforts to convince the child; all such repetitions are scored in the same category as the speech act she is repeating. Alternatively, the caregiver often drops the matter altogether, without verbalizing either her objection or acquiescence.

Appended Scores for Formal Discourse Features

The list of appended scores consists mainly of a set of formal features characteristic of baby talk, talk to the language-learning toddler. More than 100 such features have been identified (Brown, 1977) including distinctive patterns of syntax, prosody, and discourse (Snow & Ferguson, 1977). Discourse features are included in the FIS-C scoring scheme because they represent another facet of the communication process, the structure of communication. FIS-C appended scores for the discourse features of baby talk include the following:

SELF-REPETITIONS+

The caregiver repeats her preceding utterance so that both utterances serve the same communication function (i.e., the FIS-C category is the same). She may repeat the preceding utterance in its entirety, repeat a main word or phrase or add new words. Repetitions are scored only when they immediately follow the caregiver utterance being repeated. The list of these repetitions consists of an all-inclusive score, SELF-REPETITIONS, plus the following:

EXACT SELF-REPETITIONS+
 EXACT COMPLETE+ (*Hot.* [followed by] *Hot.*)
 EXACT PARTIAL+ (*That one is blue.* [followed by] *Blue.*)
 ALTERED SELF-REPETITIONS+ (*Stop that!* [followed by] *Didn't I say stop?*)

REPETITIONS-OF-CHILD+3

The caregiver repeats the preceding utterance of the child either in its entirety or she repeats a main word or phrase. New words may be added. Repetitions are scored only when they immediately follow the child utterance being repeated. The list of these repetitions consists of an all-inclusive score, REPETITIONS-OF-CHILD, plus the following:

EXACT REPETITIONS-OF-CHILD+
 EXACT COMPLETE+ (Child: *Cup.* Caregiver: *Cup?*)

---

[3]For a discussion of why we use the term "repetitions-of-child" rather the simpler term "imitations," see Appendix A.

EXACT PARTIAL (Child: *Gimme juice.*   Caregiver: *Juice?*)
ALTERED REPETITIONS-OF-CHILD[+]

EXPANSIONS[+] The caregiver adds word(s) or morphemes that are missing from the toddler's grammatically incomplete utterance while, at the same time, preserving the meaning of the child's communication. Brown (1973) suggests that expansions serve either as explications—he calls them "communication checks" (p. 105)—or confirmations. The present findings bear this out; 48.7% of maternal expansions were found to be explications and 51.3% confirmations.[4] Brown seems to limit the use of the term "expansion" to the case where the child voices a two-word utterance. Since we found that caregivers often explicate or confirm their toddler's one-word utterances making them grammatically more complete, we scored EXPANSIONS for responses to the latter as well (Child: *Ball.*   Caregiver: *You want your ball?*   or Child: *No fall.*   Caregiver: *You didn't fall?*).

OTHER ALTERED[+] This score covers all altered child-repetitions except for expansions. For instance the caregiver may alter the child's meaning by correcting, accommodating, refusing, *etc.;* she may add to a grammatically complete child utterance; she may expand the utterance and add new meaning; or she may repeat part of the child's utterance and insert the word "what" in place of part of an utterance that she cannot hear.

QUESTIONS[+]

The appended score QUESTIONS is applied to all interrogatives disregarding their communication function. That is, interrogatives can occur in any FIS-C category.

In addition to these appended scores covering discourse features characteristic of baby talk, we also scored justifying explanations, a feature of discourse that has been intensively studied in sociolinguistic research inspired by the theories of Bernstein (1970; Hess, 1969; Olim, Hess, & Shipman, 1967).

JUSTIFYING EXPLANATIONS[+]

The appended score JUSTIFYING EXPLANATIONS covers explanations, justifications, rationalizations, attempts at verbal persuasion, with the

---

[4]Note that not all expansions are explications and not all explications are expansions. Explications are far more common than expansions since explications include delayed repetitions of the child, altered repetitions that are not expansions, exact repetitions, responses to verbal communications that entail no repetition of the child's utterance, and responses to nonverbal communications.

word "because" explicit or implicit (*'cause it might break. I'm too tired.*).
Since these justifications occur mainly in conjunction with control talk,
we introduced the subscore denoting the percentage of DO's, DON'TS,
and REFUSALS qualified in this way (Subscore *p*, Category VII). In addition, some justifications occur in conjunction with categories other than
CONTROLS. For example, in seeking to alleviate the child's distress over a
cut finger, the caregiver might explain that the cold water will hurt, but
that she needs to wash the cut to keep the germs away. The appended
score JUSTIFYING EXPLANATIONS registers all occurrences no matter what
the category.

Often the speech act contains only the justification with the category
score implicit For example, *It's dirty* rather than *Don't touch it because it's
dirty*, or *Tummy ache* rather than *No more cookies because you'll get a tummy
ache if you eat too much*. In these cases the appropriate category score is
inferred from intonation or context.

Assigning and Calculating FIS-C Scores

TOTAL-TALK SCORES

Each caregiver speech act and each child communication is classified
as spontaneous or responsive in order to derive the total-talk scores.
These scores are expressed in terms of raw frequency.

COMMUNICATION-FUNCTION CATEGORY SCORES,
SUBCATEGORIES, AND SUBSCORES

Category Scores and Subcategories.   Except for the set of speech acts
classified as routines, each speech act is assigned a category score and a
subcategory. Both category scores and subcategories are expressed as a
percentage of total talk.

Occasionally, two category scores seem to apply to a single speech act,
one reflecting its primary function and the other, a secondary function.
We allow for double scoring wherever it seems indicated. In this study,
only 3.6% of maternal speech acts were assigned secondary scores. The
only secondary score to exceed the 1% frequency criteria was the category TEACHES; it accounts for two-thirds of the secondary scores. A
secondary score of TEACHES is assigned when the caregiver interpolates
some teaching into a speech act whose primary function is in another
category. For example, in confirming a child's report on a passing bus
(*Look at the bus.*), the caregiver might interpolate a lesson (*Yes, it's a
double-decker bus.*) In such a case the primary score would be CONFIRMS
REPORT, the secondary score PRESENTS KNOWLEDGE.

Since TEACHES was the only secondary score that occurred often enough in our speech sample to warrant analysis, all percent scores for categories and subcategories were calculated on the basis of the primary function of the speech act. For the teaching category, two additional percent scores were derived, one expressing the percentage of total-talk when teaching is the secondary function, and the other expressing the percentage of total-talk when teaching is either the primary or secondary function.

Subscores. A subscore is assigned to a speech act in the control category whenever indicated. We found that in talk to toddlers most mother speech acts in the control category (77%) do not require a subscore. Often the mother repeats or reformulates her command a number of times, and only a minority of these reformulations contain an explanation or some other qualification that would require a subscore. Subscores in the control category are calculated as a percentage of speech acts in each subcategory—DO'S, DON'TS, or REFUSALS.

A subscore is assigned to all speech acts in the teaching category, since the content distinctions covered by these subscores are designed to cover the variety of subject matter taught to young children (e.g., physical world, letters or numbers, fine motor tasks). Subscores in the teaching category are calculated as a percentage of speech acts in the category.

ROUTINE SCORES

Each routine is assigned a routine score. These scores are expressed as a percentage of total talk.

APPENDED SCORES FOR FORMAL DISCOURSE FEATURES

Appended scores are assigned only to category scores, not to routines. They are expressed as a percentage of the total talk in all categories. Any number of appended scores can be assigned to a speech act in any one category.

Chapter 5
Reliability Assessment and Methods of Data Analysis

Having described the scoring procedures of the FIS-C, we can now consider its reliability and the procedures employed for analyzing the data.

Reliability Assessment

The FIS-C scores cover a variety of personal and social motives (e.g., confirming, refusing, commanding, teaching). Motives are notoriously difficult to measure, since scoring is partially dependent on subjective judgment which endangers reliability. Nevertheless, psychologists have not avoided measuring motives in areas other than speech. Indeed, they have generally been willing to settle for reliability in the 70–80% range of agreement in this domain of measurement (see White, 1972). In the present study, it was important to maximize reliability because a black recorder–scorer was to observe all the black mother–toddler dyads and a white recorder–scorer would observe all the white dyads. To augment reliability, we undertook a preliminary study for the purpose of identifying scorer discrepancies, and also to see if these discrepancies were associated with differences of race between scorer and mother.

Preliminary Reliability Study

The preliminary sample consisted of four white and four black advantaged mother–toddler dyads from the Barnard College Toddler Center. Data on each dyad were collected for 24 3-minute observation intervals in the everyday setting of the home. Each protocol was scored by both our black and white scorers. The data were collected by other observers.

The results showed no significant relationship between scorer discrepancies and race differences between scorer and mother, that is, black and white scorers applied the scores in similar fashion whether mothers were black or white. A number of scores, however, did show significant discrepancies between scorers, independent of the mother's race. It was these discrepancies that suggested refinements and revisions in the scoring scheme: Some new scores were introduced; some were omitted; and others were redefined. These discrepancies also formed the basis for the set of supplementary scoring instructions to be found in Appendix A. Finally, to decrease the difficulty and to increase the reliability of scoring, the set of scores that could be identified solely on the basis of formal features was assigned to a scorer aide. This set includes the appended scores for self-repetitions and repetitions of the child, as well as all questions with grammatical markers.

Final Reliability Study

After this period of preliminary testing and revision, a final reliability assessment was undertaken. Agreement between recorder–scorers was assessed, as well as the consistency of mother speech on two successive mornings.

RECORDER–SCORER RELIABILITY

To assess recorder–scorer agreement, both observers collected data simultaneously in the everyday home setting. Data were collected for six 3-minute intervals from one black advantaged mother with a 22-month-old girl and from one white advantaged mother with a 33-month-old boy. Reliabilities were calculated by deriving the mean percentage of agreement for scores based on manual recording, and those based on manual recording plus audiotaping. There were over 200 speech acts in the sample with either system of recording.

Recorder reliability for speech acts plus context was found to be 91.0%. Scorer reliability was 84.8% for total-talk scores; 80.0% for category scores, 91.0% for subcategories (given category agreement), 86.3% for subscores, 71.5% for routine scores, and 85.3% for appended scores.

These reliabilities were higher than those attained in our previous study of teachers (Schachter *et al.*, 1976), indicating that our efforts to increase recorder–scorer agreement had succeeded.

CONSISTENCY OF MOTHER SPEECH

Consistency of mother speech was evaluated using all the data for the 30 mothers in the present study, 24 3-minute observations on each of two mornings. Correlations for consistency between the two mornings were calculated for all major FIS-C scores: total-talk scores, category scores, and subcategories. The Spearman–Brown formula was applied because the correlations were based on only 24 observation intervals rather than the 48 used in the study itself.

The mean intercorrelations were .91 for total-talk scores, .67 for category scores and .64 for subcategories. The findings are similar to those of our previous study of teachers. It is interesting to find that the verbal environment both at home and school is substantially consistent from day to day. This suggests that if we can have an impact on the child's environment, it will be felt day in and day out. The consistency in mother speech was also important for the design of our study. Had there been a low day-to-day correlation, we would have had to analyze the results for each day separately. As it turned out, the correlation was high enough to justify combining the data of both days, thereby providing a larger and more reliable picture of the mother's everyday speech.

Methods of Data Analysis

Analyses of FIS-C Scores

The basic statistical procedure employed in analyzing the data was two-way analysis of covariance, with socioeducational group and sex as the main factors and age-of-toddler as the covariate. Although the toddler groups were matched in age (see Table 2.3), our previous study comparing teacher talk to toddlers versus 3- and 4-year-olds (Schachter *et al.*, 1976) suggested that the age of the child might affect the mother's speech. It seemed advisable to partial out the variance due to the age of the toddler when comparing group differences in mother speech. Because the groups were matched for age-of-toddler, means adjusted for age were the same as unadjusted means, so that actual means will be reported.

The basic statistical procedure was modified in the case of appended scores for SELF-REPETITIONS and REPETITIONS-OF-CHILD because research on baby talk has demonstrated a significant correlation between these formal features of mother speech and the language level of the child (Cross, 1977; Harkness, 1977; Newport 1976). For these scores, we used mean length of toddler utterance (MLU) as the covariate rather than age-of-toddler. Mean length of utterance is widely applied as a measure of language maturity among toddlers (Brown, 1973). It may be noted that it is not possible to covary both MLU and age-of-toddler simultaneously, because the two are significantly correlated; using both as covariates in the same analysis would cancel out the effect of each. The correlation between MLU and age-of-toddler in the present total sample was .60; in the advantaged sample it was .66. Both correlations are significant.

We considered using the child's MLU as the covariate in analyzing the results for all scores, not just the mother's repetition scores. However, we found that MLU correlated with the main variable under study, socioeducational status. Advantaged toddlers are more advanced in MLU than disadvantaged toddlers, just as we found them to be more advanced in their mental age (see Table 2.3). Mental age correlated .56 with MLU in the total sample of toddlers, .52 in the advantaged sample. Both correlations are significant.

Since it violates the assumptions of analysis of covariance to apply the procedure when covariate and main variable are correlated, we used

TABLE 5.1

Percentage of Responsive and Spontaneous Mother Speech Acts in Each FIS-C Category

	Speech acts	
FIS-C Category scores	Responsive	Spontaneous
Predominately responsive categories		
RESPONDS TO CH[a]. EXPRESSIVE	96.0	4.0
RESPONDS TO CH DESIRE	97.8	2.2
RESPONDS TO CH EGO-ENHANCING	56.2	43.8
RESPONDS TO CH COLLABORATIVE	99.6	.4
RESPONDS TO CH REPORT	99.6	.4
RESPONDS TO CH LEARNING	92.3	7.7.
Predominately spontaneous categories		
CONTROLS, RESTICTS–COMMANDS	40.7	59.3[b]
TEACHES, PROVIDES KNOWLEDGE	32.1	67.9
REPORTS ON CH	7.6	92.4
REPORTS ON SELF, OTHERS, THINGS	8.3	91.7

[a] CH denotes CHILD.

[b] 76.4% excluding REFUSALS.

MLU as a covariate only where previous research indicated that it would be advisable (i.e., for the repetition scores). Even for the repetition scores, we reanalyzed the data using age-of-toddler as the covariate to see if the differences between socioeducational groups were the same as when MLU was the covariate. The results were similar, except for the child-repetition score EXPANSIONS. As Snow *et al.* (1976) have pointed out, the caregiver cannot expand the toddler's utterances when the child speaks in whole sentences; there is nothing to expand. To compare differences in EXPANSIONS, it is obviously necessary to control for toddler differences in language maturity. Since EXPANSIONS require adjustment for the MLU of the child, and since the results for the other repetition scores are similar whether MLU or toddler age is the covariate, the results for all repetition scores will be reported using MLU as the covariate.

In addition to the analyses for each of the FIS-C scores, the following two sets of supplementary analyses were carried out.

Supplementary Analyses for Predominately Responsive and Predominately Spontaneous Categories

Because speech acts scored in the predominately responsive categories were occasionally spontaneous while those scored in the predominately spontaneous categories were occasionally responsive, we examined the percentage of the mother's responsive and spontaneous speech acts in each category. Table 5.1 shows these percentages.

It can be seen that, except for RESPONDS TO CHILD EGO-ENHANCING COMMUNICATION, more than 92% of the scores in each predominately responsive category were assigned to responsive speech acts. The high incidence of spontaneous speech acts in the category RESPONDS TO CHILD EGO-ENHANCING COMMUNICATION is probably due to the low incidence of boasting among children below the age of 3. Few such ego-enhancing statements were found among toddlers both in our previous study in preschool settings (Schachter *et al.*, 1974) and in the present home sample; boasting seems to emerge at high levels around age 3. On this basis, we expected few mother responses to such boasts in mother talk to toddlers and this was indeed found to be the case. The incidence of RESPONDS TO CHILD EGO-ENHANCING COMMUNICATION in mother speech was the lowest of the 10 main categories, barely exceeding the 1% frequency criteria. Furthermore, as shown in Table 5.1, almost half of these ego-boosting speech acts were not responses to the toddler's own boasts, but were spontaneously generated by the mothers themselves. For example, with no prior boast on the part of the child, a mother might spontaneously exclaim *Boy, that was great!* or *That was so grown* while observing the child's performance.

For the predominately spontaneous categories, Table 5.1 shows that REPORTS ON CHILD and REPORTS ON SELF, OTHERS, THINGS were almost always assigned to the mother's spontaneous speech acts. On the other hand, the categories CONTROLS and TEACHES were often assigned to her responsive speech acts. The high incidence of responsive speech acts in the category CONTROLS is due mainly to the inclusion of REFUSALS in this category; 96.8% of REFUSALS are responsive. DO's and DON'TS are largely spontaneous, 79.8% and 74.5%, respectively, although they also occur in responsive speech. Regarding teaching talk, the mother sometimes interpolates a teaching speech act into a sequence of responses to the child's communication, just as she sometimes interpolates some teaching into a speech act whose primary function is not teaching. The latter interpolation is assigned a secondary score for teaching; the former is scored as a responsive speech act whose primary function is teaching. For example, the child might ask for juice, the mother might explicate the desire (*You want some juice?*), fulfill the desire (*Here you go* [gives].) and then add, *See, it's apple juice* [points to apple on label], in which case the added comment would be scored as a responsive speech act in the teaching subcategory PRESENTS KNOWLEDGE.

Since several of the categories are substantially represented in both responsive and spontaneous speech, supplementary analyses were undertaken excluding all spontaneous speech acts from the predominately responsive categories and all responsive speech acts from the predominately spontaneous categories. We wanted to assess whether the results based on excluding these speech acts would be the same as those based on all speech acts in the category.

For the predominately responsive categories (I–VI), we also examined the percentage of Ch:S → C:R and Ch:R → C:R responses of the mother. Table 5.2 shows these percentages. It can be seen that Ch:S → C:R speech acts in these categories were three to four times as common as Ch:R → C:R responses, with the exception of the category RESPONDS TO CHILD LEARNING COMMUNICATION. For the latter category, many Ch:R → C:R responses occur because toddlers often produce a word label in imitation of mothers' words or in response to a request for a label. The mother confirms or corrects this learning communication of the child in the same way that she responds to the child's spontaneous word-labeling.[1] The mother's response is scored Ch:R → C:R with a subcategory

---

[1]Moerk (1975) has recently described the same sequences in mother talk to toddlers.

TABLE 5.2
Percentage of Ch:S → C:R and Ch:R → C:R Mother Speech Acts in Predominately Responsive Categories

	Speech acts	
Predominately responsive categories	Ch:S → C:R	Ch:R → C:R
RESPONDS TO CH[a] EXPRESSIVE	78.3	17.7
RESPONDS TO CH DESIRE	81.6	16.2
RESPONDS TO CH EGO-ENHANCING	40.2	16.0
RESPONDS TO CH COLLABORATIVE	71.4	28.3
RESPONDS TO CH REPORT	77.7	21.9
RESPONDS TO CH LEARNING	50.8	41.5

[a] CH denotes CHILD.

score of CONFIRMS LEARNING or CORRECTS LEARNING, the same subcategory applied to the child's spontaneous word labeling.

Because most of the responses in the predominately responsive categories are Ch:S → C:R responses, supplementary analyses were undertaken to see if the results for these responses were the same as for all speech acts in the category.

Supplementary Analyses to Study the Effect of Child Communication Initiatives on Mother Speech

In addition to scoring the mother's speech, we also scored the child's communication initiatives in order to assess the effect of these initiatives on variations in mother talk. Each of the child's communications was identified as spontaneously initiated or responsive, and each spontaneous communication was scored using the FIS-P child category system. Following the procedure of Clarke-Stewart (1973), we then examined the rate of maternal responses per child initiative, that is, the rate of maternal FIS-C scores per child FIS-P score.

To study the impact of variations in the quantity of the child initiatives, we calculated the mean rate of maternal response per child initiative for total-talk scores, category scores, and routine scores. To study the impact of qualitative differences in the child's communication initiatives, the rate of maternal response in each of the predominately responsive FIS-C categories was examined in relation to the frequency of the child's initiatives in each of the corresponding FIS-P categories. For example, the rate of maternal responses in the category RESPONDS TO CHILD DESIRE COMMUNICATION was examined in relation to the frequency of the child's desire requests and the rate of maternal responses in the category RESPONDS TO CHILD REPORT was examined in relation to the frequency of the child's reports. Mean rates were calculated for each of the groups under study and the basic two-way analysis of covariance was applied—socioeducational group by sex, with age-of-toddler as a covariate.

In concluding our discussion of methodology, we should like to review our efforts to avoid the methodological pitfalls that have beset previous studies of the disadvantaged. Such studies, especially those applying to the black disadvantaged, have come under severe attack for a number of serious methodological limitations (Baratz & Baratz, 1970; Labov, 1970; Sroufe, 1970). First, a black advantaged sample has typically been omitted; black disadvantaged have been compared with white advantaged, the latter usually from highly educated university-based populations. In the present study, a highly educated black-advantaged sample is included. Second, in studies of black samples, observers have often been from the white community so that questions have been raised about trust and tension affecting the data. In the present study, the observer for the black dyads was black; for the white dyads, white. Third, preliminary tension-reducing measures have rarely been introduced, although they are especially needed in studies of the disadvantaged who are typically unfamiliar with research procedures. Such preliminary measures were instituted in the present study. Fourth, the laboratory setting has been typical of previous studies, although the disadvantaged are likely to find it alien and inhibiting. In the present study, we conducted observations in the familiar setting of the home. Finally, the mother's behavior has rarely been examined in relation to the child's behavior so that the extent to which the mother's behavior is independent of the child's behavior was not evaluated. In the present study, variations in mother speech are examined in relation to variations in the child's communication initiatives.

Part III

Everyday Mother Speech Acts to Toddlers: Findings

Chapter 6
Total-Talk Scores

The development of a comprehensive classification scheme for care-giver speech acts made it possible to undertake our microanalytic study of everyday mother talk in three socioeducational groups. We asked the following questions:

1. Are there group differences in total-talk scores? Do the mothers differ in how much they talk to or with their toddlers? These findings are reported here in Chapter 6.
2. Are there group differences in communication–function category scores, subcategories, and subscores? Do the mothers differ in the kinds of speech acts they address to their toddlers? These results are presented in Chapter 7.
3. What about group differences in routines scores and in appended scores? Do the mothers differ in their use of routines, or in their use of formal discourse features? These results are presented in Chapter 8.
4. What is the impact of the child's initiatives on the mother's speech? What is the relationship between FIS-C scores and FIS-P scores? Analyses bearing on this question are reported in Chapter 9.
5. What about the effects of the age and sex of the child on the mother's speech? The effects of these variables are reported in Chapter 10.

6. Finally, a chapter providing illustrative case material, Chapter 11, concludes the report of our findings.

Results of the mother's total verbal productivity cover the following scores: TOTAL TALK; TOTAL RESPONSIVE TALK, both Ch:S → C:R and Ch:R → C:R; and TOTAL SPONTANEOUS TALK. An introductory discussion of the findings for the entire sample of mothers precedes the report on differences among the three groups.

Total Talk: Entire Sample of Mothers

The 24,192 speech acts of the present sample can be expressed as a mean rate of 5.6 per minute per mother; the rate for advantaged mothers is 6.8. These results on the overall quantity of mother talk in the natural setting of the home should be of interest to both educators and researchers because they provide base rates allowing comparisons with other caregivers and/or other settings. Heretofore, such base rates have been unavailable.[1]

For the educator, the most cogent comparison is that between the mother's verbal productivity at home and the teacher's at school. Increasing demand for infant day care is generating growing concern that group settings may not afford sufficient adult verbal stimulation during the formative years (Provence, Naylor, & Patterson, 1977). In half-day nursery programs, teacher talk need not necessarily be as frequent as mother talk at home, since the classroom offers rich opportunities for both child–child and child–material interaction as well as adult–child interaction. Indeed, many middle-class parents enroll their preschool · children in half-day programs to provide peer experience. In full-day care, however, there should probably be many episodes throughout the day when teacher talk equals the quantity of mother talk at home.

At the Barnard College Toddler Center where children attend two mornings a week, and at the Columbia University Greenhouse Nursery in a half-day program for 3- and 4-year-olds, teacher talk during free play has been found to average about four speech acts per minute (Schachter et al., 1976), somewhat less than at home. Comparable data for full-day care are not yet available.

---

[1]Previous naturalistic studies in the home provide data on the rate of maternal vocalization to infants (e.g., Tulkin & Kagan, 1972) and on the number of time units (White & Watts, 1973) or behavior episodes (Schoggen & Schoggen, 1976) with maternal verbalizations, but no data on the rate of maternal speech acts. Previous research on baby talk has not been conducted in the everyday setting of the home.

For the researcher, perhaps the most timely comparison is that between the everyday home setting and the constrained setting typical of research. Stimulated by Bronfenbrenner's (1977) call for an ecologically valid developmental psychology, Belsky (1977) has demonstrated that social interaction between mother and child is much higher in the laboratory setting than in the naturalistic setting of the home. Research on baby talk shows a similar increment with respect to verbal interaction, when compared with the present findings. Even during free play in the laboratory setting, rates of about 11.4 maternal utterances per minute have been reported in the baby-talk literature (Seitz & Stewart, 1975). This is considerably higher than our findings for the everyday setting. Furthermore, when the researcher visits the home with a bag of toys and limits mother and child to the room with the toys and the tape recorder, a common practice in baby-talk research (e.g., Newport, 1976; Shatz, 1977), the mother still talks much more than in the everyday setting. For example, extrapolating[2] from Shatz (1977), we find a rate of 10.8 utterances per minute. It seems that mothers at home alone with their toddlers talk more than preschool teachers and less than mothers in constrained laboratory settings.

The findings in the categories of TOTAL RESPONSIVE TALK and TOTAL SPONTANEOUS TALK for the entire sample of mothers are no less interesting than those reported for TOTAL TALK. A large proportion of mother talk was found to be responsive to the communications of the child—more than half for the advantaged mothers, less so for disadvantaged mothers (see Figure 6.1 to be discussed in the next section). The results are consistent with research on mother-child social interaction (Schaffer, 1977; Stern, 1977). It appears that the early verbal environment, like the early social environment, is largely responsive.

Total Talk: Group Differences

Figure 6.1 shows the total frequency of mother speech acts and the total frequency of responsive and spontaneous speech for each of the three groups of mothers (i.e., black disadvantaged, black advantaged, and white advantaged) and for the advantaged groups combined. Throughout this report the findings for advantaged groups will be combined whenever there is no significant difference between them. Recall that we are mainly interested in differences shared by advantaged as against disadvantaged mothers, whatever their ethnic background, as it is these differences that should reflect their distinct advantages, their

---

[2]Extrapolation is necessary because data on verbal productivity are rarely reported in research on baby talk.

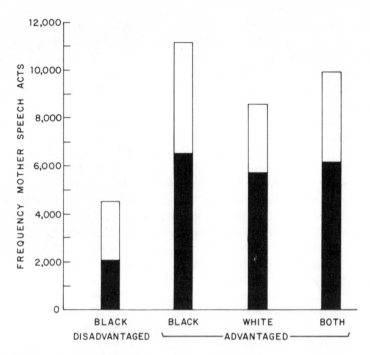

FIGURE 6.1.   *The bar graph illustrates the frequency of mother speech acts for black disadvantaged, black advantaged, and white advantaged groups.* (■) = *responsive speech;* (□) = *spontaneous speech.*

superior educational opportunities, their ready access to child development information, and their freedom from the heavy burdens of poverty.

Figure 6.1 shows a striking difference between disadvantaged and advantaged mothers in total talk, with no significant difference between the two groups of advantaged mothers. Educated mothers talk twice as much as the less educated. Based on the total frequency data of Figure 6.1, the mean number of speech acts is 985.3 for the educated, compared to 448.6 for the less educated mothers (difference significant).

Despite the wide discrepancy in TOTAL TALK, there is no significant difference among the groups in TOTAL SPONTANEOUS TALK. Only TOTAL RESPONSIVE TALK shows a significant effect of maternal education, a threefold increment for educated mothers. These differences, when viewed as proportions of total speech, show that a significantly larger percentage of the educated mothers talk is responsive as compared with that of the less educated. The actual means obtained were 63.3% for educated mothers and 46.2% for less educated mothers. On the other hand, a significantly larger percentage of the less educated mother's speech is spontaneous, a mean of 53.8% as against a mean of 36.7% for educated mothers.

When we further examined the significant increment in responsive speech of advantaged mothers to see if it held for responses to both the child's spontaneous and responsive communications, we found that it did. TOTAL Ch:S → C:R RESPONSIVE TALK and TOTAL Ch:R → C:R RESPONSIVE TALK both show a significant increment for educated mothers with no significant differences between educated groups.

What of the frequency of the child's communications to which the mother responds? For each group of children, Figure 6.2 shows the total frequency of communications, both responsive and spontaneous. Advantaged groups again show a twofold increment as compared with the disadvantaged, and again there is no significant difference between advantaged groups. The mean number of communications is 394.8 for advantaged toddlers and 193.6 for the disadvantaged (difference significant). Furthermore, the twofold increment holds for both spontaneous and responsive child communications. As may be noted in Figure 6.2, the three groups of children do not differ significantly in the proportion of their communications that are spontaneous or responsive. The mean percentage for spontaneous communications is 59.6% for advantaged groups and 62.0% for the disadvantaged, whereas comparable percentages for responsive communications are 40.4% and 38.0%.

Figures 6.1 and 6.2 together indicate that the total frequency of mother speech acts and child communications are highly correlated. For the

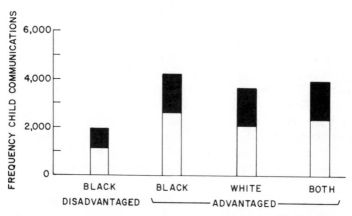

FIGURE 6.2. *The bar graph illustrates the frequency of child communications for black disadvantaged, black advantaged, and white advantaged groups. (■) = responsive communications; (□) = spontaneous communications).*

sample as a whole, the correlation is .85 with a mean rate of 2.5 maternal speech acts per child communication. There are a number of possible sources of this correlation. To the extent that the child's spontaneous initiatives evoke responses in the mother, as, for example, when the child produces a desire request and she responds to the request—scored Ch:S → C:R response—the correlation would be increased. To the extent that the mother's spontaneous initiatives elicit responses in the child, as, for example, when she elicits a report and the child responds with a report, the correlation would also be increased. To the extent that the mother responds to the responses she elicits from the child, as, for example, when she confirms a report that she herself elicits—scored Ch:R → C:R response—this would further increase the correlation. Finally, some of the correlation may be due to the child's imitations of the mother's speech; these imitations make up 8.5% of the sample of child communications, with no significant difference between the groups.[3]

Whatever the sources of this correlation, the crucial question for our purposes is whether the significant increment in total responsive speech for advantaged mothers is due merely to the tendency for advantaged toddlers to initiate more conversations, thereby evoking more responses in their mothers. Because this question concerning the effects of the child's initiatives on mother speech applies to all four sets of FIS-C scores, not just to total-talk scores, we will deal with it fully in a separate chapter (Chapter 9). At this point, we will discuss the findings for total-talk scores disregarding the input of the child.

The results clearly indicate that differences in total verbal productivity are related to maternal educational level and not to race. Black mothers with educational and economic advantages speak just as much to their toddlers as do whites with similar advantages. Indeed, Figure 6.1 shows that verbal productivity is higher for the black advantaged sample than for the white, though the increment is not statistically significant. The present findings are of special importance because, although a number of studies of the early verbal environment have shown no differences between black mothers and white mothers who are poor and uneducated (e.g., Wachs et al., 1971), there have been none comparing highly educated blacks and whites. The present data, showing that black educated mothers talk even more to their children than do comparably educated whites, should serve to combat racial stereotypes and to chal-

---

[3]Group differences in the frequency of maternal responses to the child's imitations are the same as those obtained for maternal responses to the child's other responsive communications.

lenge genetic explanations of the school problems of inner-city blacks (e.g., Jensen, 1969).

With respect to the effects of socioeducational status, the findings for total talk are consistent with previous comparisons in the natural setting of the home (Schoggen & Schoggen, 1976; Tulkin & Kagan, 1972; Wachs *et al.*, 1971), showing that advantaged mothers verbalize or vocalize significantly more often than disadvantaged mothers. Moreover, there seems to be a consensus concerning the magnitude of this difference—a twofold increment for advantaged mothers. Tulkin and Kagan report a twofold increment comparing maternal vocalizations to infants, and in a little known naturalistic study of talk in a pediatric waiting room, Greenberg and Formanek (1974) show a similar twofold increment when comparing maternal statements.

The more important finding of the present study, with implications for early intervention, is that the increment for educated mothers applies only to responsive speech; there are no significant differences among the groups with regard to the quantity of the mother's spontaneous speech. This finding would seem to undermine any theory of a generalized verbal or language deficit for lower-class mothers, as suggested by advocates of the didactic approach to early intervention. Disadvantaged mothers do not appear to be "deficient" in the quantity of their spontaneous speech; only their responsive speech is less frequent.

Rather than suggesting an overall decrement in verbal stimulation in the homes of disadvantaged children, the results point up a difference in the social or emotional aspects of communication. Educated mothers appear to adopt a responsive communication style; they talk **with** rather than **to** their children. The present microanalytic study of everyday speech acts should help to identify the kinds of communication strategies characterizing the responsive communication style of educated mothers.

Chapter 7

Communication-Function Category Scores, Subcategories, and Subscores

This chapter covers the findings obtained on the 10 main categories of caregiver talk, the 10 main kinds of speech acts, and their subcategories and subscores. Since the FIS-C represents a first attempt at a taxonomy of speech acts in everyday mother talk to young children, the findings for the sample as a whole should interest both educators and researchers. Does the mother's speech consist mainly of control talk or of teaching talk? What proportion of caregiver speech consists of responses to the child's desire requests or responses to the child's reports? An introductory discussion of the findings for the entire sample of mothers will precede the report on group differences.

Entire Sample of Mothers

Figure 7.1 shows the percentage of mother speech acts in each of the main categories of the FIS-C for the entire sample. These categories account for almost all of mother speech, 93.3%. Another 3.3% is accounted for by routines, and the remaining 3.4% of mother talk occurs in categories of inadequate frequency.

For the predominately responsive categories, it can be seen that those occurring most frequently are RESPONDS TO CHILD DESIRE COMMUNICA-

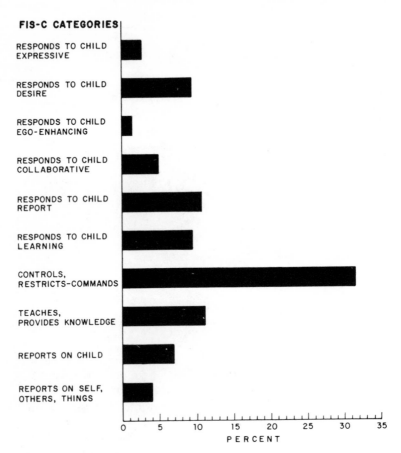

FIGURE 7.1   *The graph illustrates the percentage of mother's speech acts in each of the 10 main FIS-C categories for the entire sample.*

TION, RESPONDS TO CHILD REPORT, and RESPONDS TO CHILD LEARNING COMMUNICATION, each representing about 10% of mother speech. It is perhaps not surprising to find that the incidence of these responsive FIS-C categories in mother speech tends to mirror that of the FIS-P categories in the child's spontaneous communications to which the mother responds. Figure 7.2 shows the percentage of the child's spontaneous initiatives in each FIS-P category for the entire sample of toddlers. It can be seen that the most common FIS-P categories are DESIRE COMMUNICATION, REPORT, and LEARNING COMMUNICATION; they account for 77.8% of the child's initiatives, 32.3, 29.6, and 15.9%, respectively.

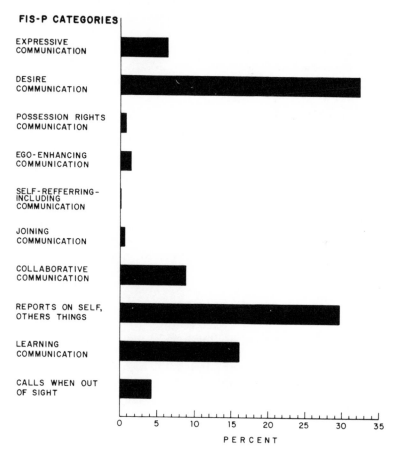

FIGURE 7.2.   *The graph shows the percentage of child's spontaneous communications in each FIS-P category for the entire sample.*

Note that the child's spontaneous learning communications occur far less frequently than do desire requests or reports, whereas the mother's responses to learning are about as frequent as her responses in the other two categories. This disparity no doubt results from the fact that mother speech acts scored in the category RESPONDS TO CHILD LEARNING COMMUNICATION often occur in response to the child's responsive communications, after she herself evokes a learning communication (mother's response scored Ch:R → C:R), whereas mother responses scored in the categories RESPONDS TO CHILD DESIRE COMMUNICATION and RESPONDS TO CHILD REPORT more often occur in reaction to the child's spontaneous initiatives (mother's responses scored Ch:S → C:R) as shown in Table 5.2.

For the predominately spontaneous categories, Figure 7.1 shows that the two occurring most frequently are CONTROLS and TEACHES, the former accounting for more mother speech than any other category, 31.6%, whereas the latter accounts for 11.2%. The mother's reports make up the remainder of her speech in the predominantly spontaneous categories, with REPORTS ON CHILD occurring twice as often as REPORTS ON SELF, OTHERS, AND THINGS.

It appears that control talk, DO'S, DON'TS, and REFUSALS, dominates the mother's speech, constituting about one-third of it. Yet it clearly does not make up the whole of it. The desire requests, reports, and learning communications that dominate the child's communications evoke a range of responses in the mother (e.g., explications, confirmations, accommodations), and these responses also account for about one-third of her speech. In addition, one-fifth of the mother's speech is concerned with teaching and learning; the categories involved are TEACHES and RESPONDS TO CHILD LEARNING COMMUNICATION. Together with control talk, the categories RESPONDS TO CHILD DESIRE COMMUNICATION, RESPONDS TO CHILD REPORT, RESPONDS TO CHILD LEARNING COMMUNICATION, and TEACHES, each representing about 10% of the speech sample, account for almost all of the everyday talk of mothers to their toddlers.

For the educator, it is of special interest to compare these findings on mother speech acts at home with those in our previous study of teacher talk in a free-play setting (Schachter et al., 1976), particularly in view of Cazden's claim (1972b) that the verbal environment in the homes of children developing well resembles that in unstructured preschool settings rather than didactic ones. Table 7.1 compares the percentage of speech acts in the 10 main FIS-C categories for our middle-class mothers of toddlers with the results for the middle-class teachers of toddlers in our previous study. It can be seen that the speech act profiles of these teachers and mothers are quite similar, despite recent revisions of the FIS-C and although observer–scorers were different in the two studies. In contrast, descriptions of teacher communication in didactic settings (e.g., Bereiter & Engelmann, 1966; Becker, Engelmann, & Thomas, 1971) suggest marked differences from mother talk at home, with almost all of the teacher's talk in the categories CONTROLS and TEACHES. Cazden's claim appears to be substantiated by the data.

For the researcher, the FIS-C could provide a comprehensive taxonomy of speech acts in early caregiver talk. Although it would be premature to claim validity for the instrument, some confidence in its

TABLE 7.1

Percentage of Teacher versus Mother Speech Acts in Each FIS-C Category

FIS-C Category scores	Caregivers[a]	
	Teacher	Mother
Predominately responsive categories		
RESPONDS TO CH[b] EXPRESSIVE	1.7	3.1
RESPONDS TO CH DESIRE	16.3	10.4
RESPONDS TO CH EGO-ENHANCING	3.2	1.6
RESPONDS TO CH COLLABORATIVE	2.4	5.7
RESPONDS TO CH REPORT	11.8	11.3
RESPONDS TO CH LEARNING	7.7	9.9
Predominately spontaneous categories		
CONTROLS, RESTRICTS–COMMANDS	24.6	27.5
TEACHES, PROVIDES KNOWLEDGE	10.2	11.1
REPORTS ON CH	11.8	7.2
REPORTS ON SELF, OTHERS, THINGS	5.3	4.3

[a] Educated mothers only compared with teachers of toddlers.
[b] CH denotes CHILD.

validity derives from the finding that it can be applied in varied settings (e.g., home and school) and to varied dialects (e.g., Black English as well as Standard English). The FIS-C could be particularly useful in research on the special baby-talk code used in addressing the language-learning toddler. While studies of baby talk have focused on form rather than communication-function, there is some initial evidence suggesting that there may be a distinctive pattern of speech acts in addressing toddlers, just as there is a distinctive pattern of formal features (Gleason, 1977; Schachter *et al.*, 1976). We will examine this issue in Chapter 10, which summarizes the findings on the effects of the toddler's age on mother speech.

Group Differences

Table 7.2 shows the mean percentage of speech acts in each of the 10 main FIS-C categories for each group of mothers, as well as the combined mean for the advantaged groups whenever there is no significant difference between them. The results can be summarized as follows:

1. There are extensive differences in mother talk between disadvantaged and advantaged groups and almost no significant differences be-

TABLE 7.2
FIS-C Category Scores:
Mean Percentage of Mother Speech Acts for Groups

	Groups			
	Disadvantaged	Advantaged		
FIS-C Category scores	Black	Black	White	Both
Predominately responsive categories				
RESPONDS TO CH[a] EXPRESSIVE	1.5	2.9	3.1	3.0
RESPONDS TO CH DESIRE	5.5	8.8	12.4*	10.6*
RESPONDS TO CH EGO-ENHANCING	.3	1.7*	1.8*	1.7*
RESPONDS TO CH COLLABORATIVE	1.5	5.5	4.4	5.0
RESPONDS TO CH REPORT	6.6	12.5*	10.0	11.3*
RESPONDS TO CH LEARNING	7.6	8.8	12.4	10.6
Predominately spontaneous categories				
CONTROLS, RESTRICTS–COMMANDS	53.4	31.1*	28.1*	29.6*
TEACHES, PROVIDES KNOWLEDGE	8.6	9.6	11.0	9.8
REPORTS ON CH	5.1	8.0*	5.1	—†
REPORTS ON SELF, OTHERS, THINGS	2.5	3.8	4.5	4.2

[a] CH denotes CHILD.
*$p < .05$ Scheffé comparing disadvantaged versus advantaged group(s).
†$p < .05$ Scheffé comparing advantaged groups.

tween black and white advantaged groups. Disadvantaged and advantaged groups differ significantly in four of the category scores, RESPONDS TO CHILD DESIRE COMMUNICATION, RESPONDS TO CHILD EGO-ENHANCING COMMUNICATION, RESPONDS TO CHILD REPORT and CONTROLS. These categories represent 53.3% of the total sample of mother speech. On the other hand, black and white advantaged groups differ significantly in only one category, REPORTS ON CHILD, representing 6.9% of mother speech, with more such reports for the black advantaged mothers. As with total-talk scores, and as we will find throughout the study, category scores show striking differences between mothers of disparate educational levels and almost no race differences.

2. There are no significant group differences for the categories concerned with teaching and learning, what we ordinarily view as the cognitive aspect of the verbal environment. Table 7.2 shows that group means for TEACHES and RESPONDS TO CHILD LEARNING COMMUNICATION are similar. Even when we combine the means for these two categories, no significant group differences are obtained.

3. Rather than showing differences in the cognitive domain, advantaged and disadvantaged mothers show extensive differences in the social and emotional aspects of the verbal environment. Significantly more of the speech of the educated mothers is concerned with responding to their child's desires, responding to their reports, and enhancing their egos, while significantly more of the speech of less educated mothers involves controlling their child.

Supplementary analyses. The means for Table 7.2 are based on all mother speech acts in each category, whether responsive or spontaneous. Supplementary analyses were undertaken, as planned (see Chapter 5), comparing means for responsive speech acts in the predominately responsive categories and for spontaneous speech acts in the predominately spontaneous categories, that is, comparing the predominant mode in each category. Table 7.3 shows these means. In addition, for the predominately responsive categories, supplementary analyses were undertaken based on Ch:S → C:R responses alone, excluding the less

TABLE 7.3
Responsive Speech in Predominately Responsive Categories and Spontaneous Speech in Predominately Spontaneous Categories:
Mean Percentage of Mother Speech Acts for Groups

	Groups			
	Disadvantaged	Advantaged		
FIS-C Category scores	Black	Black	White	Both
Predominately responsive categories				
RESPONDS TO CH[a] EEPRESSIVE	1.4	2.7	3.0	2.8
RESPONDS TO CH DESIRE	4.8	8.5	12.4*	10.4*
RESPONDS TO CH EGO-ENHANCING	.2	1.1	1.0	1.0
RESPONDS TO CH COLLABORATIVE	1.5	5.2	4.4	4.8
RESPONDS TO CH REPORT	6.6	12.5*	10.0	11.3*
RESPONDS TO CH LEARNING	6.9	8.0	11.6	9.8
Predominately spontaneous categories				
CONTROLS, RESTRICTS–COMMANDS	35.4	19.3*	13.8*	16.6*
TEACHES, PROVIDES KNOWLEDGE	7.4	6.1	6.2	6.2
REPORTS ON CH	4.8	7.2	4.8	6.0
REPORTS ON SELF, OTHERS, THINGS	2.3	3.4	4.2	3.8

[a] CH denotes CHILD.
*$p < .05$ Scheffé comparing disadvantaged versus advantaged group(s).

common Ch:R → C:R responses. Table 7.4 shows these means for Ch:S → C:R speech.

Results for Tables 7.3 and 7.4 are the same. They indicate that the findings for the predominately responsive categories are not affected by including Ch:R → C:R responses in the analysis. Results for Tables 7.2 and 7.3 are the same for all categories except RESPONDS TO CHILD EGO-ENHANCING COMMUNICATION and REPORTS ON CHILD. The former fails to show a significant increment for advantaged mothers when spontaneous ego-boosts, a large proportion of speech in this category (see Table 5.1), are excluded from the analysis. Spontaneous ego-boosts are probably required to attain significance because toddlers rarely produce the boasts that elicit responsive ego-boosts. The latter category, REPORTS ON CHILD, fails to show a significant increment for black advantaged mothers relative to the other groups when responsive reports, a small proportion of speech in this category (see Table 5.1), are excluded from the analysis. The variability in results for REPORTS ON CHILD may be due to the unreliability of the finding. As this is the only one of the 10 main categories showing significant race differences, significance may have been achieved solely on the basis of chance.

At any rate, the supplementary analyses reported in Tables 7.3 and 7.4 do not affect the three major conclusions based on Table 7.2, which covers all mother speech acts in each category. In fact, the supplementary analyses underscore the conclusion that differences in mother speech are based on educational level rather than race, as the only find-

TABLE 7.4
Ch:S → C:R Speech Acts in Predominately Responsive Categories:
Mean Percentage of Mother Speech Acts for Groups

	Groups			
	Disadvantaged	Advantaged		
Predominately responsive categories	Black	Black	White	Both
RESPONDS TO CH[a] EXPRESSIVE	1.3	2.3	2.1	2.2
RESPONDS TO CH DESIRE	4.2	7.4	8.9*	8.2*
RESPONDS TO CH EGO-ENHANCING	.2	.7	.8	.7
RESPONDS TO CH COLLABORATIVE	1.4	4.2	2.3	3.3
RESPONDS TO CH REPORT	4.4	9.9*	7.4	8.7*
RESPONDS TO CH LEARNING	4.5	4.6	6.0	5.3

[a] CH denotes CHILD.
*$p < .05$ Scheffé comparing disadvantaged versus advantaged group(s).

ing showing race differences—for Reports on Child—is found to be somewhat unstable.

Category scores provide an overview of differences in communication among mothers of diverse socioeducational backgrounds. For a micro-level description of specific communication strategies, we need to examine the findings on subcategories and subscores as well as the results of some additional analyses suggested by the data.

Predominately Responsive Subcategories

Table 7.5 shows the mean percentage of mother speech acts in each group for all predominately responsive subcategories of adequate frequency.

TABLE 7.5
Predominately Responsive Subcategories:
Mean Percentage of Mother Speech Acts for Groups

	Groups			
	Disadvantaged	Advantaged		
Predominately responsive subcategories	Black	Black	White	Both
Responds to Ch[a] Expressive				
ACCOMODATES: COMFORTS DISTRESS	.5	1.4	1.5	1.5
Responds to Ch Desire				
EXPLICATES DESIRE	2.1	3.4	3.8	3.6*
ACCOMODATES: FULFILLS DESIRE	2.0	4.3*	6.4*	—†
ASSISTS Ch FULFILL OWN DESIRE	1.0	.7	1.2	.9
Responds to Ch Ego-Enhancing				
EGO-BOOSTS	.3	1.6*	1.5*	1.6*
Responds to Ch Collaborative				
ENGAGES IN COLLABORATIVE DRAMATIC PLAY	.5	3.3	2.3	2.8
Responds to Ch Report				
EXPLICATES REPORT	1.6	3.5*	3.1	3.3*
CONFIRMS REPORT	3.1	6.6*	4.6	5.6*
Responds to Ch Learning				
CONFIRMS LEARNING	3.6	4.7	5.3	5.0
ACCOMODATES: SUPPLIES LEARNING	1.7	1.4	2.7	2.0
CORRECTS LEARNING	2.1	2.3	3.5	2.9

[a] Ch denotes Child.
*$p < .05$ Scheffé comparing disadvantaged versus advantaged group(s).
†$p < .05$ Scheffé comparing advantaged groups.

CATEGORY I: RESPONDS TO CHILD
EXPRESSIVE COMMUNICATION

For this category with no significant group differences, Table 7.5 shows that the results are the same for the only subcategory of adequate frequency, ACCOMMODATES: COMFORTS DISTRESS. Although this subcategory shows substantial differences in the means for advantaged and disadvantaged mothers, the variability within groups is so large that the difference in the means is not significant.

Note the relative low incidence of this category and subcategory in mother talk to toddlers. Infant research (Tulkin & Kagan, 1972) suggests that comforting distress is a more prominent feature of mother–child interaction during the first year of life than it is for toddlers. The lower incidence in talk to toddlers can be accounted for by the fact that many of these maternal speech acts occur in response to the child's frets and tears. Since these nonverbal expressions of generalized distress are likely to decline as toddlers learn to express their needs in words, maternal responses would also be expected to decline.

CATEGORY II: RESPONDS TO CHILD DESIRE COMMUNICATION

For this category with a significant increment for advantaged mothers, Table 7.5 shows similar results for the subcategories EXPLICATES DESIRE and ACCOMMODATES: FULFILLS DESIRE. The combined mean of the advantaged groups for EXPLICATES DESIRE is significantly higher than that of the disadvantaged and the mean of each advantaged group is significantly higher for ACCOMMODATES: FULFILLS DESIRE. The subcategory ASSISTS CHILD TO FULFILL OWN DESIRE, which occurs rarely in talk to toddlers, shows no significant differences among the groups.

These findings are important for everyday experience because desire requests are so common in the child's communications and responses to them are so frequent in the mother's speech (see Figures 7.1 and 7.2). A considerable proportion of mother talk to toddlers is concerned with efforts by the mothers to help their children attain the goals they set for themselves. Educated mothers are more likely to assume this facilitating role.

The results also provide some insight into the reason why educated mothers show more total responsive speech than do the less educated. More of the educated mothers' speech consists of responding to their children's desires, explicating and fulfilling them. Often the mother explicates the desire request, checking to make sure she has understood it (*You need some soap?*), before she proceeds to fulfill the desire (*I'll get some.*).

Additional analysis. Note that ACCOMMODATES: FULFILLS DESIRE also shows a significant difference between the advantaged groups. Since these two groups of mothers are similar in educational background, we examined this discrepancy further to see if it might be attributable to differences in the frequency of desire communications among their toddlers.[1] The mean rate of the mother's desire fulfilling responses for each of the child's spontaneous desire communications was calculated for each group. The rates obtained were .16, .59 and .51 for black disadvantaged, black advantaged, and white advantaged groups, respectively. These results show a significant disparity between disadvantaged and advantaged groups and no significant difference between the advantaged groups. The results indicate that the educational level of the mother is a key correlate of the way she responds to her child's desire requests. When we control for variations in the frequency of the child's desire communications, the disparity between black and white educated mothers disappears, while the disparity between educated and less educated mothers remains.

CATEGORY III: RESPONDS TO CHILD
EGO-ENHANCING COMMUNICATION

For this category almost all mother speech acts fall in the subcategory of EGO-BOOSTS, so that the results for the subcategory are the same as those for the category as a whole, a significant increment for advantaged mothers (see Table 7.5).

The low frequency of ego-boosting in the total speech sample merits attention. Since praise or approval are among the most widely discussed caregiver speech acts in the lay literature, we might have expected a higher frequency of ego-boosts. Our data suggest two possible explanations for this discrepancy. First, ego-boosting is only one among many forms of caregiver approbation, one which entails prideful, self-conscious praise, often expressed with exaggerated emphasis (*Wow! Aren't you something!*). The FIS-C identifies another set of caregiver approbations in the various subcategories for confirmation. In contrast to ego-boosts, confirmations are expressed in a matter-of-fact manner, often by simply repeating or echoing the child's message (*Right, you put it back.; Uh huh.; Good.*). As can be seen in Table 7.5, the subcategories CONFIRMS REPORT and CONFIRMS LEARNING are far more common in mother speech than is the subcategory EGO-BOOSTS. Confirmations of one kind or another are seven times more frequent than are ego-boosts, fre-

---

[1]See Table B.1 of Appendix B (page 197) for mean FIS-P scores for the child's spontaneous communications.

quent enough to warrant the attention accorded to praise and approval in the lay literature.

Second, as our previous work (Schachter *et al.*, 1974, 1976) and the work of others (Gleason, 1973) suggest that child boasting and caregiver ego-boosting are more common in verbal interaction with older children, there may be developmental factors contributing to the low incidence of ego-boosting praise in the present sample. We have noted that toddlers rarely boast. In the present sample, only three black disadvantaged toddlers, nine black advantaged toddlers, and five white advantaged toddlers boasted at all, so that opportunities for responsive ego-boosting were very limited. In addition, the mothers produced very few spontaneous ego-boosts, as compared to confirmations. It may be that mothers sense that their toddlers are not yet ready for this kind of self-conscious approval.

Additional Analysis. RESPONDS TO CHILD EGO-ENHANCING COMMUNI-CATION is one of three categories substantially represented in both the responsive and spontaneous speech of the mother; the others are TEACHES and CONTROLS (see Table 5.1). For these categories, additional analyses were undertaken to see if the findings are the same for both responsive and spontaneous speech acts. We have seen in Table 7.3 that RESPONDS TO CHILD EGO-ENHANCING COMMUNICATION fails to show significant group differences when only responsive speech acts are analyzed. Analysis based on spontaneous speech acts only does show a significant increment for educated mothers, with means of .1, .6 and .7% for black disadvantaged, black advantaged, and white advantaged mothers, respectively. The findings indicate that the significance of the increment for educated mothers in this category depends on the significance of the increment for spontaneous speech acts.

CATEGORY IV: RESPONDS TO
CHILD COLLABORATIVE COMMUNICATION

For this category with no significant group differences, Table 7.5 shows similar results in the case of the only subcategory of adequate frequency, ENGAGES IN COLLABORATIVE DRAMATIC PLAY. While the mean for advantaged mothers is considerably higher than for the disadvantaged, there is so much variability within groups that differences between groups are not significant. The chief factor accounting for the variability in this subcategory, as well as for the category as a whole, is that collaborative sequences are among the longest in our entire speech sample, as mother and child assume their roles alternately in the collaboration. A few such long sequences can sharply raise the mother's mean, significantly augmenting the range of scores for the total sample.

Note that there was far more dramatic play than playful participation of other kinds, such as collaborative joint projects or collaborative chanting; the latter did not reach the 1% frequency criterion. Perhaps the most common type of dramatic play was the separation fantasy, where the child pretends to hide and the mother says, *I wonder where Tony is. Just can't find my Tony. Oh, there he is.* Sometimes the child pretends to be leaving to go to the store or to work, and the mother enters into the fantasy, waving goodbye, etc.

Additional Analysis. Collaborative talk when instigated by the mother is assigned the child category score COLLABORATIVE COMMUNICATION, rather than RESPONDS TO CHILD COLLABORATIVE COMMUNICATION (see Appendix A). These mother-initiated collaborations were rare, less than 1% of speech, and additional analysis showed no significant differences among the groups. Nor were there significant group differences in the mother's total collaborative talk, whether instigated by the child or the mother.

CATEGORY V: RESPONDS TO CHILD REPORT

For this category with a significant increment for advantaged mothers, Table 7.5 shows similar results for the subcategories, EXPLICATES REPORT and CONFIRMS REPORT. These subcategories often occur in sequence, with the mother first explicating the child's report (*You gonna fix it?*) and then confirming it (*Okay.*).

As was the case for the category RESPONDS TO CHILD DESIRE COMMUNICATION, these findings have importance for everyday experience because reports make up a large portion of the child's communications. They are second only to desire requests, and the mother's responses to them make up a large portion of her talk.

How are we to understand the prevalence of these reports and of these responses to them? It seems that the speech acts we classify as reports are the same kind as those Piaget calls the "collective monologue," which, together with the monologue and repetitions, make up what he refers to as the young child's "egocentric speech" (Piaget, 1926). Collective monologues differ from true dialogues in that although "everyone is supposed to be listening," which distinguishes them from pure monologue, the child is, nevertheless, merely talking "aloud to himself in front of others ... thinking ... aloud [Piaget, 1926, pp. 18, 19]."

It seems that young children often share their inner thoughts, their own experiences and observations with others. Piaget's data on two 6-year-olds in a preschool classroom shows that 23–30% of their speech consists of collective monologues. We have seen that 29.6% of the toddler's spontaneous communications at home consists of these reports (see Figure 7.2). Most of the toddlers' reports, like those of Piaget's preschoolers, are about the self (*I'm bye-bye. Fall down.*), although some are about others (*Daddy bye-bye.*) and things (*Look at the bus.*).

While there has been considerable research on the young child's egocentric collective monologues, there have been no data on how the caregiver responds to them. Our findings suggest that mothers of toddlers typically explicate these reports, making sure they understand them, and that they then proceed to confirm them. They rarely correct them or seek further elaboration. In explicating these reports, especially when they are presented nonverbally or in the immature syntax of the toddler, mothers seem to be putting into words the child's inner thoughts. In confirming these reports, mothers seem to provide what the psychoanalyst Harry Stack Sullivan (1953) calls "consensual validation" of the child's experiences and observations.

Educated mothers assume this role more often than do less educated mothers. As was the case with the category RESPONDS TO CHILD DESIRE COMMUNICATION, these findings shed light on why educated mothers produce more total responsive speech. More of their speech consists of explicating and confirming their child's reports, their collective monologues.

CATEGORY VI: RESPONDS TO CHILD
LEARNING COMMUNICATION

For this category with no significant group differences, Table 7.5 shows the same results for the subcategories CONFIRMS LEARNING, SUPPLIES LEARNING, and CORRECTS LEARNING. Note that confirming and correcting the child's learning communications are mutually exclusive, much like positive and negative reinforcement. Table 7.5 demonstrates that confirming is more frequent than correcting for all three groups of mothers. SUPPLIES LEARNING sometimes precedes a confirmation of learning. For example, the child may seek to learn a new word (*What's this?*); the mother may supply it (*That's a bear.*); the child may then repeat the word (*bear*) and the mother may confirm the learning (*Right, a bear.*).

Again, as in the case of responding to the child's desire requests and reports, these findings are of practical everyday importance. The child's learning communications, both requests for new learning (*What that say?*) and pronouncements of recently acquired learning (*That's a cookie-*

cutter.), make up a large portion of the child's messages, and the mother's responses to them make up a large portion of her talk. The set of caregiver responses we have identified can be recognized as representative of the set of didactic techniques traditionally applied in learning tasks. CONFIRMS LEARNING represents positive feedback or reinforcement; CORRECTS LEARNING negative feedback or reinforcement; and SUPPLIES LEARNING knowledge-supplying feedback. The data of Table 7.5 indicate that the groups do not differ in the proportion of their speech devoted to these traditional didactic techniques.

COMBINED SUBCATEGORY SCORES

Table 7.6 shows the results for the combined subcategories of adequate frequency. It can be seen that significantly more of the speech of educated mothers consists of ALL EXPLICATIONS, ALL CONFIRMATIONS, and ALL ACCOMMODATIONS. The results of Table 7.6 in conjunction with those of Table 7.5 indicate that educated mothers do more explicating mainly because they more often explicate their toddler's desire requests and reports; they do more confirming mainly because they more often confirm their toddler's reports; and they do more accommodating mainly because they more often fulfill their toddler's desires.

Explications, confirmations, and accommodations are common in mother talk to toddlers, each accounting for about 10% of the mother's speech. Explications have been noted in previous research on baby talk. They seem to serve two functions. Brown (1973) stresses their function as communication checks; the caregiver seems to check to see if what she has said is what the child means. Additionally, Gleason (1977) and Schachter *et al.* (1976) have suggested that in explicating the child's communications, the caregiver seems to assume the child's role in the

TABLE 7.6
Combined Subcategories:
Mean Percentage of Mother Speech Acts for Groups

Combined subcategories	Groups			
	Disadvantaged	Advantaged		
	Black	Black	White	Both
ALL EXPLICATIONS	4.7	8.3*	9.2*	8.8*
ALL CONFIRMATIONS	7.0	12.2*	10.3	11.2*
ALL ACCOMMODATIONS	5.2	8.6	11.6*	10.1*
ALL CORRECTIONS	2.5	3.0	4.0	3.5

*$p < .05$ Scheffé comparing disadvantaged versus advantaged group(s).

conversation; she speaks for the child. Such role-taking has also been observed in talk to aphasics and other listeners with limited conversational abilities (Gleason, 1977). Not surprisingly, Table 7.5 shows that the mother most often explicates what the toddler most often communicates, desire requests and reports.

Confirmations have also been discussed in previous research on baby talk (Brown, 1973: Gelman & Shatz, 1977). Brown has suggested that EXPANSIONS function either as communication checks or confirmations, as noted earlier. Table 7.5 shows that confirmations typically occur in response to the toddler's reports and learning communications. In confirming the toddler's reports, the caregiver seems to be validating the child's experiences and observations; in confirming the toddler's learning communications the caregiver provides positive reinforcement for correct learning.

Although the category of accommodations has not been discussed in the literature on baby talk, Tables 7.5 and 7.6 show that a good deal of mother talk to toddlers occurs in the context of accommodating the child's various demands. The mother uses words to comfort distress, to fulfill desires, and to supply answers to learning questions.

In contrast to the findings for explications, confirmations, and accommodations, Table 7.6 shows no differences in group means for ALL CORRECTIONS. Nor are corrections as common in baby talk as are explications, confirmations, and accommodations. This finding is interesting in view of the debate on theories of language acquisition. Contrary to behavioristic theory, Brown and Hanlon (1970) have pointed out that mothers rarely correct the grammar of their toddlers. Our naturalistic results support their statement. Out of a total of 662 corrections in the entire speech sample, only 1 was grammatical (Child: *Tooths.* Caregiver: *Teeth.*). The most common type of correction (44.7%) entailed word learning (*That's not red; it's blue.*). There was also a substantial number of corrections involving fine-motor activity (13.9%), letters and numbers (12.5%), the truth value of the child's statement (11.6%), and social norms (9.1%). Corrections of pronunciation, the only other type related to language learning, were rare (3.6%). It seems that when mothers self-consciously teach their children language, they principally teach vocabulary or word-labeling.

Predominately Spontaneous Subcategories
and Subscores

CATEGORY VII: CONTROLS, RESTRICTS-COMMANDS

In this category, with a significant increment for disadvantaged mothers, all subcategories, DO'S, DON'TS, and REFUSALS, occur with high frequency in mother speech. Table 7.7 shows the mean percentages for each subcategory. It is clear from Table 7.7 that disadvantaged mothers show a significant increment in control talk because more of their speech consists of DON'TS than does that of advantaged mothers. Although DON'TS are common in the speech of all mothers, their incidence is 1 in 3.7 speech acts for less educated mothers and 1 in 11.5 speech acts for the educated.

In contrast, the groups show no significant differences in the means for DO's. This subcategory consists mainly of orders to perform some conventional action (*Put your toys away.*) or suggestions and directions for child activities (*You wanna play with your puzzles?*).

For REFUSALS, the statistical analysis showed a significant effect of socioeducational group as well as a significant interaction between socioeducational group and sex. Scheffé tests revealed no consistent interaction between the group variable and the sex variable; only mothers of white advantaged girls and black advantaged boys showed significantly more REFUSALS. To examine the source of this apparently meaningless interaction effect, an additional analysis was performed. It is described below, after presenting the findings on subscores of the control category.

Table 7.8 shows the results for these subscores that denote control strategies in mother talk. The following control strategies reached adequate frequency: appeals to SOCIAL NORMS, appeals to SELF NORMS, provides SUBSTITUTE GRATIFICATION, appeals to ANY NORMATIVE EXPLANATION, and appeals to JUSTIFYING EXPLANATIONS. Table 7.8 shows the incidence of these control strategies for DO's, DON'TS, and REFUSALS in each of the groups (mean percentage per subcategory).

TABLE 7.7
Subcategories of Control Category:
Mean Percentage of Mother Speech Acts for Groups

	Groups			
	Disadvantaged	Advantaged		
Subcategories	Black	Black	White	Both
DO's	16.4	13.8	12.4	13.1
DON'TS	26.8	11.5*	5.8*	8.7*
REFUSALS[a]	10.2	5.8	9.9	7.9

[a] Shows significant group by sex interaction as well as significant group effect.
*$p < .05$ Scheffé comparing disadvantaged versus advantaged group(s).

TABLE 7.8

Subscores of Controls Category—DO'S, DON'TS, REFUSALS with Subscores: Mean Percentage for Groups

	Groups			
	Disadvantaged	Advantaged		
Subscores	Black	Black	White	Both
DO'S				
SOCIAL NORMS	1.3	2.0	1.8	1.9
SELF NORMS	.9	1.2	.5	.8
SUBSTITUTION GRATIFICATION	2.3	4.4	5.6	5.0
ANY NORMATIVE EXPLANATION	2.6	4.3	3.4	3.8
JUSTIFYING EXPLANATIONS	4.6	5.9	7.3	6.6
DON'TS				
SOCIAL NORMS	4.0	4.6	8.1	6.3
SELF NORMS	3.1	5.6	5.0	5.3
SUBSTITUTE GRATIFICATION[a]	2.6	8.6	6.8	7.7
ANY NORMATIVE EXPLANATION	8.8	15.0	15.9*	15.4*
JUSTIFYING EXPLANATIONS	11.0	19.2*	19.8*	19.5*
REFUSALS				
SOCIAL NORMS	2.1	2.2	5.3	3.8
SELF NORMS	3.9	2.6	1.7	2.2
SUBSTITUTE GRATIFICATION	5.4	13.2	15.2	14.2*
ANY NORMATIVE EXPLANATION	11.6	10.7	9.7	10.2
JUSTIFYING EXPLANATIONS	23.2	21.7	29.0	25.4

[a] Shows significant group by sex interaction as well as significant group effect.

*$p < .05$ Scheffé comparing disadvantaged versus advantaged group(s).

It can be seen that the groups do not differ significantly in their use of control strategies for DO'S.[2] In the case of DON'TS, advantaged mothers are significantly more likely to use explanations, including any kind of normative explanation as well as all justifying explanations. With REFUSALS, advantaged mothers provide significantly more substitutes. There is also evidence that they provide significantly more substitutes with DON'TS. Statistical analysis for DON'TS with SUBSTITUTE GRATIFICATION showed a

[2]Note that within group variability for subscores tended to be much larger than for category scores or subcategories because the latter are based on percentage of total talk, whereas the former are based on percentage of talk within the category. For this reason, large between-group differences in subscore means occasionally fell short of statistical significance, as can be seen in Tables 7.8 and 7.10.

significant effect of socioeducational group as well as a significant interaction between socioeducational group and sex. Scheffé tests revealed that half of the advantaged mothers (black mothers of boys and white mothers of girls) provided significantly more substitutes with DON'TS than half of the disadvantaged (mothers of girls), indicating that this control strategy is significantly more common in the speech of educated mothers.

Additional Analyses. To clarify the findings for the REFUSALS subcategory, particularly the apparently meaningless interaction effect, we examined the mother's rate of refusal in relation to the frequency of the child's spontaneous desire requests. Since most refusals (69.5%) occur in response to these desire requests, variations in refusals might be due to variations in these requests. The mean rate of maternal refusal responses per child desire request was found to be .58, .67, and .69 for black disadvantaged, black advantaged, and white advantaged groups, respectively, with no significant differences between the groups and no significant interaction effects. It appears that when we take into account the frequency of the child's desire requests, we find no significant differences in the incidence of refusal responses.

Finally, because control talk is substantially represented in both the responsive and spontaneous speech of the mother, additional analysis was indicated to see if the increment for the black disadvantaged mothers obtains for both kinds of speech acts. We have seen in Table 7.3 that the increment obtains when we analyze spontaneous speech acts only. Analysis based on responsive speech acts only showed a significant group effect as well as a significant interaction between group and sex. To see if this interaction was due to variations in the frequency of the child's initiatives, we examined the mean rate of control responses per child initiative. The results show a significantly higher rate of control responses for the disadvantaged mothers as compared to the advantaged, with no significant interaction between the groups. It seems that when we take into account the frequency of the child's initiatives, disadvantaged mothers show higher levels of responsive control talk, just as they show higher levels of spontaneous control talk.

CATEGORY VIII: TEACHES, PROVIDES KNOWLEDGE

In this category, with no significant group differences, three subcategories reached adequate frequency: PRESENTS KNOWLEDGE, ELICITS KNOWLEDGE, and WORD TEACHING. Table 7.9 presents the means for these subcategories. It can be seen that none of the subcategories show significant group differences.

TABLE 7.9
Subcategories of Teaches Category:
Mean Percentage of Mother Speech Acts for Groups

	Groups			
	Disadvantaged	Advantaged		
Subcategories	Black	Black	White	Both
PRESENTS KNOWLEDGE	5.3	7.8	7.4	7.6
ELICITS KNOWLEDGE	2.3	1.6	3.6	2.6
WORD TEACHING	2.4	2.3	1.4	1.9

These subcategories, like the subcategories of the category RESPONDS TO CHILD LEARNING COMMUNICATION, are representative of traditional didactic techniques. PRESENTS KNOWLEDGE covers the common technique of modeling new knowledge; ELICITS KNOWLEDGE, the technique of practice and drill in recently acquired knowledge; and WORD TEACHING, the didactic technique frequently observed in talk to the language-learning toddler (Snow & Ferguson, 1977). Sometimes the caregiver asks a question, eliciting knowledge, and then answers it herself, presenting knowledge or teaching words (*What's that? The mommy bear.*).

The subscores in this category denote variations in the content of teaching. For each group, Table 7.10 shows the mean percentage of teaching talk for all subscores of adequate frequency, namely, PHYSICAL WORLD, SOCIAL WORLD, PHYSICAL NORMS, LETTERS AND NUMBERS, and

TABLE 7.10
Subscores of Teaches Category:
Mean Percentage for Groups

	Groups			
	Disadvantaged	Advantaged		
Subscores	Black	Black	White	Both
PHYSICAL WORLD	31.9	42.6	38.4	40.5
SOCIAL WORLD	12.3	21.0	22.0	21.5
PHYSICAL NORMS	8.3	10.3	17.4	13.9
LETTERS AND NUMBERS	23.3	8.1	4.3*	6.2*
ANY NORMATIVE EXPLANATION	18.9	16.0	19.3	17.6

*$p < .05$ Scheffé comparing disadvantaged versus advantaged group(s).

ANY NORMATIVE EXPLANATION. It can be seen that there is little difference among the groups in the content of teaching. The only significant difference that emerges is in the teaching of letters and numbers. In this area, disadvantaged mothers show significantly more teaching. That is, less educated mothers stress letters and numbers when they teach.

Additional Analyses. Additional analyses were undertaken to study the secondary score for teaching. This is the kind of teaching that is interpolated into a speech act whose primary function is scored in some other category. The results show a significant increment for advantaged mothers. The means for teaching as a secondary score are .9, 2.2, 3.3% for black disadvantaged, black advantaged, and white advantaged mothers, respectively. To see if any and all teaching, whether scored primary or secondary, would show significant group differences, we combined the means for both. As was the case for results based on primary scores alone, the combined means show no significant group differences. Although advantaged groups produce relatively more secondary teaching, the absolute amount of such teaching is too small to have a significant impact on the combined means.

Finally, because this teaching-talk category is substantially represented in both the mother's spontaneous and responsive speech, additional analysis was indicated to see if the results were the same for both kinds of speech acts. We have seen in Table 7.3 that there are no significant group differences in teaching talk when we analyzed only spontaneous speech acts. In contrast, the analysis based only on responsive speech acts shows a significant increment for advantaged mothers. The means are 1.1, 3.4, and 4.8% for black disadvantaged, black advantaged, and white advantaged groups, respectively. We shall see in Chapter 9 that this increment in responsive teaching-talk for advantaged mothers holds, even when we take into account that advantaged toddlers initiate more conversations, thus increasing the chances for responsive caregiver talk in any category. Educated mothers seem to adopt a responsive teaching style—another facet of their general responsive style of communication.

These additional analyses cover the results for the two kinds of interpolated teaching techniques, teaching assigned a secondary score (i.e., interpolated into a speech act whose primary function is scored in another category) and responsive teaching (i.e., speech acts interpolated into a sequence of responses to the child's communications, often instigated by the child's own desire requests or reports). Both kinds of interpolated teaching differ from spontaneous teaching in one important respect. In spontaneous teaching, the caregiver must mobilize the child's attention anew; in interpolated teaching the child's attention is already engaged when the mother inserts her minilesson into the stream of discourse. Educated mothers are more likely to make use of these techniques of interpolated teaching.

CATEGORY IX: REPORTS ON CHILD

In the remaining predominantly spontaneous categories, REPORTS ON CHILD and REPORTS ON SELF, OTHERS, AND THINGS, Table 7.11 shows the results for all subcategories of adequate frequency.

Recall that REPORTS ON CHILD is the only category score showing a significant race difference, a significant increment for black advantaged mothers compared to the white advantaged mothers as well as the black disadvantaged. Table 7.11 shows that the findings are the same for the subcategory PRESENTS REPORT-SPECIFIC, but not for the subcategory ELICITS REPORT-SPECIFIC. The latter shows no significant group differences. As eliciting reports is far more common than present reports and as eliciting shows no race differences, the already meager evidence of race differences now proves to be even more scanty. PRESENTS REPORT-SPECIFIC represents only 2.3% of the total sample of mother speech.

These reports on the child (e.g., questions and comments describing the child's activities, attributes, products, fantasies) often serve the function of initiating conversation between the caregiver and the relatively noncommunicative toddler. Sometimes the caregiver elicits a report with a "wh-question" (*What are you writing?*) and answers it herself with a

TABLE 7.11
Subcategories of Reports on Child and Reports on Self, Others, Things:
Mean Percentage of Mother Speech Acts for Groups

| | Groups | | | |
| | Disadvantaged | Advantaged | | |
Subcategories	Black	Black	White	Both
REPORTS ON CHILD				
PRESENTS REPORT-SPECIFIC	0.9	3.2*	1.0	—†
ELICITS REPORT-SPECIFIC	3.5	3.7	3.4	3.6
REPORTS ON SELF, OTHERS, THINGS				
SELF	1.5	2.2	2.4	2.3
THINGS	0.7	1.2	1.7*	1.4

*$p < .05$ Scheffé comparing disadvantaged versus advantaged group(s).
†$p < .05$ Scheffé comparing advantaged groups.

"yes-no question" (*An A?*) or by presenting her own report (*It looks like an A.*). In reporting on the child she seems to be speaking for the child, assuming the child's role in the conversation, just as she does when she explicates the child's own communications (Gleason, 1977; Schachter *et al.*, 1976).

The incidence of these reports in mother speech does not appear to be related to the educational level of the mother; the means for presenting reports are similar for educated white mothers and less educated black mothers and the means for eliciting reports show no significant group differences (see Table 7.11). As to the increment for black educated mothers in the mean for presenting reports, there is no obvious explanation for this race difference. The increment in this technique of reporting on the child cannot be explained on the grounds that black advantaged toddlers are less likely to report for themselves. In fact, Table B.1 of Appendix B shows that black advantaged toddlers are more likely to report than are either of the other two groups, significantly more than black disadvantaged toddlers. Perhaps the most parsimonious explanation for this race difference in presenting reports is that it is due to chance alone. With a total of 21 subcategories, one of them might be expected to show significant race differences due to scoring disagreements or some other chance factor.

CATEGORY X: REPORTS ON SELF, OTHERS, THINGS

In this category, with no significant group differences, Table 7.11 shows that results are the same for the subcategory REPORTS ON SELF, but not for the subcategory REPORTS ON THINGS. The latter occurs significantly more often in the speech of white advantaged than black disadvantaged mothers. At the same time, although there is no significant difference between the advantaged groups, the combined advantaged mean fails to show a significant increment over the disadvantaged mean.

This pattern of group differences is puzzling because the increment for advantaged whites cannot be attributed to maternal education, since the combined mean for educated mothers fails to show a significant increment. Nor can it be attributed to race, since the difference between black and white advantaged mothers is not significant. Because this is the only 1 of 21 subcategories with this particular pattern of group differences, the findings may well be due to chance factors alone.

It is interesting to note that these caregiver reports are similar to the collective monologues that are classified as reports in our FIS-P category scheme for child speech. Piaget (1926) suggests that collective monologues appear in immature adults "who are in the habit of thinking aloud as though they were talking to themselves, but are also conscious of their audience [p. 18]." The present data indicate that the overall incidence of these reports in mother talk to toddlers (3.9%) is relatively rare compared to that in the toddler's own speech (29.6%). Only to a minor extent do mothers seem to share their own thoughts and experiences with their toddlers. As with their toddlers, more of these reports are about the self (*I'm so tired.*) than about things (*There goes that faucet again* [leaking].).

Overall, the findings based on subcategory scores and subscores plus the additional analyses suggested by the data add substance and detail to the three major conclusions based on category scores alone.

1. As was the case for category scores, subcategories and subscores show extensive differences between advantaged and disadvantaged mothers with almost no differences between the advantaged groups. Six subcategories, accounting for 28.8% of mother speech, show significant effects of maternal education. The incidence of EXPLICATES DESIRE, AC-COMMODATES: FULFILLS DESIRE, EGO-BOOSTS, EXPLICATES REPORT, and CONFIRMS REPORT is significantly higher in the speech of educated mothers; that of DON'TS is significantly higher in the speech of the less educated. For the combined subcategories, the speech of educated mothers shows a higher incidence for ALL EXPLICATIONS, ALL CONFIR-MATIONS, and ALL ACCOMMODATIONS which together account for about 30% of the total speech sample. Furthermore, a number of subscores show significant effects of maternal education; DON'TS with ANY NORMA-TIVE EXPLANATION, with SUBSTITUTE GRATIFICATION, as well as REFUSALS with SUBSTITUTE GRATIFICATION are more common among educated mothers, whereas the teaching of LETTERS AND NUMBERS is more com-mon among the less educated.

In contrast, none of the combined subcategories, none of the subscores, and only two of the individual subcategories show significant dif-ferences between black and white advantaged mothers. Furthermore, the race difference obtained for one of these subcategories, ACCOMMO-DATES: FULFILLS DESIRE, can be accounted for by variations in the fre-quency of their toddler's desire requests rather than variations in the mother's responses to these requests. Only one subcategory, PRESENTS REPORT-SPECIFIC, accounting for 2.3% of mother speech, shows an un-qualified difference between black and white educated mothers with more such speech for blacks. Given the large number of subcategories under study, one significant difference between black and white mothers would be expected on the basis of chance alone. The findings underscore the communality of different racial groups, challenging theories of inherited psychological racial differences such as Jensen's

(1969). In the natural setting of their own homes, in the microscopic details of everyday communication, highly educated black and white mothers provide their young children with almost identical environments.

2. There are no significant group differences in the subcategories concerned with teaching and learning (Categories VI and VIII). These subcategories cover the broad range of techniques for "cognitive enrichment" that are the earmark of didactic programs, techniques for both spontaneous teaching—modeling, practice and drill, and word-labeling—and for responding to the child's learning communications—positive or negative feedback and knowledge-supplying feedback. In these programs, it is assumed that the early environment of disadvantaged children is deficient in these cognitive aspects. Our results fail to support this assumption. Less educated mothers do not appear to be deficient in their use of traditional didactic techniques; the incidence of such techniques in mother speech seems unrelated to the level of the mother's education.

Nor do less educated mothers appear to be deficient in the content of their teaching. Subscores in the teaching category show no significant differences among the groups in the proportion of teaching talk concerned with the physical world or the social world. Groups are also similar in the proportion of teaching that involves explanations. The only significant group differences in the content of teaching indicate that the less educated mothers emphasize the teaching of letters and numbers. In view of the importance of learning these skills in our culture, this emphasis can hardly be judged a deficiency in the cognitive aspects of the environment.

Educated mothers are more likely to interpolate teaching into a speech act whose main function is in another category. However, even when we include this interpolated teaching in the analysis, there is no significant difference among the groups in the total percentage of teaching talk. There is also another technique of interpolated teaching that is characteristic of the speech of educated mothers; they tend to insert their teaching into the flow of their everyday responsive talk, talk mainly initiated by the child. This technique of interpolated teaching appears to point up a difference in the social or emotional aspects of communication, rather than the cognitive. Educated mothers seem to teach their children at a moment when the child's interest and motivation are already engaged in the communication process, increasing the likelihood that the children will attend to what their mothers are trying to teach.

3. Instead of finding group differences in what is ordinarily viewed as the cognitive aspect of the early verbal environment, we found extensive

differences between educated and less educated mothers in the social and emotional aspects of communication. In their everyday talk, educated mothers seem to consistently support and facilitate their child's own actions. More of their speech is concerned with explicating and fulfilling their child's desire requests, with helping their children attain the goals they set for themselves. More of the speech of educated mothers is concerned with explicating and confirming their child's constant reports or collective monologues, so that they seem to help their toddlers put their inner thoughts into words and to provide consensual validation for these thoughts. Educated mothers are also more likely to boost their child's ego. Moreover, they seem to minimize inhibitions of their child's actions. Although DON'TS appear often in the speech of all mothers, they make up a far smaller proportion of the speech of educated mothers, less than 10% as compared to more than 25% of the speech of the less educated. Furthermore, when DON'TS are necessary, educated mothers provide justifications or they offer substitute means for the children to attain their goals. Similarly, when REFUSALS are necessary, highly educated mothers tend to offer substitutes, so that the children can attain their goals to some degree. Even in their teaching, educated mothers are more likely to follow the child's lead, interpolating their lessons into the stream of discourse when the child's attention is already engaged in communication.

These communication strategies of educated mothers acquire special significance in the light of developmental theory, more particularly, theories of early affective or ego development. Both Piagetian and psychoanalytic theory describe the developmental stage before age 3 as a time when differentiation between the self and the other is not yet complete. Piaget and Inhelder (1969) posit a primordial state of lack of differentiation between self and other, "the initial adualism [p. 22]," and suggest that significant ego-differentiation takes place by age 3, when self-assertion and self-valorization erupt in full force. Similarly, psychoanalytic ego psychologists describe an initial state of oneness (Kaplan, 1978) between self and other, the state of "primary narcissism," and they too suggest that the self emerges by age 3. For example, Mahler, Pine, and Bergman (1975) define the "psychological birth" of the child as a period of separation and individuation spanning the years from birth until 3; Erikson (1963) describes the toddler stage as the time of emerging autonomy.

Our results indicate that educated mothers take this affective development of their toddlers into account. They support their toddlers' emerging autonomy, helping them attain their own goals; validating their own observations and experiences; boosting their nascent egos;

minimizing prohibitions and providing justifications or substitutes when restrictions are necessary; and teaching when the child's interest is engaged.

Theories of early ego development also help to illuminate our diverse findings on the much-discussed caregiver strategy of praise or approval. The results indicate that there are three main kinds of caregiver approbation, EGO-BOOSTS, CONFIRMS REPORT, and CONFIRMS LEARNING, and that confirmations are far more frequent in talk to toddlers than are ego-boosts. Ego theory can account for the relatively low incidence of ego-boosts in our sample, since mothers might well delay this strategy until the self of the child is sufficiently differentiated to grasp the full meaning of the self-conscious pride expressed in this kind of praise. More important for our study of group differences is the finding that educated mothers are significantly more likely to boost their toddlers' egos and confirm their reports, whereas there are no significant differences among the groups in the incidence of confirmations of learning. Ego theory suggests a plausible explanation for this differential pattern of approbation. Whereas confirmation of the child's learning merely provides reinforcement for learning specific skills, the pride expressed in the caregiver's ego-boosts and the validation of the child's own experiences expressed in the caregiver's confirmation of reports, seem to signal a generalized affirmation of the child's whole being. Educated mothers tend to supply this generalized kind of affirmation.

The responsive communication style of our educated mothers seems to consist of a set of strategies that support the burgeoning selfhood of the toddler. How these communication strategies might serve to enhance the educational potential of the child will be discussed after all of the results are presented.

Chapter 8
Routines and Appended Scores for Formal Discourse Features

The category scores discussed in the preceding chapter account for almost all of the mother's speech to her toddler. As noted earlier, only 3.3% of the mother's total speech sample consists of routines (e.g., WHAT? HI, GOD BLESS YOU) and only one of these routines reaches the 1% frequency criterion, namely, WHAT? After reporting the results for the relatively infrequent routine scores, we will turn our attention to the appended scores which occur with high frequency in talk to toddlers.

Routine Scores

Table 8.1 summarizes the results for the percentage of mother speech devoted to routines. For each group under study, it shows the means for all routine scores, as well as the mean for the routine score WHAT? The vast majority of WHAT? utterances (two-thirds) signify 'What did you say?' and occur when the mother cannot hear the child's message. WHAT? can also signify 'What do you mean?' This usage is relatively rare, however, because mothers usually explicate the toddler's message when they can hear it but are unsure of its meaning; they simply guess at the meaning. Explications make up 8.7% of the total sample of mother

TABLE 8.1
Routine Scores:
Mean Percentage of Mother Speech Acts for Groups

| | Groups | | | |
| | Disadvantaged | Advantaged | | |
Routine scores	Black	Black	White	Both
All routines	3.4	2.9	3.5	3.2
WHAT?	2.6	1.6	2.1	1.9

speech, while WHAT? scores signifying 'What do you mean?' make up less than 1%.

It can be seen in Table 8.1 that the incidence of all routines as well as the incidence for the routine score WHAT? is similar for all groups; there are no significant differences among the means. Apparently the incidence of these routines is unrelated to the mother's educational level or ethnicity.[1]

Appended Scores for Formal Discourse Features

The appended scores include the set of discourse features characteristic of baby talk, SELF-REPETITIONS, REPETITIONS-OF-CHILD, and QUESTIONS (Snow & Ferguson, 1977), as well as another feature, JUSTIFYING EXPLANATIONS, that has been studied in research inspired by Bernstein's (1970) sociolinguistic theories (Hess, 1969). For both kinds of features, we will report the results for the entire sample of mothers before presenting the results on differences between the socioeducational groups.

Discourse Features of Baby Talk

ENTIRE SAMPLE OF MOTHERS

The results of discourse features of baby talk for the total sample are of interest for two reasons. First, although a number of studies have shown that these features occur very often in talk to the language-learning

---

[1]There is another kind of "What?" utterance which occurs in response to the child's CALL WHEN OUT OF SIGHT (see Appendix A). This score did not reach adequate frequency, and there were no significant differences between the groups.

toddler (Cross, 1977; Newport, 1976; Snow, 1972; Snow et al., 1976), suggesting that they may play a role in the acquisition of language, none of the previous data have been collected in the everyday setting of the home. The present study provides everyday data to compare with previous findings. Second, and more pertinent to our concern with the effects of socioeducational status, group differences in these formal features may reflect differences in the kinds of speech acts articulated by mothers; that is, form may be related to communication-function. If this is so, it is important to examine the data for the total sample to determine which communication functions are associated with each of these formal features.

Present versus Previous Findings.   Table 8.2 compares the percentages of self-repetitions, child-repetitions, and questions from the present sample with those reported by Snow et al. (1976) from a study based on free-play observations in a laboratory setting. Snow's data were selected for comparison because her sample is similar to the present one, both with respect to socioeducational status and age-of-toddler. It can be seen in Table 8.2 that the findings of the two studies are quite comparable. Although the percentages obtained for SELF-REPETITIONS and QUESTIONS are slightly lower in the present study than in the study by Snow et al., the differences can probably be accounted for by variations in details of methodology, criteria for scoring, composition of the groups (the present sample has more educated mothers), and the fact that Snow's sample was Dutch-speaking. The findings for REPETITIONS-OF-CHILD were also similar to those of Snow et al.

Overall, the similarity in the results obtained in the everyday and in the laboratory setting indicate that these discourse features of baby talk are no mere artifact of the constraining situational context of previous research. Although there is evidence that mothers talk more in contrived

TABLE 8.2
Discourse Features of Baby Talk:
Mean Percentage in Present Study versus Snow Study

Discourse features of baby talk	Studies	
	Present	Snow
SELF-REPETITIONS	14.9	18.9
REPETITIONS-OF-CHILD	11.5	11.0
QUESTIONS	23.6	27.0

TABLE 8.3
Discourse Features of Baby Talk:
Percentage in Each Category and Subcategory

Categories and subcategories	Self-Repetitions	Repetitions-of-Child	Questions
Predominately responsive categories			
RESPONDS TO CH[a] EXPRESSIVE	18.7	14.9	38.9
ACCOMODATES: COMFORTS DISTRESS	21.9	2.2	14.0
RESPONDS TO CH DESIRE	12.2	22.6	40.6
EXPLICATES DESIRE	12.5	44.6	87.7
ACCOMODATES: FULFILLS DESIRE	10.4	10.1	6.3
ASSISTS CH FULFILL DESIRE	19.3	3.3	17.1
RESPONDS TO CH EGO-ENHANCING	11.0	7.1	8.6
EGO-BOOSTS	11.7	6.2	3.2
RESPONDS TO CH COLLABORATIVE	21.8	21.3	22.4
ENGAGES IN COLLABORATIVE DRAMATIC PLAY	22.8	14.2	22.5
RESPONDS TO CH REPORT	13.9	33.2	32.8
EXPLICATES REPORT	13.3	46.4	89.5
CONFIRMS REPORT	11.4	31.7	1.8
RESPONDS TO CH LEARNING	13.1	27.5	9.1
CONFIRMS LEARNING	9.6	35.4	1.6
ACCOMODATES: SUPPLIES LEARNING	16.0	16.4	3.8
CORRECTS LEARNING	17.4	14.7	8.5
Combined Subcategories			
ALL EXPLICATIONS	13.0	42.8	89.4
ALL CONFIRMATIONS	10.7	33.6	1.8
ALL ACCOMMODATIONS	14.4	11.0	6.4
ALL CORRECTIONS	18.8	16.4	8.3

Predominately spontaneous categories

CONTROLS, RESTRICTS–COMMANDS	17.1	3.9	15.2
DO'S	18.2	.7	19.8
DON'TS	17.7	2.3	11.2
REFUSALS	14.3	11.5	13.2
TEACHES, PROVIDES KNOWLEDGE	17.3	2.2	27.5
PRESENTS KNOWLEDGE	10.0	.6	4.8
ELICITS KNOWLEDGE	17.1	4.6	79.3
WORD TEACHING	23.5	2.2	7.0
REPORTS ON CHILD	13.7	.6	61.4
PRESENTS REPORT-SPECIFIC	5.4	.2	.4
ELICITS REPORT-SPECIFIC	13.6	.8	97.5
REPORTS ON SELF, OTHERS, THINGS	7.9	.4	10.1
REPORTS ON SELF	6.9	.2	4.7
REPORTS ON THINGS	8.6	.9	13.9

[a]CH denotes CHILD.

settings than in the everyday home setting (see Chapter 6),[2] the relative frequency of these discourse features seems virtually the same in both situations. Furthermore, it may be noted that the present results are also consistent with previous research findings which show that self-repetitions as well as exact and expanded child-repetitions decrease as the toddler's MLU increases, and that both exact and expanded child-repetitions decrease with increasing age (Cross, 1977; Harkness, 1977; Newport, 1976). Data on the effect of toddler MLU and age on discourse features of baby talk in the present sample can be found in Table B.2 of Appendix B.

Speech Acts and the Formal Features of Baby Talk. What are the communication functions associated with these discourse features? Table 8.3 (pp. 98–99) shows the percentage of self-repetitions, child-repetitions, and questions in each of the 10 main categories of the FIS-C and also in each subcategory of adequate frequency, individual and combined. It can be seen that SELF-REPETITIONS is the score which is most evenly distributed among the speech act categories ranging from 7.9 to 21.8% of speech in any one category. Within this range, the categories with the highest percentage of self-repetitions (> 17.1%) include RESPONDS TO CHILD COLLABORATIVE COMMUNICATION, RESPONDS TO CHILD EXPRESSIVE COMMUNICATION, CONTROLS, and TEACHES; those with the lowest percentage (< 12.2%) include RESPONDS TO CHILD DESIRE COMMUNICATION, RESPONDS TO CHILD EGO-ENHANCING COMMUNICATION, and REPORTS ON SELF, OTHERS, THINGS.

In contrast, the REPETITIONS-OF-CHILD score is selectively distributed among the categories. These repetitions occur mainly in conjunction with explications and confirmations of the child's messages—42.8% of ALL EXPLICATIONS and 33.6% of ALL CONFIRMATIONS are child-repetitions—so that the individual subcategories with the highest percentage of such repetitions are EXPLICATES DESIRE, EXPLICATES REPORT, CONFIRMS REPORT, and CONFIRMS LEARNING. By definition, the mother cannot repeat the child's communication when she is speaking spontaneously, so that child-repetitions rarely occur in the predominately spontaneous categories.

QUESTIONS show yet another pattern of distribution among the speech act categories. They occur mainly in conjunction with explications and elicitations—89.4% of the former and 89.3% of the latter—so that the individual subcategories with the highest percentage of questions are

---

[2]Snow *et al.* (1976) do not report on frequency of mother speech acts. Comparisons of frequency in everyday and constrained settings (Chapter 6) are based on other studies.

ELICITS REPORT, EXPLICATES REPORT, EXPLICATES DESIRE, and ELICITS KNOWLEDGE.

It can be seen that each of these formal features is associated with a different set of communication functions or speech acts. In the following section, we will discuss how this differential pattern of speech acts might help to account for group differences in the incidence of these formal features.

GROUP DIFFERENCES

Table 8.4 presents the group means for the discourse features of baby talk. It can be seen that disadvantaged mothers show a significantly higher percentage of EXACT SELF-REPETITIONS; advantaged mothers show a significantly higher percent of REPETITIONS-OF-CHILD, ALTERED REPETITIONS-OF-CHILD, and EXPANSIONS; and there are no significant differences in repetition scores for the advantaged groups. The significant increment in child-repetitions for advantaged mothers was not due solely to the increment in expansions. As we shall see in Chapter 9, when

TABLE 8.4
Discourse Features of Baby Talk:
Mean Percentage of Mother Speech Acts for Groups

	Groups			
	Disadvantaged	Advantaged		
Discourse features of baby talk	Black	Black	White	Both
SELF-REPETITIONS	16.6	15.4	12.8	14.1
EXACT SELF-REPETITIONS	8.6	6.7	4.3*	5.5*
EXACT COMPLETE	6.0	4.6	2.9	3.8
EXACT PARTIAL	2.6	2.1	1.3	1.7
ALTERED SELF-REPETITIONS	8.0	8.7	8.5	8.6
REPETITIONS-OF-CHILD[a]	8.9	12.6	12.9*	12.8*
EXACT REPETITIONS-OF-CHILD	2.6	2.8	2.7	2.8
EXACT COMPLETE	2.2	2.0	2.3	2.2
ALTERED REPETITIONS-OF-CHILD	6.3	9.8	10.2*	10.0*
EXPANSIONS	.6	2.2*	2.2*	2.2
OTHER ALTERED	5.7	7.6	8.0	7.8
QUESTIONS	19.2	20.9	30.7	—†

Note: Means for repetitions are adjusted for MLU of toddler.
[a] Exact Partial of inadequate frequency.
*p < .05 Scheffé comparing disadvantaged versus advantaged group(s).
† < .05 Scheffé comparing advantaged group(s).

child-repetitions are calculated as a percentage of the child's utterances, mothers also show a significant increment for other altered repetitions of the child. It seems that educated mothers tend to repeat and expand what their children say, whereas less educated mothers tend to repeat exactly what they themselves say.

With respect to QUESTIONS, Table 8.4 shows a significant increment for the white advantaged mothers as compared to either of the black groups, advantaged or disadvantaged; nor do the black groups differ significantly from each other. As this is the only FIS-C score with this particular pattern of race differences independent of educational level, and also the only score concerned with syntax, the results may well reflect discrepancies between Black English and Standard English. Perhaps syntactic features of Black English baby talk differ from those of Standard English baby talk in some respects.

These findings are strikingly consistent with those of Snow *et al.* (1976), who compared mothers of diverse social background in their Dutch-speaking sample. Snow *et al.* found that academic middle-class mothers were significantly more likely to repeat and expand their child's speech and working-class mothers were more likely to repeat their own speech, although the latter finding was not significant. Regarding QUES-TIONS, these groups showed no differences.

In discussing the results for discourse features, one can take the view that the baby-talk code entails a set of linguistic skills, with more profi-cient mothers more likely to foster language development in their toddlers. If we adopt such a view, we find that the data fail to support a deficit theory for the less educated mothers. Indeed, less educated mothers would be rated as more proficient in providing self-repetitions; educated mothers would be rated as more proficient in providing repeti-tions of the child; and proficiency in providing questions would be re-garded as unrelated to the educational level of the mother.

Instead of suggesting that less educated mothers are deficient in baby-talk skills, the results of Table 8.4, when examined in relation to those of Table 8.3, suggested that the difference in repetition scores between mothers of disparate educational levels reflect variations in the ways they communicate. Recall that less educated mothers show a higher percent of DON'TS in their speech (see Table 7.7). Table 8.3 shows that maternal self-repetitions often occur in conjunction with DON'TS; 17.7% of the speech acts in this subcategory are self-repetitions, more than for most other subcategories. Moreover, the percentage of DON'TS that are exact self-repetitions is 17.9%, more than for any other subcate-gory excepting DRAMATIC COLLABORATIVE PLAY. It seemed likely that the increment in exact self-repetitions among less educated mothers was due to the prevalence of DON'TS in their speech. Regarding child-repetitions, Table 8.3 shows that they occur mainly in conjunction with explications and confirmations; EXPLICATES REPORT, EXPLICATES DESIRE, and CONFIRMS REPORT are among the four subcategories with the highest percentage of child-repetitions. Since more of the speech of educated mothers occurs in these subcategories (see Table 7.5), it seemed probable that the increment in child-repetitions for educated mothers was due to the prevalence of these explications and confirmations in their speech.

Because the data of Table 8.3 merely provided evidence of covariation between communication-function scores and formal discourse features, additional analyses were required to determine the direction of the effect. The data for exact self-repetitions were reanalysed excluding DON'TS from the analysis; and the data for DON'TS excluding all exact self-repetitions. Similarly, the data for child-repetitions were reanalyzed excluding ALL EXPLICATIONS and ALL CONFIRMATIONS, and the data for ALL EXPLICATIONS and ALL CONFIRMATIONS excluding all child-repetitions. The results show no significant differences between the groups in exact self-repetitions excluding DON'TS and no significant group differences in child-repetitions excluding ALL EXPLICATIONS and ALL CONFIRMATIONS. In contrast, the increment in DON'TS for disadvantaged mothers and the increment in ALL EXPLICATIONS and ALL CONFIRMATIONS for advantaged mothers remain significant, even when these repetitions are excluded from the analysis. Thus, what the mothers are saying seems to account for group differences in the formal features of discourse; communication-function seems to account for form.

From the perspective of our finding on speech acts, then, it appears that group differences in these formal discourse features of baby talk represent another aspect of the advantaged mother's responsive communication style. Educated mothers seem to support and facilitate their toddler's efforts to communicate. They repeat their toddler's primitive messages, explicating them to make sure they understand their meaning and also confirming their truth value (i.e., providing consensual validation).

Justifying Explanations

ENTIRE SAMPLE OF MOTHERS

The pattern of speech acts associated with JUSTIFYING EXPLANATIONS is different from those associated with the baby-talk features described in Table 8.3; control talk accounts for 85.4% of the mothers' justifications. Table 8.5 lists the percentage of justifying explanations in the subcategories of control talk and also in all other categories. It can be seen

TABLE 8.5
Justifying Explanations:
Percentage in Subcategories

Subcategories	Justifying Explanations
DO'S	5.6
DON'TS	14.9
REFUSALS	25.4
OTHER	1.0

that more justifications occur in conjunction with REFUSALS and DON'TS than any other speech acts. Mothers seem to feel the need to justify their negative commands. Perhaps we all feel this way when we interfere with the autonomy of another.

In all, 5.1% of the mother's speech is qualified by justifying explanations, an unexpectedly high figure in view of the limited cognitive capacities of toddlers, especially their primitive grasp of causality (Piaget & Inhelder, 1969). Perhaps the term "explanation" is a misnomer. We have called these qualifications "justifying explanations" in order to distinguish them from the teaching explanations of Category VIII; both seem to involve the concept of cause and effect. However, the high incidence of the justifying explanations in contrast to the low incidence of teaching explanations (only 1.7% of the entire speech sample) prompted a reexamination of justifications. This showed that justifying statements often take the form of predictions or warnings (*You'll hurt yourself. It's gonna fall.*) Since young children can predict phenomena long before they can explain them—even as early as the first 18 months of life (Piaget, 1970)—the toddler's understanding of predictions could account for the mother's use of justifications. By helping toddlers predict the consequences of their actions, these maternal statements could influence the child's behavior. Such justifications would reduce the necessity for repeated prohibitions and admonitions, even though the child may have little understanding of cause and effect.

Whether the term "justifying explanations" or "predictions" is used to denote their form (we will use the former for consistency), the data of Table 8.5 indicate that these statements generally serve as adjuncts to control talk. More particularly, they seem to modulate or soften the impact of a bald command (*No! Stop that! Pick that up!*). In supporting the autonomy of the toddler, modulation of DON'TS would appear to serve a special interpersonal function; they are likely to diminish the coercive power of the adult and enhance the relative power of the child, reducing the enormous power differential between the two.[3]

GROUP DIFFERENCES

The mean percentage of JUSTIFYING EXPLANATIONS in the mother's speech is shown in Table 8.6 for each group. No significant differences appear between the groups. To see whether the same results held for the percentage of mother speech with justifications in the control category, an additional analysis was undertaken. The results of this analysis, presented in Table 8.6, also show no significant groups differences.

At first glance, these findings might appear to contradict the previously reported finding that educated mothers are more likely to justify their DON'TS (see Table 7.8). In fact, the findings are not contradictory. Because less educated mothers produce at least twice as many DON'TS (see Table 7.7), and educated mothers produce roughly twice as many explanations for their DON'TS, the percentage of justifying explanations in the mother's total speech remains the same for all groups.

The finding that educated mothers tend to justify their DON'TS is consistent with that of Hess (1969; Hess & Shipman, 1965; Olim, Hess, & Shipman, 1967) who finds that middle-class mothers are more likely to use cognitive–rational or personal–subjective explanations in conjunction with control talk (*Would you keep quiet a minute? I want to talk on the phone*), whereas lower-class mothers use imperative–normative appeals (*Be quiet. Shut up.*).[4] Hess's interpretation of this finding, however, differs somewhat from our own. Drawing upon Bernstein's (1970) sociolinguistic theories, Hess views the middle-class control strategies as a manifestation of an "elaborated linguistic code," a code that appeals to universal principles like the rational and personal considerations entailed in justifications. In contrast, lower-class speech is said to be characterized by a "restricted linguistic code"; one that is particularistic, stereotyped, and condensed. The findings of Table 8.6 do not support this interpretation. If less educated mothers were generally deficient in their use of an elaborated linguistic code, we would expect to find a decrease in the percentage of justifying explanations in their total speech, not just in the percentage of DON'TS with justifications. We might also expect them to show a decrease in the percentage of teaching talk with explanations, since such explanations, like those accompanying DON'TS, reflect an elaborated code. We have seen, however, that the groups do not differ

---

[3]In Schachter *et al.* (1974, 1976) justifying explanations were called "Modulations."
[4]These examples are from Hess and Shipman (1965, p. 872).

TABLE 8.6
Justifying Explanations:
Mean Percentage of Mother Speech Acts for Groups

	Groups			
	Disadvantaged	Advantaged		
Justifying Explanations	Black	Black	White	Both
All categories	6.4	5.4	6.4	5.9
Control category	6.0	4.3	4.9	4.6

in the subscore for these teaching explanations (see Table 7.10). There are also no significant group differences for the percentage of teaching explanations in the mother's total speech.

Rather than suggesting that less educated mothers are deficient in their linguistic code, the present findings suggest that the increment in DON'TS with JUSTIFYING EXPLANATIONS is one of many manifestations of the educated mother's responsive communication style, her strategy of support for the child's own actions. The educated mother mitigates the coercive impact of her prohibitions either by providing an explanation or by suggesting a suitable substitute (increment for DON'TS and REFUSALS with SUBSTITUTE GRATIFICATION). She not only mollifies her DON'TS when they do occur, she also shows a lower incidence of DON'TS in the first place. Finally, not only are educated mothers less inhibiting of the child's own actions, they are also more supportive of them, helping their children to attain their goals (increment for RESPONDS TO CHILD DESIRE COMMUNICATION), validating their childrens' own experiences and observations (increment for RESPONDS TO CHILD REPORT), and boosting their egos (increment for RESPONDS TO CHILD EGO-ENHANCING COMMUNICATION).

It should be noted that both Hess and Bernstein have described a very similar pattern of middle-class support in theorizing on the social context for the development of the elaborated linguistic code. For example, Hess and Shipman (1965) describe middle-class mothers as "person-oriented" in their control strategies, taking into consideration the child's individuality and encouraging initiative, whereas lower-class mothers are described as "status-oriented," fostering compliance to group norms and traditions. By emphasizing social-class differences in linguistic codes, however, both Hess and Bernstein have tended to obscure what, in the perspective of the present findings, appears to be their more important contribution—a recognition of the critical role of social and emotional factors in mother–child communication. As was the case for the baby-talk code, the data on justifying explanations do not support the theory that less educated mothers are deficient in their mastery of a linguistic code, in this case the elaborated code. What the results do indicate is that educated mothers using a variety of communication strategies—not only elaborated explanations—are more likely to support the individuality and autonomy of their young children.

Chapter 9

Effects of the Child's Communication Initiatives on Mother Speech

We have now reported the results for all of the mothers' FIS-C scores. To evaluate these findings, it is necessary to determine whether they are independent of the communication initiatives of their toddlers—their spontaneous communications. For example, it could be that advantaged mothers show significantly more responsive talk merely because their toddlers initiate more conversations, thereby stimulating the mothers to respond more often. Or it could be that advantaged mothers show a significantly higher percentage of talk in the category RESPONDS TO CHILD DESIRE COMMUNICATION merely because their toddlers initiate more desire requests. It was to investigate these kinds of questions that we scored the toddlers' communications, noting which were spontaneously initiated and which were responsive, and also classifying each spontaneous communication according to the FIS-P category scheme (Schachter et al., 1974).

By scoring the child's communications, we were able to examine the direct effect of their initiatives on the sample of mother's speech evoked by these initiatives, the mother's Ch:S → C:R speech. Apart from such direct effects, the child's initiatives may have indirect effects on the mother's spontaneous speech or on her Ch:R → C:R speech. For example, if the child tends to initiate conversations frequently, the mother might be inclined to reduce her own spontaneous initiatives; or she might reduce the number of responses she elicits from the child so that her own Ch:R → C:R speech would decrease. Although such indirect effects of the child's initiatives are a distinct possibility, there is no way of estimating their prevalence given our present knowledge of early verbal interaction. Our analysis of the impact of the child's initiatives on mother speech must be limited, therefore, to an examination of direct effects on the mother's Ch:S → C:R speech.

The procedure we adopted was, first, to examine group differences in the mean rate of maternal response per child initiative—thus controlling for the child's spontaneous input. We then compared these findings with the results based on our previous analyses where variations in the child's initiatives were not controlled. If the findings for the controlled analyses were the same as those for the previous uncontrolled analyses, it seemed reasonable to infer that the previous findings were independent of variations in the child's initiatives. Analyses of mean rates of maternal response per child initiative were undertaken for total-talk scores, category scores, and routines. Additionally, all of the appended scores for repetitions of the child were recalculated as a percentage of the child's speech to provide a comparison with the findings based on the percentage of mother speech.

Effects on Total-Talk Scores

Each of the child's initiatives can evoke more than one speech act from the mother. For example, a mother might explicate a report, confirm it, and then seek further elaboration of the report. Therefore, three maternal responses would be evoked by a single initiative of the child. Figure 9.1 shows the mean number of speech acts evoked by each of the child's initiatives for each group under study—the mean rate of response per initiative. It can be seen that while the mean was virtually the same for the two advantaged groups, the disadvantaged mothers responded at a lower rate. The increment for the advantaged mothers was significant.

Not all of the child's initiatives elicited responses from their mothers; some were ignored. Figure 9.2 shows the proportion of the child's initiatives that were ignored by the mother for each group. It can be seen that disadvantaged mothers ignored a considerably higher proportion of their toddler's initiatives than did the advantaged. The increment for the disadvantaged was significant, whereas there was no significant difference between the advantaged groups.

The findings presented in Figures 9.1 and 9.2 are similar to those obtained for the frequency of total-talk (see Figure 6.1, p. 62). Recall that

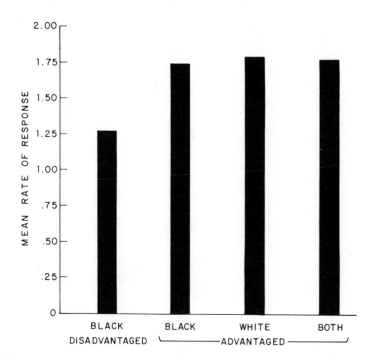

FIGURE 9.1.   *The graph shows the mean rate of mother speech-act responses to child initiatives in black disadvantaged, black advantaged, and white advantaged groups.*

advantaged mothers showed a significant increment in TOTAL RESPON-SIVE TALK compared to the disadvantaged, whereas there were no signif-icant differences between black and white advantaged groups. The re-sults of Figures 9.1 and 9.2 indicate that the advantaged mothers did not show significantly more total responsive speech merely because their toddlers initiated more communications. Even when we control for vari-ations in the quantity of these initiatives, we find that advantaged mothers produce significantly more responsive speech. They rarely ig-nore their toddler's spontaneous communications and produce almost two verbal responses for every one of the child's initiatives. Nor do variations in the quantity of child initiatives account for the similarity between the two advantaged groups in their TOTAL RESPONSIVE TALK scores. When we control for these child variations, we find black and white advantaged mothers similar in their total verbal responses.

Although the significance of the increment in TOTAL RESPONSIVE TALK for advantaged mothers appears to be independent of the child's initia-tives, the initiatives may, to some extent, account for the size of the

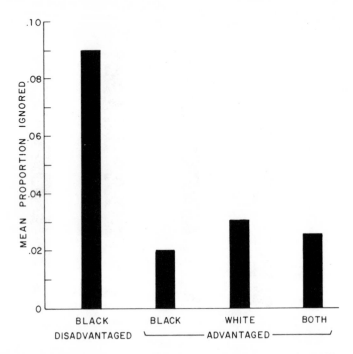

FIGURE 9.2.   *The graph illustrates the mean proportion of child initiatives ignored by mothers in black disadvantaged, black advantaged, and white advantaged groups.*

increment. Whereas the increment in the mother's total responsive talk is threefold (see Figure 6.1), the increment in her mean rate of response to the child's initiatives is considerably smaller (see Figure 9.1). This suggests that some of the increment in TOTAL RESPONSIVE TALK can be accounted for by the higher frequency of initiatives among advantaged toddlers. However, it may be that the advantaged mother's greater responsiveness generates higher rates of initiatives in their toddlers. If so, the mother would be contributing to the increment in her total responsive talk at two levels: first, by responding to her child's initiatives at a higher rate; second, by fostering higher levels of these initiatives which, in turn, instigate higher levels of maternal response. Experimental research on infant babbling (Rheingold, Gewirtz, & Ross, 1959) indicates that the more the infant's babbling is responded to, the more it is likely to occur. The same effect may apply in the case of responses to the toddler's communications.

Effects on Category and Routine Scores

The most common response to the child's initiatives is a speech act in the responsive FIS-C category corresponding to the FIS-P category of the child's initiative. For example, the child reports and the mother confirms the report (FIS-P category: REPORTS ON SELF, OTHERS, THINGS; FIS-C category: RESPONDS TO CHILD REPORT) or the child communicates a desire request and the mother explicates the desire (FIS-P category: DESIRE COMMUNICATION; FIS-C category: RESPONDS TO CHILD DESIRE COMMUNICATION). We called these "matching responses." When scored in the predominantly responsive categories, responses to the child's initiatives were virtually all matching responses, 95.7%. It was rare, for example, for a mother to confirm a report when the child communicated a desire request, or for her to explicate a desire in response to the child's report.

However, these matching responses in the predominately responsive FIS-C categories were not the only kinds of speech acts evoked by the child's initiatives. The next most common response was a speech act in the predominantly spontaneous category CONTROLS. It was not unusual for the child's initiatives to evoke REFUSALS, DON'TS, and DO'S. Another common response was a speech act in the predominately spontaneous category TEACHES. Mothers often interpolated a teaching statement into a sequence of responses to the child's communications, as was noted earlier. Finally, the child's initiatives often evoked the routine score WHAT?, when the mother could not hear or understand the communication.

These four kinds of responses, matching responses, CONTROLS, TEACHES, and WHAT?, together with ignoring the child's communication altogether, account for virtually all of the mother's responses to the child's initiatives. For each of these maternal responses, Table 9.1 shows the mean rate of maternal response per child initiative for all groups under study. Results are shown for both the first maternal response evoked and for the total number of maternal responses evoked per child initiative. The findings for the first response are similar to those for the total responses evoked, except that interpolated teaching rarely occurs as the first response. Mothers tend to react first with a matching response, for example, explicating or fulfilling the child's desire, explicating or confirming the child's report. They then add some teaching later in the sequence of responses.

It can be seen in Table 9.1 that advantaged mothers are significantly more likely than the disadvantaged to respond to their toddler's initia-

TABLE 9.1
Summary of Mother Responses to Child Initiatives:
Mean Rate of Response for Groups

		Groups		
	Disadvantaged	Advantaged		
Responses	Black	Black	White	Both
First response evoked				
Predominately Responsive Categories Matching Responses	.51	.73*	.73*	.73*
Predominately Spontaneous Categories				
Controls, Restricts–Commands	.31	.14*	.16*	.15*
Teaches, Provides Knowledge	.00	.01*	.02*	.02*
Routines: WHAT?	.08	.05	.05	.05
Ignored	.09	.02*	.03*	.03*
Total responses evoked				
Predominately Responsive Categories Matching Responses	.63	1.17*	1.13*	1.15*
Predominately Spontaneous Categories				
Controls, Restricts–Commands	.48	.29*	.40	.34*
Teaches, Provides Knowledge	.02	.09	.14*	.12*
Routines: WHAT?	.08	.06	.05	.05
Ignored	.09	.02*	.03*	.03*

*$p < .05$ Scheffé comparing disadvantaged versus advantaged group(s).

tives with a matching response or by interpolating some teaching talk into a sequence of responses. In contrast, disadvantaged mothers are significantly more likely to respond with control talk or by ignoring the initiative of the child.

The findings of Table 9.1 are similar to those we have reported for FIS-C scores based on the percentage of mother speech. The results for mean rate of matching responses correspond with the finding that advantaged mothers show higher percent scores for several of the predominately responsive categories (see Table 7.2). The higher mean rate of control talk responses for disadvantaged mothers is consistent with the higher percent score for the control category (see Table 7.2). The higher mean rate of teaching-talk responses for advantaged mothers corresponds to the finding based on percent scores that advantaged mothers do more interpolated responsive teaching (see Chapter 7). The mean rate of WHAT? responses shows no significant group differences, just as the percent scores showed no such differences (see Table 8.1). Finally, none of the mean rates of Table 9.1 show significant differences between the advantaged groups, just as there were no such differences in percent scores for any of the predominantly responsive categories or for CONTROLS, TEACHES, and WHAT? (see Tables 7.2 and 8.1). Altogether, the data of Table 9.1 indicate that the findings we have reported for those FIS-C scores often evoked by the child's initiatives are not affected by variations in the quantity of the child's initiatives.

What about effects of variations in the quality of the child's initiatives? As was noted at the beginning of this chapter, the results reported for the predominately responsive categories based on the percentage of mother speech may depend to some extent on variations in the FIS-P score that corresponds to a given responsive FIS-C score (e.g., the increment for advantaged mothers in percentage of speech in the category RESPONDS TO CHILD REPORT may be due merely to a higher incidence of reports in their toddler's speech). To examine this issue, we calculated the mean rate of matching FIS-C responses for each category of FIS-P score (e.g., EXPRESSIVE COMMUNICATION, DESIRE COMMUNICATION). We then compared the results based on these rates, which control for qualitative variations in the child's initiatives, with results for the previously reported percent scores that leave the child's initiatives uncontrolled.

Table 9.2 shows the mean rates of matching maternal FIS-C responses for each type of child FIS-P score. Omitted from the table are the mother's responses to the child's ego-enhancing boasts, because only 17 toddlers produced these kinds of initiatives. Any analysis of variations in maternal responses to these boasts will require either a larger sample

TABLE 9.2
Matching Maternal FIS-C Responses to Child FIS-P Initiatives:
Mean Rate of Response for Groups

	Groups			
	Disadvantaged	Advantaged		
Matching responses	Black	Black	White	Both
Expressive—CH[a] EXPRESSIVE	.79	1.23	1.69*	1.46
Desire—CH DESIRE	.41	1.09*	1.06*	1.08*
Collaborative—CH COLLABORATIVE	.75	1.57*	1.05	1.31
Report—CH REPORT	.74	1.12*	1.09*	1.11*
Learning—CH LEARNING	1.02	1.19	1.22	1.21

[a] CH denotes CHILD.
*$p < .05$ Scheffé comparing disadvantaged versus advantaged group(s).

of toddlers or an older group of children, since boasting occurs so rarely among children below 3, as we have noted before.

Turning to the data presented in Table 9.2, it can be seen that the findings for these predominately responsive categories, based on mean rate of matching maternal responses, are similar to those previously reported, based on percentage of mother speech (see Table 7.2, p. 72). Recall that the results of the previous analyses were as follows:

1. Advantaged mothers showed a significantly higher percentage of their speech in the categories RESPONDS TO CHILD DESIRE COMMUNICATION and RESPONDS TO CHILD REPORT.
2. For the other categories listed in Table 9.2, there were no significant differences between advantaged and disadvantaged groups.
3. There were no significant differences between the advantaged groups for any of the responsive categories.

The mean rates of Table 9.2 show similar results as follows:

1. Advantaged mothers, as compared to disadvantaged mothers, show significantly higher mean rates of matching responses to their child's desire requests and also to their child's reports.

2. For those categories with no significant group differences in percent scores, the mean rates of Table 9.2 show no consistent differences between advantaged and disadvantaged groups. In the case of the category RESPONDS TO CHILD LEARNING COMMUNICATION, there are no significant group differences in the mean rate of matching maternal responses. For the categories RESPONDS TO CHILD EXPRESSIVE COMMU-

NICATION and RESPONDS TO CHILD COLLABORATIVE COMMUNICATION, one or the other advantaged group shows an increment in mean rate compared to the disadvantaged, but the combined mean for the advantaged groups shows no significant increment.

3. There are no significant differences between advantaged groups in mean rate of matching maternal responses for any of these categories.

The results indicate that group differences in percent scores for predominately responsive FIS-C categories are not due merely to variations in the toddler's FIS-P scores. When we control for these qualitative variations in child communications, we obtain the same findings as in the analyses based on percent scores.

In addition to examining the impact of the child's initiatives on responsive category scores, we also studied their effects on the mothers' responsive subcategory scores. Combined subcategories were studied rather than individual subcategories, because the mean rates of maternal response for the latter were sometimes quite low.

Table 9.3 shows the mean rates for the combined subcategories for all groups under study. Comparing these results with those for the percent scores presented in Table 7.6, it can be seen that the findings are the same. In both cases, advantaged mothers show a significant increment for ALL EXPLICATIONS, ALL CONFIRMATIONS, and ALL ACCOMMODATIONS, whereas there are no significant group differences for ALL CORRECTIONS. Also, in both cases, there are no significant differences between the advantaged groups. It appears that the results obtained for

TABLE 9.3

Maternal Combined Subcategory Responses to Child Initiatives: Mean Rate of Response for Groups

| | Groups | | | |
| | Disadvantaged | Advantaged | | |
Combined subcategory responses	Black	Black	White	Both
ALL EXPLICATIONS	.14	.28*	.29*	.28*
ALL CONFIRMATIONS	.15	.32*	.23	.27*
ALL ACCOMMODATIONS	.15	.32*	.36*	.34*
ALL CORRECTIONS	.05	.06	.07	.06

*$p < .05$ Scheffé comparing disadvantaged versus advantaged group(s).

the combined subcategories, like those obtained for the category scores, are independent of the child's initiatives.[1]

Effects on Appended Scores for Formal Discourse Features

Assessing the impact of the child's communications on the findings for appended scores is a more complex matter than assessing their impact on the other FIS-C scores. For SELF-REPETITIONS, QUESTIONS, and JUSTIFYING EXPLANATIONS, the effect of the child's initiatives is bound to vary depending on the subcategory score to which these scores are appended. For example, questions that occur when the caregiver is eliciting reports are likely to be less dependent on the child's initiatives than those that occur when the caregiver is explicating the child's communication; the former are generally spontaneous, the latter responsive. Similar considerations apply to SELF-REPETITIONS, and JUSTIFYING EXPLANATIONS. That is, the impact of the child's initiatives on these appended scores is mediated by what the mother is saying. Given the complexity of these relationships, it seemed premature to speculate on the relationship between the child's initiatives and results on these appended scores.

In contrast, for the appended score REPETITIONS-OF-CHILD, the literature on baby talk suggested a straightforward procedure for controlling for the effects of the child's communications. Since the mother cannot repeat a child's utterance unless the child produces one, several investigators (Nelson, 1973; Newport, 1976; Seitz & Stewart, 1975) have noted that there are two possible procedures for calculating repetitions of the child: one as a percentage of the child's utterances, and the other as a percentage of the mother's utterances. Although the latter procedure is standard in research on baby talk (e.g., Nelson, 1973; Newport, 1976), the crucial question for our purposes is whether the group differences we obtained for child-repetitions as a percentage of the mother's speech merely reflect differences in the frequency of their toddler's speech.

To answer this question, we recalculated each of the child-repetition scores as a percentage of the child's utterances and compared the findings with those based on the percentage of mother speech. Table 9.4 shows the means for the recalculated percentages for each group under study. Comparing the results of Table 9.4 based on the percentage of

---

[1]Note also that all subscores are independent of the child's initiatives because they are expressed as a percentage of talk within category.

TABLE 9.4
Maternal Repetitions-of-Child as Percentage of Child Utterances:
Mean Percentage for Groups

| | Groups | | | |
| | Disadvantaged | Advantaged | | |
Repetitions-of-child	Black	Black	White	Both
EXACT REPETITIONS[a]	7.0	7.3	8.0	7.7
EXACT COMPLETE	6.0	6.1	7.1	6.6
ALTERED REPETITIONS-OF-CHILD	14.9	24.4*	27.1*	25.8*
EXPANSIONS	1.3	6.1*	6.1*	6.1*
OTHER ALTERED	13.7	18.9	21.0*	19.9*
ALL REPETITIONS-OF-CHILD	21.6	31.6	35.3*	33.4*

Note: Means are adjusted for MLU of toddler.
[a] Exact Partial of inadequate frequency.
*$p < .05$ Scheffé comparing disadvantaged versus advantaged group(s).

child speech with those of Table 8.4 based on the percentage of mother speech, it can be seen that both ways of calculating child-repetitions show significant increments for advantaged mothers for the scores REPETITIONS-OF-CHILD, ALTERED REPETITIONS-OF-CHILD, and EXPANSIONS. The data indicate that the increments reported in Table 8.4 were not due merely to the higher frequency of talk among advantaged children.

Table 9.4 also shows an increment for advantaged mothers in OTHER ALTERED REPETITIONS-OF-CHILD. Whereas Table 8.4 shows a similar increment based on the percentage of mother speech, the latter failed to reach significance. This failure can be accounted for by the relatively low frequency of speech among disadvantaged mothers. The incidence of these repetitions in their speech was relatively inflated, therefore, as compared to the incidence in the speech of advantaged mothers, thus decreasing the difference between the groups. When we disregard how much the mothers talk, and calculate child-repetitions as a percentage of the child's utterances, advantaged mothers show an increment for all kinds of altered child-repetitions, EXPANSIONS as well as OTHER ALTERED REPETITIONS-OF-CHILD.

Overall, to the extent that we are able to investigate the effect of the child's communication initiatives on the mother's speech, the findings point to a single conclusion. For each set of FIS-C scores, total-talk, category, routine, and appended, the findings based on the percentage of mother speech appear to be independent of the child's initiatives.

Chapter 10
Effect of Age and Sex of Child on Mother Speech

In studying the effect of socioeducational status on mother's speech, age and sex of the child were control variables. In the present chapter, we will examine their independent effects.

Effect of Age of Child

Having assembled a vast array of formal features distinctive of baby talk, developmental psycholinguistics are beginning to ask *why?* and *how?* Why do we use baby talk in addressing toddlers, and how might it help in language acquisition? Gleason (1977) has recently suggested that what adults do in talking to toddlers is speak **for** the child, "filling the child's role [p. 203]" in conversation. As she describes it, "The developmental history of conversation begins with prelinguistic infants and competent adults. In the beginning, all of the conversation is provided by adults, and only slowly do children assume their conversational roles. Until they do, the adults **speak for them** as well as for themselves [Gleason, 1977, p. 203; emphasis added]."

Gleason's hypothesis, based on intuitive impressions, is strikingly similar to the one we derived from our statistical analysis of FIS-C scores in teacher talk (Schachter *et al.*, 1976). Comparing teacher talk to toddlers with their talk to 3- and 4-year-olds, we found that the following speech act scores occurred significantly more often in speech to toddlers: EXPLICATES DESIRE, REPORTS ON CHILD, WORD TEACHING, and TOTAL SPONTANEOUS TALK. It appeared that talk to toddlers mirrors the talk of the toddlers themselves, their frequent desire requests, their constant reports about themselves, and their persistent word learning. Where toddlers assert their desires, caregivers explicate them; where toddlers report on themselves, caregivers report on them; where toddlers are learning words, caregivers are teaching words; and where toddlers are speechless, caregivers speak spontaneously. This reciprocal or complementary character of the caregiver's speech pattern suggested the hypothesis that the caregiver adopts the role of the child's alter ego in communicating with toddlers. Like Gleason, we concluded that the caregiver seems to be "**speaking for the toddler** [Schachter *et al.*, 1976, p. 238, emphasis added]." We called this speech pattern "alter-ego speech."

Both Gleason's hypothesis and our own suggested that there is a distinctive pattern of communication in talk to toddlers, a characteristic pattern of speech acts, just as there is a distinctive pattern of formal features. If so, then the communication functions in baby talk might help to explain *why* baby talk takes the form that it does and *how* it serves to facilitate the acquisition of language.

The present data can contribute to research in this important area in the following ways:

1. The validity of the hypothesis that there is a distinctive pattern of speech acts in baby talk can be assessed by examining whether the effects of the age of the children in the present study are similar to those found in the previous study of teacher talk.

2. Since the FIS-C provides data on both the incidence of formal discourse features in baby talk as well as the incidence of speech acts, we can examine whether the former are associated with the latter, whether form and function are interrelated.

Comparison of Age-of-Child Effects: Teacher Study versus Mother Study

Although the typical strategy in identifying the distinctive features of baby talk has been to compare talk to toddlers with talk to older children or adults, an alternative strategy has been to compare talk to younger, communicatively immature toddlers and older mature toddlers (Cross, 1977; Newport, Gleitman & Gleitman, 1977; Phillips, 1973). Applying

TABLE 10.1

Age-of-Toddler Effects in Mother Study for Scores with Increments for Toddlers in Teacher Study: F-Ratio and Direction of Covariate Effect

Increment for toddlers: Teacher study	Age-of-toddler effects: Mother study	
	F	Direction
Category and subcategory scores		
EXPLICATES DESIRE	3.51*	−
REPORTS ON CHILD	3.50*	−
WORD TEACHING	15.36*	−
Total-talk score		−
TOTAL SPONTANEOUS TALK	4.99*	−

*$p < .05$, one-tailed test.

the latter strategy to the data of the present study, we can examine whether differences in maternal speech acts to younger and older toddlers are consistent with our previously reported differences in teacher talk to toddlers and older children.

Table 10.1 compares the age-of-child effects for the two studies. For each speech act score with significant increments in talk to toddlers in the teacher study, Table 10.1 shows the F-ratios for the age-of-toddler covariate in the present sample as well as the direction of the age effect.[1] Probability values for the covariate are based on one-tailed tests since the teacher study provided predictions for age-of-toddler effects.

It can be seen that the findings of the present study are consistent with those of the previous one. Caregivers of younger as compared to older toddlers, like caregivers of toddlers as compared to older children, show significant increments for EXPLICATES DESIRE, REPORTS ON CHILD, WORD

[1]Note that one other speech act score showed an increment in talk to toddlers in the teacher study, CONTROLS with SUBSTITUTE GRATIFICATION. However, because the definition of this score has since been revised, there is no mother data to compare with the teacher data. Note also that appended scores, as well as speech acts scores, show significant effects of age-of-child, as discussed in Chapter 8 (also see Table B.2). Additionally, in both the teacher and the mother study, there were speech acts scores with significant increments in talk to older children. In teacher talk to 3- and 4-year-olds, these scores include ASSISTS CHILD TO FULFILL OWN DESIRE; EGO-BOOSTS; CONTROLS with PHYSICAL NORMS; CONTROLS with SOCIAL NORMS ENCOURAGES PERSISTENCE; and PRESENTS KNOWLEDGE—NOT WORDS (see Schachter *et al.*, 1976). In mother talk to older toddlers, these scores include DON'TS and TEACHES ANY NORMATIVE EXPLANATION.

TEACHING, and TOTAL SPONTANEOUS TALK. The data support the hypothesis that baby talk is alter-ego speech—that the caregiver talks for the toddler.

Speech Acts and the Formal Features of Baby Talk

Is there any basis for inferring that this distinctive pattern of speech acts can help to account for the distinctive pattern of formal features in baby talk? The data of Table 8.3 (see Chapter 8), summarizing our findings on the relationship between speech acts and the formal features SELF-REPETITIONS, REPETITIONS-OF-CHILD and QUESTIONS, suggests that this might be the case.

Table 8.3 shows that maternal self-repetitions often occur in conjunction with WORD TEACHING; 23.5% of speech acts in this subcategory are self-repetitions, more than for any other subcategory. It seems likely that word teaching contributes to the high incidence of self-repetitions in baby talk. Regarding child-repetitions, Table 8.3 shows that they often occur in conjunction with EXPLICATES DESIRE; 44.6% of speech acts in this subcategory are repetitions of the child's preceding utterance, more than any other subcategory except EXPLICATES REPORT. It seems probable that child-repetitions are common in baby talk because of the prevalence of these explications. Similarly, the data of Table 8.3 suggest that questions may be common in baby talk because of the prevalence of speech acts in the category REPORTS ON CHILD. Virtually all (97.3%) of the speech acts in the main subcategory of this category, ELICITS REPORT, take the interrogative form. In addition, explications are almost always questions (89.4%), so that the prevalence of EXPLICATES DESIRE in talk to toddlers might also help explain the frequency of questions.

Altogether, the evidence suggests that communication function and form are interrelated in baby talk. Whether this relationship is one of cause and effect, that is, whether function accounts for form, is a matter for further investigation. Further analysis using the present sample of mother speech did not seem appropriate given the differential effects of maternal education on the scores for communication function and form.

Just as the data show an association between specific speech acts in baby talk and specific formal features, there also seems to be a relationship between the general nature of alter-ego speech and the overall form of baby talk. It has become apparent that adult talk to babies (BT) is similar in its overall form to the talk of babies to adults (TB) (Brown, 1977; Cross, 1977; Snow, 1977). For example, both BT and TB show high fundamental pitch, low MLU, frequent self-repetitions, and frequent repetitions of others. Though there are some differences between BT and TB, the overall similarity between the two is so extensive that Brown (1977) has suggested that BT originated in TB. The hypothesis that BT serves as alter-ego speech is consistent with Brown's suggestion. In adopting the conversational role of the baby, the caregiver is likely to mimic the form of the baby's talk, just as we mimic form in assuming anyone's role. In this way, the intention of the caregiver to speak for the child could account for the overall similarity in the form of BT and TB, just as Table 8.3 suggests that specific speech acts in baby talk might account for specific formal features.

These findings are of special interest because, in attempting to explain why we use baby talk, various investigators (Brown, 1977; Snow, 1977) have pointed out how finely tuned it is to the cognitive and linguistic development of the toddler. The hypothesis that baby talk serves as alter-ego speech suggests that it is also finely tuned to the affective development of the toddler. We noted earlier that both Piagetian and psychoanalytic theory posit a primary phase of lack of differentiation between the self and the other, called "the initial adualism" by Piaget and "primary narcissism" by psychoanalysts. With respect to the caregiver's role during this primary undifferentiated state, Piaget (1926/1959) describes the child as tending to view the adult "as a glorified omnipresent 'alter ego' [p. 257]," while the psychoanalyist Spitz (1951) suggests that the caregiver acts as the child's "external ego [p. 256]." Clearly one might expect a theory of why we use baby talk to take into account these developments in the underlying structure of self–other (speaker–listener) differentiation, as does the hypothesis that baby talk is alter-ego speech.

The hypothesis might also help to explain how baby talk facilitates the acquisition of language in that the complementary nature of alter-ego speech would seem to provide an optimum curriculum for language learning. By speaking for the toddler, the caregiver is demonstrating just how toddlers can say what they would say if they could speak for themselves.

Effect of Sex of Child

The question of whether mothers speak differently to male and female toddlers is of special significance in view of the evidence that girls talk earlier than boys. A study at the Barnard College Toddler Center (Schachter, Shore, Hodapp, Chalfin, & Bundy, 1978), showing that MLU and "upper bound" (UB) (the child's longest utterance [Brown, 1973]) are higher in female toddlers, provides supporting evidence for older studies of the 1930s and 1940s which found that girls talk earlier than boys (Day, 1932; McCarthy, 1930; Smith, 1935, 1939). Are there differences in the early verbal environment of boys and girls that might account for this apparent sex difference in language acquisition? On the basis of their thorough review of the literature, Maccoby and Jacklin (1974) concluded that previous research shows no consistent differences in mother talk to boys and girls. Among the studies reviewed by Maccoby and Jacklin was a microanalytic investigation of formal syntactic features in baby talk by Phillips (1973). Phillips's study was well designed to test sex differences with a large sample from a homogeneous social background. She found no significant effect of sex-of-toddler for her findings on the mother's syntax. The present data on FIS-C scores make it possible to examine the effect of sex-of-toddler on the mother's speech acts and on formal features of discourse.

The results show few sex differences. There were no significant effects of sex-of-toddler on any of the total-talk scores, category scores, individual subcategories, routine scores, or appended scores.

Table 10.2 lists the only FIS-C scores with significantly different means in talk to boys and girls. The combined subcategory score ALL CONFIRMATIONS shows a significantly higher mean for boys, while the subscores DON'TS with ANY NORMATIVE EXPLANATION and DON'TS with JUSTIFYING EXPLANATIONS show a significantly higher mean for girls. Since these subscores are highly intercorrelated—the latter subsumes the former—there are essentially only two scores with significant differences in talk to boys and girls. Given the large number of scores under study, it is highly probable that these two significant effects were obtained solely on the basis of chance.

It should be noted that this study was not designed to examine the effect of the toddler's sex on mother speech. The socioeducational

TABLE 10.2
Effect of Sex of Toddler on Mother Speech:
Mean Percentage for Scores with Significant Effects

	Sex of toddler	
Scores	Girls	Boys
ALL CONFIRMATIONS	8.1	11.5*
DON'TS with ANY NORMATIVE EXPLANATION	15.9*	10.6
DON'TS with JUSTIFYING EXPLANATIONS	19.0*	14.4

$*p < .05.$

heterogeneity of the sample could easily obscure any such effects. Sex differences in MLU for the toddlers themselves were probably obscured because MLU among the disadvantaged toddlers was similar for girls and boys (i.e., means were 2.01 and 2.06, respectively). Although the advantaged toddlers showed the expected increment in MLU for girls ($M = 2.67$ versus 2.22 for boys), the sex difference for the sample as a whole fell somewhat short of significance ($p < .10$, one-tailed test).

A better design for testing the effect of the toddler's sex on mother FIS-C scores would be to study a sample of adequate size consisting of boys and girls from a homogeneous background, as did Phillips in her study of syntax in baby talk. Until such data are available, the question of differences in early maternal speech acts addressed to boys and girls remains open.[2]

As we review the findings for all of the variables under study, socioeducational status, race, age-of-toddler, and sex, it becomes apparent that the variable with by far the greatest impact on mother speech is socioeducational status. It shows significant effects on a large number of FIS-C scores of every kind (total-talk scores, category scores, individual and combined subcategories, subscores and appended scores). The results would appear to have important implications for our early intervention efforts. Educated mothers, as compared to less educated mothers, seem to provide their young children with very different kinds of early verbal environments, and these differences may well account for the disparities in the later school performance of their children. Implications for both theory and practice in early intervention will be discussed in the final section of the book, after the presentation of illustrative case material in the next chapter.

[2]A recent study by Cherry and Lewis (1978) of mother speech acts of 12 toddlers (6 male and 6 female) from a homogeneous middle-class background shows some interesting trends, but the small sample size demands replication.

Chapter 11
Illustrative Case Material

To illustrate the findings for the three socioeducational groups, we present samples of mother–toddler talk for the three oldest girls in each group, Rhonda, black disadvantaged; Felicia, black advantaged; and Sarah, white advantaged. Their names have been changed and all identifying data withheld to preserve comfidentiality.

These cases were selected primarily because they exemplify much of the speech pattern that is typical of the groups they represent, although no three toddlers matched for age and sex could be found where data demonstrated all the trends found in their groups. The age of the toddlers was another factor in their selection. Interpretation of the speech of older toddlers is less dependent on context than that of younger ones, so that context notes can be kept at a minimum. In addition, all three cases were part of our taped sample, so that the records are as complete as possible.

Because the advantaged mothers spoke roughly twice as much as the disadvantaged, we report five 3-minute intervals for the former and ten for the latter. The protocols cover the first set of intervals on the first morning of observation. There are at least 50 maternal speech acts in each protocol. In order to illustrate scoring procedures, FIS-C scores are noted as footnotes for the first speech act in each protocol.

RHONDA'S PROTOCOL

FIRST INTERVAL

[Both in Mother's bedroom: Rhonda with head on Mother's knee; Mother reading mail while sitting on bed]

RHONDA	MOTHER
	[leaves room]
[plays with toy phone]	
	[returns]
	Get your finger out your mouth. [1]
	[leaves room]
[goes into her adjoining roomette and briefly manipulates items, drinking glass, clothes, etc.]	
[returns to Mother's room]	
	[returns]
I'm not getting on. [the bed]	
	What you say, Peaches?
I'm not getting on.	
	Huh?
I said, I'm not getting.	
	You don't what?
I'm not get, Mom.	
	[ignores]
	[sits on bed, works on mail]

SECOND INTERVAL

[Both in Mother's bedroom: Rhonda sitting on floor at foot of bed, squatting, sucking thumb; Mother reading mail while sitting on bed]

[wanders around room sadly]

RHONDA	MOTHER
	What's wrong?
	Throw this in the trash for mama. [envelope]
	Then you and Joan [neighbor] *is going out, okay?*
	All right?
All right.	

THIRD INTERVAL

[Both in Mother's bedroom: Rhonda looking under bed; Mother reading mail while sitting on bed]

[1]Total-talk score: TOTAL SPONTANEOUS TALK
Category score and subcategory: CONTROLS, DON'TS

RHONDA	MOTHER
[sees shoes under bed]	
You got shoes.	
	I don't want those shoes.
	They not my shoes.
Get shoes, you got?	
[picks up shoes and plays with them]	
	[gives pile of clothes]
	Put these on the bed.
	These, Angel.
[takes, puts on bed]	
[briefly manipulates items in room, clothes, envelopes]	
[puts fingers in mouth]	
	Take your finger out your mouth.
	Thank you. [persuading]
[removes fingers]	
	Thank you. [acknowledging]
[puts fingers in mouth]	
	Don't put it back in there. [finger]
	You aren't going with me there. [ominous tone]

FOURTH INTERVAL

[Both in Mother's bedroom, sitting on bed: Rhonda files Mother's nail; Mother watches]

RHONDA	MOTHER
[pushes Mother's finger away]	
Give. [finger]	
Give, Momma.	
	Oh, you finished with this one. [gives other finger]
Not that. [finger]	
That.	
	[gives other finger]
[files Mother's nails]	
Do mine.	
	[files Rhonda's nails]
	How old you gonna be?
Three.	
	Your birthday's three months from now.
	How old you gonna be?
	How old you gonna be?
	You're gonna be . . .
Three.	
	That's right.
	Count.
	Put three fingers up.

I can't do it.

           [fixes hand as it should be]
           What's that say?
           What's that say?

Um?

           How much is that?

Three.

           That's right.
           That's how old you're gonna be.
           One, two, three. [counts child's fingers]
           One, two, three. [counts child's fingers]

One, two, three.
One, two, three.
One, two, three.
One, two, three.
One, two, three.

FIFTH INTERVAL

[Both in Mother's bedroom]

      RHONDA   MOTHER

Three.
Five.

           You didn't get that age yet.
           [walks out of room]

[briefly manipulates items in room, clothes,
   shoes]
[goes to living room]

           [in kitchen, washing dishes]

[plays with bottom of bedroom door]

           [goes to child] *Come on, Angel.*
           Didn't I tell you not to go down there? [bottom
             of door]
           Come on, stay away from this door before the
             splinter goes in your hand, girl.
           [returns to dishes]

[goes into kitchen, watches Mother do
   dishes]

SIXTH INTERVAL

[Both in kitchen: Rhonda takes broom to living room, sweeps living room playfully;
Mother collects ashtrays in living room and returns to kitchen; washes ashtrays and
dishes]

      RHONDA   MOTHER

Get off. [talking to broom]
Get off. [talking to broom]
Get off. [talking to broom]

           [washing dishes]

RHONDA	MOTHER
[in living room, playfully sweeping]	
	[enters living room]
I sweep up.	
	[ignores]
[sweeps playfully]	
	[straightening up house]
Mop up that. [to self]	
	Pick the broom up and sweep the trash.
[does]	
Oops. [to self, after hitting broom on table]	
Cleaned.	
	Sweep it in here.
	Sweep the trash in here.
[picks up some papers]	
	You don't need those papers.

[Both in living room]

RHONDA	MOTHER
Sweep in here.	
	Take it in the kitchen.
[takes dustpan into kitchen]	
[returns]	
	[cleaning table]
[taking sweater off]	
	Don't take your sweater off.
	Keep it on.
I hot.	
	You keep it on.
I hot.	
Shoot.	
	Don't take it off.
I hot.	
I hot Mommy.	
	[takes Rhonda's sweater off]
[in bedroom playfully sweeping under bed]	
	[cleaning in kitchen]

[Both in bedroom; Rhonda near radiator]

RHONDA	MOTHER
	Come from behind there.
	Before you get burned.
	Bring the sweater and put it in the room.

Don't want the sweater.
I hot. [puts away]
[sweeping up the trash]

Leave it.
Sweep it up later.

Ma.

[ignores]
I cut my hand right there and I ain't got no Band-Aid.
See, I cut my hand.

[looks]
How you cut your hand?

I don't know how I cut it.

Go doctor, Mommy.

The doctor send me home with this little cut.

The doctor send you home cut?

Yeah, I buy some Band-Aids.
You remember me buy some Band-Aids when we go out?

Yeah.

Okay.
Cause you may cut your hands one of these days.
Need Band-Aids.

Mommy, chewing gum.
Mommy.

I don't have no more.

Um hum.

No I don't.

Um hum.

I don't have none,
I got to buy some.

TENTH INTERVAL

[Both in bedroom]

RHONDA	MOTHER
	[taking Rhonda's pile of trash away]
Mommy, don't touch that.	
	I'm going to put it outside.
Outside?	
	Uh huh. [leaves room taking trash]
[briefly manipulating items in room] [sucks thumb]	
	[returns with glass of soda] *Stop sucking your finger.* *Buy you some red stuff.* [bad tasting fluid to prevent thumb sucking] [sitting on bed drinking soda]
[watches Mother]	
	[sets soda on table]

[takes soda and drinks]

All gone.

All gone.

[sits on bed]

          [watches child drink]

          Didn't I tell you to ask for things?

          Didn't I tell you to ask for things?

FELICIA'S PROTOCOL

FIRST INTERVAL

FELICIA	MOTHER
[In her bedroom playing with doll and dollhouse, talking to self, playing with phone]	[In the dining area drinking coffee, reading newspaper]

SECOND INTERVAL

[In her bedroom playing with doll, looking at books]	[In dining area drinking coffee, reading newspaper]

FELICIA	MOTHER
Mommy, I got something.	
	What book you got, Hon? [2]
Red book.	
White book.	
Blue book.	
	What's that in there?
Me, my Daddy, and my Mommy.	
	Oh.
Are you?	
Are you my Mommy?	
	Huh?
Are you Daddy's Mommy?	
	No, only your Mommy.
	Nobody else.
[sits on sofa, examing book]	
	[at table reading newspaper]

THIRD INTERVAL

[Both in dining area: Felicia singing and dancing; Mother reading newspaper]

FELICIA	MOTHER
	[goes into kitchen; washes dishes]
[goes into kitchen]	

[2]Total-talk score: TOTAL RESPONSIVE-TALK, TOTAL Ch:S → C:R RESPONSIVE TALK
   Category score and subcategory: RESPONDS TO CHILD REPORT, SEEKS FURTHER ELABORATION OF REPORT
   Appended scores: REPETITION-OF-CHILD, ALTERED REPETITIONS-OF-CHILD, OTHER ALTERED; QUESTIONS

Mommy.
Mommy.
I got the little baby on my back. [doll]

There's a baby on your back?
You want me to tie the baby on your back?

Uh huh.

Uh huh.

Uh huh.

Uh huh.

I want you to tie her on my back.
With scarf.

Okay. [ties]
This is the scarf that we use to tie the baby on the back.
[ties]

The little baby is gonna ride.

Okay.

[goes into living room–dining area]

See you later, Hon.

I got the baby on me. [to self, walking around room]

[washing dishes in kitchen]

FOURTH INTERVAL

FELICIA   MOTHER

[in kitchen washing dishes]

[enters kitchen]
Mommy, you know.
Mommy, know.
The baby sleeping.

She sleeping back there?

Yeah.

You better go put her in her bed.
If she's asleep, don't you want to put her in her bed?

[takes doll off]

You gonna take her off now?

[taking bubble water into living room–dining area]

You remember.
Don't pour it on the floor, you hear?
Huh?

Okay, I won't.
Mommy, can I pour it in that?
Mommy, can I pour it in that?

[goes to her in living room–dining area]
Where?
Pour it in what?

That.

                                                          Why don't you . . . [considers substitute]
                                                          You want to put it in there?
Uh huh.

                                                          Okay.
                                                          Be careful.
                                                          That's enough, Hon.
                                                          That's enough, Hon.
                                                          You always go too much, Hon.
                                                          When I say that's enough you should stop.
                                                          You know what you're doing?
                                                          Wasting it.
                                                          And then it's gonna be all gone.
                                                          Now that's enough now.
                                                          I'm gonna put it away now.
                                                          [takes it away]
                                                          Okay, 'cause you're wasting it now.
                                                          *You think you're in the bathtub playing with
                                                              water.*
                                                          Why you want to waste your bubbles?
                                                          We have to buy that from the store.
                                                          That's not water from the water fountain.
                                                          Felicia, that's for making bubbles anyhow.
                                                          *That's not for pouring from one container to
                                                              another.*

[throws papers that were on coffee table on
    floor]

                                                          You know I happen to be cleaning up.
                                                          I'm cleaning up, Felicia.

[throws papers on floor]

                                                          Why you doing that?
                                                          Huh?
                                                          Are you angry?
                                                          Are you angry?
Yes.

                                                          How come?

FIFTH INTERVAL

FELICIA	MOTHER
[In her bedroom playing with doll, talking to self]	[Cleaning up living room-dining area]
Mommy, Lee is going to sleep. [doll]	
	[goes to Felicia's bedroom]
	What is it, Hon?
Lee is going to sleep. [doll]	
	Do what?

Lee is gone to sleep.

She's gone to sleep?
You want to put her to bed now?

No.
I want her stay.

You gonna let her sleep on your back?

Uh huh.
I gonna let her sit on my . . .
[hugs doll]

You love Lee?
You want me to give you a glass of water?
Huh?

Glass of water?
Okay.

[Both go to kitchen]

[gives her water]

[looks at water]
It's coffee.
It's coffee.

It's not coffee.
It's water.

It's water.
It's coffee.
It's coffee.

When you gonna get dressed again?

Huh?

Huh?
Huh?
When you gonna get sharp?
Get your hair all pretty.

[wants roll of scotch tape]

Huh?

Who used that all up?

Used what all up?

This.

You must of moved it.
Here. [gives scotch tape]

[taking tape off roller]

Try not to waste it.
Hear?

SARAH'S PROTOCOL

FIRST INTERVAL

[Both in playroom: Sarah setting up toy bed and dolls in doll house; Mother knitting]

SARAH	MOTHER
It's not all finished, Mommy.	
	Okay.[3]
This is the bed, Mommy.	
	Um hum.
[inaudible]	
It's all set, Mommy.	
	Okay.
It's all set.	
Mommy, my other people.	
[dolls]	
	Okay.
These are my other people.	
	Um hum.
I'm using my people, my people.	
	Okay.
Those are my people.	
Those are my people.	
	Um hum.
That's my dress.	
	[ignores]
I like to stay with my mother.	
I like to stay with my mother.	
	Yes, you do.
I like to stay with my mother.	
I didn't do the show yet.	
I didn't do the show yet, Mommy.	
	Shall I introduce you?
	Shall I say, ladies and gentlemen?
No.	
	No?
	Sarah presents. . .?
What, Mother?	
	Did you start your show yet?
No.	
	You're just setting it up?
[inaudible]	
I'm fixing my show.	
	Um hum.
	[goes into kitchen when tea kettle whistles]

[3]Total-talk score: TOTAL RESPONSIVE TALK, TOTAL Ch:S → C:R RESPONSIVE TALK
Category score and subcategory: RESPONDS TO CHILD REPORT, CONFIRMS REPORT

[follows Mother]

[making tea in kitchen]

I can drink coffee.

That's tea.
You want some tea?

I can drink tea.

[ignores]

[Mother offers observer tea; observer accepts. Observation is interrupted until teatime is over and mother and child have resumed their activities excluding the observer]

SECOND INTERVAL

[Both back in playroom: Sarah playing with pieces that insert into slots in toy castle; Mother knitting]

SARAH	MOTHER
	Here's your dragon. [piece for toy castle]
Dragon.	
	Um hum.
Where does the dragon go? [trying to put in slot]	
	Does he fit in there?
No.	
	No?
	Wanna put the people inside? [dolls]
I want to put the frog.	
	If you squeeze real hard you can get him in.
He goes in here. [puts frog in castle]	
	Very good.
In there.	
	In there?
	That's a good place.
That's a good place.	
	Um hum.
	[bell rings] *What's that, Sarah?*
The castle.	
	No.
	That's my timer.
	I have to shut off my hard-boiled eggs, Sarah.
	Be right back.
	[goes to kitchen, shuts off eggs]
[runs after]	
	[returns to playroom]
[follows Mother]	

THIRD INTERVAL

[Both in playroom: Sarah playing with dollhouse family; Mother knitting]

SARAH	MOTHER
[inaudible]	
	Hum?

They have the same mouth.
[two toys]

                              Right, they do.

I have a mouth.
Kiss there, Mommy. [toy]

                              Hum?

Kiss there, Mommy.

                              [kisses]

He has the same mouth.

                              Um hum.

Would you put this back on, Mother?
    [animal-toy parts that snap together]

                              [does]

Mommy, fix this. [snap toy]

                              Put it down, Sarah.
                              [shows how to snap two parts together]
                              Put it down, Sarah.
                              Put it down, Sarah.

Now put this?

                              Now put this in. [snap toy]

I can't.

                              Um hum.

[snaps] *I did it!*

                              Sure you can.

                              Good.
There he goes. [pushing snap toy]   *You did it yourself.*

                              Where's he going, Sarah?

FOURTH INTERVAL

[Both in playroom: Sarah getting plane; Mother knitting]

SARAH   MOTHER

I need my airplane.

                              Um hum.

That too big. [toy can't fit in dollhouse]

                              Um hum.

Can the people go in? [doll house]

                              Well, try.

Can the people go in?

                              Sure.

Yes, they could, Mommy.

                              Um hum.

She doesn't have a hat. [doll]

                              No, she doesn't.

She has hair.
It's only make believe.

                              Um hum.

People make believe.
She's only a people.

                              Make-believe person.
                              Make-believe lady, huh?

[talking to self, playing]
That's an airplane, Mommy.

                [ignores]

I'm locking that door now. [dollhouse]

                Okay.

FIFTH INTERVAL

[Both in playroom]

SARAH	MOTHER
Can I ride on the horsey, Mother?	
	Um hum.
Look, Mommy. [on rocking horse]	
	Very good, Sarah.
Now climb.	
I'm climbing on the roof.	
[on climber]	
	Do your trick?
Do the trick?	
	Yeah, I wanna see you do the trick.
That's not the way.	
	What's the way you're gonna do it?
[does trick]	
	Very good, Sarah.
	Very good.
I hurt myself.	
	Your head?
I can reach.	
	Reach the top?
	You have to climb up, don't you?
	Hey, hey, you're stepping on my knitting.
I am?	
	Yeah.
Look. [on climber]	
	That's a good trick.
	That's a "bird's nest." [type of trick]
That's an exercise.	
	Yeah, that's a "bird's nest."
Yeah.	
	[inaudible], *Sarah.*
Look. [on climber]	
	That's a "bird's nest."
That's my "bird's nest."	
	Yeah.
I'm gonna make my own "bird's nest."	
[inaudible]	
	Go on the other side.
Other side, Mommy?	
	Um hum.
I'm on my side. [of climber]	
	No, you're on my side.

Commentary

Mother talk to Rhonda contrasts sharply with mother talk to Felicia and Sarah. Although the two advantaged girls are different in personality—Felicia, more independent, often leaving her mother's side; Sarah, more dependent, remaining near her mother at all times—the speech samples of their mothers share a great deal in common compared with that of Rhonda's mother.

Total-Talk Scores

Much of the talk of Rhonda's mother is spontaneous (e.g., telling her daughter to move away from the door, to discard the trash, to take her finger out of her mouth, to say how old she is). On the other hand, the mothers of Felicia and Sarah talk mainly in response to their daughters' communications. Felicia shows her mother a book, and her mother asks for elaboration of the child's report; or she reports a fantasy about a sleeping doll, and her mother explicates, confirms, and adds a suggestion of her own. Sarah tells her mother about a show she is organizing, and the mother confirms the child's reports; or she asks her mother to fix a broken toy, and her mother shows her how to do so.

Felicia and Sarah talk so much more than Rhonda that this accounts for some of the increment in responsive speech for the educated mothers. But it does not account for all of it. Note how the educated mothers support the flow of conversational initiatives of their children with explications, confirmations, and accommodations, often with more than one response per child initiative. On the other hand, the flow of Rhonda's conversational initiatives is often cut short. For example, Sarah's stream of reports on her show is greeted with a stream of confirmations by her mother, and Felicia's request for her mother to tie the doll on her back evokes as many as six maternal speech acts. In contrast, Rhonda's initiatives are often rebuffed with control talk, DON'TS or REFUSALS, or they are simply ignored. For example, when she offers her mother some shoes, the offer is abruptly rejected (*I don't want those shoes.*), and when she announces she is finished drinking some soda (*All gone.*), she is scolded for forgetting to ask if she could have some. A number of Rhonda's other communications are ignored, including her first comment (*I'm not getting on.*). After her mother makes two attempts to understand the comment, she gives up and ignores it. Felicia's mother too has difficulty understanding one of her daughter's comments (*Lee is going to sleep.*), but she persists until she knows how to respond.

Note that, despite the marked contrast in total responsive speech, Rhonda's mother shows no decrement in total spontaneous speech. That is, there is no generalized deficit in verbal productivity.

Communication-Function Category Scores,
Subcategories, and Subscores

Control talk dominates the speech of Rhonda's mother, as it does for the less educated sample as a whole. More specifically, there is a large proportion of DON'TS in her speech (*Get your finger out your mouth. Don't take your sweater off. Come away from there.*). While Felicia's mother produces a series of DON'TS as she tries to regulate her child's play with bubble water, these DON'TS do not dominate her speech; there is a variety of speech acts in other categories as well.

The other frequent categories in Rhonda's protocol are TEACHES and RESPONDS TO CHILD LEARNING COMMUNICATION, as represented in the sequence where the mother tries to teach the child her age. In this respect, Rhonda's protocol does not differ from Sarah's. Sarah's mother also shows a number of speech acts in these two categories as she teaches her child about the timer ringing in the kitchen; corrects her about the name for "tea"; prompts her to practice a gross motor skill (*Do your tricks?*); teaches her the name of the skill (bird's nest); and confirms her word learning.

The categories that occur often in the protocols of the educated mothers and rarely in Rhonda's protocol, reflecting group differences we have obtained, are RESPONDS TO CHILD DESIRE COMMUNICATION, RESPONDS TO CHILD REPORT, and for Sarah, RESPONDS TO CHILD EGO-ENHANCING. For example, Felicia's mother shows several scores in the subcategories EXPLICATES DESIRE and ACCOMMODATES: FULFILLS DESIRE when, in response to her child's requests, she ties the doll to the child's back, grants permission to use a container, and provides scotch tape. Sarah's mother shows a long series of scores in the subcategory CONFIRMS REPORT (*Um hum., Okay., Okay., Um hum.*) in response to Sarah's long series of reports on her show. Sarah's mother also shows several EGO-BOOSTS (*You did it yourself.; Very good!*).

Additionally, the protocols illustrate stylistic differences in control talk and in teaching talk that were found to be characteristic of educated and less educated mothers. When Felicia's mother attempts to regulate her child's play with bubble water, she demonstrates the way educated mothers provide justifying explanations when they say DON'TS. She gives two different explanations for taking the bubble water away from Felicia, first, that the child is wasting it so it will soon be gone, and second, that it is not ordinary bathtub water but special water that needs to be purchased in a store. Felicia's mother also justifies another prohibition; she points out that when the child throws paper on the floor it is obstructing her efforts to clean up. On only one occasion does she admonish Felicia without providing an explanation (i.e., when she reminds the child not to get the floor wet). Felicia's protocol also contains an example of offering the child a substitute with a refusal. When Felicia asks if she can pour her bubble water into a particular container, the mother starts to suggest a different container, but then seems to allow the child her original choice.

In contrast, although Rhonda's mother, like Felicia's, provides justifications for DON'TS on two occasions, explaining that the child may splinter her hand playing with the door or burn herself touching the radiator, there are a large number of DON'TS with no explanations at all—nor is there any substitute gratification offered.

Similarly, Sarah's protocol illustrates the style of teaching that is common in the educated sample, while Rhonda's illustrates the style typical of the less educated. Sarah's mother interpolates her teaching into the flow of responsive speech acts. When Sarah pridefully displays her climbing ability, her mother responds with an ego-boost and then adds a second response giving the name of her trick (*That's a bird's nest.''*). On the other hand, Rhonda's mother spontaneously initiates the teaching sequence about her daughter's age, eliciting knowledge from the child and presenting new knowledge. There are also characteristic group differences in the content of teaching. Rhonda's mother teaches her numbers, while Sarah's mother teaches about the social world (e.g., how to introduce a play), about the physical world (e.g., the timer), about gross motor activity (e.g., the bird's nest trick). There is no teaching of numbers in the protocols of the advantaged girls.

Routine Scores and Appended Scores for Formal Features

As in the sample as a whole, routines are relatively infrequent in these protocols. The only routine score that appears in all three protocols is WHAT?

In contrast, the protocols illustrate the high frequency of repetitions and questions in talk to toddlers. Also illustrated is the finding that educated mothers show more repetitions of the child. Note also that repetitions of the child occur mainly in conjunction with explications and confirmations. For example, Felicia says, *The baby sleeping,* and her mother explicates, *She sleeping back there?*; Sarah says, *She doesn't have a hat,* and her mother confirms, *No, she doesn't.*

Altogether, these protocols serve to illustrate the main conclusions from our statistical findings, namely, that advantaged and disadvantaged mothers differ mainly in the social and emotional aspects of their communication with their young children, not in the linguistic and cognitive aspects.

Part IV

Implications for Theory and Practice in Early Intervention

Chapter 12

A Cognitive-Affective Theory of the Caregiver Role in Early Intervention: Beyond the Difference-Deficit Controversy

Confronted with the crisis in our inner-city schools, Wilson Riles, the black school superintendent of Los Angeles, formulates the problem of the relationship between poverty and poor school performance as follows: "I am not talking about poverty, but about what poverty brings with it. What we have are parents beset with all kinds of difficulties, not able or don't know how to take care of their youngsters."[1] As a result, he concludes, these children are not prepared for their school experience.

Riles's formulation that the early home environment of poor children provides less than optimal conditions for the development of educability is widely accepted among preschool educators holding diverse educational philosophies (Bereiter & Engelmann, 1966; Biber, 1977). It was this view, buttressed by the evidence compiled by Hunt (1961) and Bloom (1964), that formed the basis of early intervention efforts, both in education and research. And it was this view that formed the basis of the present research project.

Nevertheless, this early environment hypothesis has not been accepted universally. Indeed, it has given rise to considerable controversy, most prominently, the heredity–environment controversy and the difference–deficit controversy. Proponents of the heredity position (e.g., Jensen, 1969) have argued that heredity and not the early home environment accounts for the poor school performance of low-income children—more particularly, low-income black children. When early intervention was in its infancy, Jensen (1969) had already pronounced it doomed to fail in the face of presumed biological limitations.

Proponents of the difference theory (e.g., Cole & Bruner, 1971; Labov, 1970) have argued that the early environment of low-income minority children, who make up a large proportion of our disadvantaged population, does provide optimal conditions for development. However, it offers a culturally different set of teaching and learning experiences, different but not deficient—as Cole, Gay, Glick, and Sharp (1971) put it, "different but equal [p. 222]." Difference theorists reject early intervention and propose instead that the schools learn to accommodate more effectively to cultural diversity. Because proponents of both the heredity theory and the difference theory have challenged the basic rationale for early intervention, it is important to examine the merits of their positions carefully.

Jensen's heredity theory has come under attack from all quarters (Cronbach, 1969; Fehr, 1969; Hall & Freedle, 1975; Kagan, 1969). There is little point in reviewing all the criticisms here once again. We need only note that our findings are consistent with the major thrust of the argument against Jensen, namely that it is poverty and not race that accounts for the poor school performance of the low-income black child. Our findings show almost no race difference in the everyday speech acts of mothers to their toddlers, whereas they show extensive differences associated with the mother's educational and economic status. Similarly, while all of our advantaged toddlers, both black and white, were found to perform at mental ages exceeding their chronological age, only 3 of the 10 low-income toddlers did so. It is class, rather than race, that accounts for the differences that emerged in the early home environment as well as in the child's cognitive performance.

In contrast to the heredity theory, the difference theory has met with general approval—no doubt because it appeals to the egalitarian ideals of a democratic and pluralistic society, just as Jensen's theory is totally repugnant to these ideals. However, if the difference theory threatens to undermine support for educational programs that aim to achieve equality for low-income minorities (e.g., early intervention), it may prove to be equalitarian only in spirit and not in substance. The difference–deficit controversy demands close scrutiny.

When we examine the history of the difference–deficit controversy, we note that the difference theory is a form of cultural relativism (see

Cole & Bruner, 1971), that arose as a reaction against the doctrine of cultural deprivation or environmental deficit. This doctrine proposes that the environment of the child of poverty is deficient in its linguistic and cognitive aspects, is bereft of adequate teaching and learning experiences in these areas. It is this concept of cultural deprivation or deficit that has provided the rationale for didactic programs designed to supply the training in intellectual skills that is missing. Indeed, the difference theory had its origin in an attack by the sociolinguist Labov on Bereiter and Engelmann's didactic language training program. Bereiter and Engelmann (1966) claimed that poor black children are deprived of language. Labov (1970) retorted that, in fact, these children are "bathed in verbal stimulation from morning to night [p. 163]." However, the dialect they are exposed to is Black English rather than Standard English, and it is expressed in different ways and contexts (i.e., more eloquently on the streets than in school).

We have since learned that poor black children are not "bathed in verbal stimulation from morning to night" (Schoggen & Schoggen, 1976; Wachs et al., 1971; and the present data). Furthermore, the present findings suggest that the quality of verbal stimulation is probably far more important than its quantity. In addition, we have since learned that the dialect spoken in the home, even the language spoken, has little or no effect on the child's school performance when it is not associated with differences in socioeducational status. For example, it has become apparent that affluent English-speaking children suffer no special academic problems when they are transferred to French-speaking schools in Quebec. Also, in Israel, where few immigrant children arrive at school speaking Hebrew, it is only those from educationally disadvantaged backgrounds who have special academic problems.

Nevertheless, the difference–deficit controversy survives, mainly because the emphasis of the difference theorists has shifted from a concern with language (Labov, 1970) to a concern with cognition (Cole et al., 1971; Cole & Schribner, 1974). The focus of attack continues to be the doctrine of cultural deprivation. By analogy with linguistic relativism (i.e., the theory that all languages of the world are functionally equal although they may express their power in different contexts), Cole has proposed a theory of cognitive relativism. Generalizing from data collected mainly in Liberia to low-income minority subcultures in this country, Cole argues that no culture can be described as deficient in cognitive competence. Rather, different cultures express their competence in different contexts and situations. The only deficits that exist in comparing cultures are performance deficits with respect to particular situations, and these deficits are defined by each culture. A Yale sophomore, for example, would be viewed as deficient in estimating volumes of rice by the standards of a Liberian rice farmer, while the latter would be viewed as deficient in estimating distances by the standards of an educated American (Cole & Bruner, 1971).

The argument that only deficits in performance exist across cultures is untestable, because it is impossible to measure deficits in underlying competence, as Cole *et al.* (1971) rightly point out. We can only assess how a child performs in a given situation; estimates of competence are always a matter of speculation. In view of the diminishing support for all government programs for the poor, it seems counterproductive to waste time and energy on an unresolvable controversy. Apart from the few who claim that cultural deficits are inherited, both difference and deficit theorists agree that disadvantaged children show environmentally induced, and therefore potentially reversible, performance deficits in our schools and that some form of educational remedy is indicated to deal with the problem. What form this educational remedy should take depends on how we come to view the cause of this performance deficit.

As to whether the cause is a cultural deficit or a cultural difference, the data we have assembled suggest that it is neither. From the perspective of the present findings, it becomes clear that, despite the continuing debate, both difference and deficit theorists share in common an exclusive concern with the linguistic and cognitive aspects of the environment of poverty. Both views neglect the role of social or emotional factors in promoting the development of educability. The present microanalysis of the everyday verbal environment shows extensive social-class differences in the social and emotional domains, and almost no difference in what might be viewed as the intellectual aspects of the environment. They challenge the facile polarity of the difference–deficit controversy and raise questions about preschool educational recommendations derived from either of these theories—the didactic approach from the deficit theory and the "no early intervention" position from the difference theory. Instead, the findings suggest a third theory to account for the school problems of low-income children, a cognitive–affective theory, one consistent with the whole-child or Piagetian approach to early intervention.

Cultural Deficit Theory: Didactic Early Intervention

The data do not support the theory that the early environment of disadvantaged children is culturally deprived or deficient. Let us review the evidence.

Total-talk Scores.   While advantaged mothers talk twice as much as disadvantaged, there is no difference between the two groups in the amount of spontaneous talk, only in the amount of talk responsive to the child's communications. Rather than suggesting an overall deprivation in verbal stimulation or a generalized linguistic deficit, the results suggest a difference in the social or emotional aspects of everyday communication. Advantaged mothers adopt a responsive communication style. (See Chapter 6.)

Category Scores, Subcategories, and Subscores.   The findings also cast doubt on a theory of early cognitive deprivation in the disadvantaged environment. The two speech act categories concerned with teaching and learning, what we ordinarily view as the cognitive aspects of the verbal environment, show no significant differences among the groups. Mothers of toddlers, whether advantaged or not, devote about 10% of their speech to teaching new knowledge and a similar percentage of their speech responding to their child's learning communications. Furthermore, in teaching new knowledge, advantaged and disadvantaged mothers use the same didactic communication techniques in the same proportion, presenting or modeling the new knowledge, eliciting practice, and word teaching. The techniques used in responding to the child's learning communications, confirming or correcting recently acquired knowledge and supplying answers to learning questions, also show the same incidence for all groups. Additionally, with the exception of teaching letters and numbers, the content of teaching is the same for all groups, mainly covering facts about the physical or social world and normative explanations. A significantly higher proportion of the disadvantaged mother's teaching focuses on letters and numbers. However, in view of the cultural pressures for school success, this can hardly be viewed as a sign of a culturally deprived environment. On the contrary, this finding suggests that disadvantaged mothers are more attentive to teaching their young children the skills of the majority culture than are advantaged mothers.

The only other significant group difference in the mother's teaching talk is a greater emphasis on interpolated teaching among the advantaged mothers. Whereas the proportion of spontaneous teaching is similar for both disadvantaged and advantaged mothers, the latter are significantly more likely to interpolate their teaching speech acts into a series of responses to the child's communication. Advantaged mothers are also more likely to interpolate a teaching component into a speech act whose primary function is not teaching. Since the overall percentage of teaching talk is the same for both the advantaged and disadvantaged, these findings seem merely to represent another manifestation of the advantaged mother's responsive communication style. (See Chapter 7.)

Appended Scores. Disadvantaged mothers were not found to be deficient in their mastery of the baby-talk code. They showed a higher percentage of exact self-repetitions, whereas advantaged mothers showed a higher percentage of repetitions of the child. In addition, the findings question Bernstein's (1970) theory of a restricted linguistic code among the disadvantaged since the percentage of explanations in the mother's speech, justifying explanations as well as teaching explanations, was found to be similar for all groups. Only when we examine the percentage of DON'TS with justifications do the advantaged mothers show a significant increment. (See Chapter 8.)

The lack of support for a theory of cultural deprivation or deficit raises questions about didactic programs based on this theory. Indeed, in many respects the disadvantaged mother resembles the caregiver in didactic programs. Like the teacher in programs cast in the Bereiter and Engelmann model (1966) or in the Becker *et al.* model (1971), she initiates most of the daily verbal interaction with the child; her speech is dominated by control talk and teaching talk; she makes frequent use of negative commands; she emphasizes the teaching of letters and numbers; and she often uses the technique of exact self-repetition. Like these teachers, she generally talks **to** the child rather than responsively **with** the child.

Cultural Difference Theory: No Early Intervention

The data do not support a theory of cultural differences to account for the later school problems of minority children any more than they support a theory of cultural deprivation. Highly educated mothers, whether members of the minority black culture or the majority white culture, seem to provide their young children with almost identical everyday verbal environments, and the similarity holds for both the linguistic and cognitive aspects of the environment and the social and emotional aspects. For each set of FIS-C scores—total-talk, category, routine, and appended—significant differences between black and white advantaged mothers are so few that they might well be accounted for by chance variation alone. Most important for a theory suggesting that black and white children are exposed to different kinds of teaching and learning experiences at home are the findings that educated black and white mothers show no significant difference in amount of total talk, either spontaneous or responsive, and no significant differences for any of the category scores, subcategories, and subscores concerned with teaching and learning talk.

It could be argued that we might have found cultural differences had we included a comparison of disadvantaged black and white mothers. However, such comparisons of early maternal social interaction in the home have been carried out (Schoggen & Schoggen, 1976; Wachs et al., 1971) and produced no significant differences between black and white mothers. The present data support and extend these previous findings by providing data comparing the maternal verbal interaction of highly educated black and white mothers. Moreover, as noted earlier, even when we compare the teaching and learning talk of disadvantaged black mothers with that of advantaged white mothers, we find almost no differences.

The results are consistent with the recent analysis of the black economist Thomas Sowell. Sowell (1972) has compiled an impressive array of historical data demonstrating that educational problems are by no means unique to our current low-income minorities. Poor school performance and low scores on tests that correlate with school success have been a persistent characteristic of all our previous low-income minorities—Irish, Italian, Jewish, and others. As each minority group achieved economic and educational equality, the problems disappeared. That is, the school problem of our current low-income minorities does not seem to be a matter of cultural differences or deficits but of economic and educational disadvantage. Although early intervention programs were not available to promote the educational advancement of previous minority groups, such programs are now needed because our economy provides few of the opportunities for unskilled work formerly available to less educated groups. Limited employment opportunities perpetuate lower-class status, which in turn perpetuates the school problems of our current minorities. In addition, for nonwhite minorities, there is the moral obligation to make amends for their legacy of racial discrimination and exclusion.

In this connection, note that in the various debates concerning early intervention efforts, black identity is sometimes treated as a matter of race (e.g., the heredity–environment controversy) and other times as a matter of culture (e.g., the difference–deficit controversy). Whatever terminology is applied, our results show almost no differences in the everyday verbal environment that can be attributed to black versus white identity, whereas there are extensive differences related to socioeducational status.

Cognitive-Affective Theory: A Whole-Child Piagetian Approach to Early Intervention

When we examine the significant differences in the everyday talk of advantaged and disadvantaged mothers to their toddlers, a single unifying theme seems to integrate all of the findings. Advantaged mothers, both black and white, appear to support and facilitate the actions of their toddlers. Let us review the evidence.

Total-Talk Scores.   While disadvantaged mothers generally talk **to** their children, advantaged mothers generally talk responsively **with** their children; they show a threefold increment in responsive speech. (See Chapter 6.)

Category Scores, Subcategories, and Subscores.   A significantly larger proportion of advantaged mothers' speech consists of responses to the two main types of child communication, desire requests and reports. These mothers explicate and fulfill their children's desires, helping them to attain the goals that the children have set for themselves. They also explicate and confirm the children's reports, providing consensual validation for the child's own observations and experiences. Additionally, advantaged mothers are more likely to express pride in their child's actions, and less likely to prohibit them. They minimize DON'TS and when they do inhibit the child, they feel the need to justify the prohibition with an explanation or to suggest a substitute for the prohibited action. When they refuse the child, they suggest substitute means of gratification at the same time. Finally, when advantaged mothers teach, they do so responsively when their children are already engaged in communication with them, often at their own initiative rather than at a moment of the mother's choosing. (See Chapter 7.)

Appended Scores.   Advantaged mothers are more apt to repeat the child's utterances, explicating them to make sure that the child's meaning is clearly understood and also confirming the validity of the message. (See Chapter 8.)

Whether advantaged mothers are responding to the child's communications, minimizing or modulating prohibitions, or repeating the child's speech, they seem to persistently adapt and adjust their communications to support the child's own actions. Furthermore, this unifying theme serves not only to integrate the present findings; it also serves to synthesize the results of several recent observational studies designed to identify the early antecedents of effective linguistic and cognitive performance. The results of these studies in a variety of disciplines are congruent with our own.

The findings on total responsive speech are consistent with recent studies on the effect of early social interaction apart from considerations of social class. Clarke-Stewart (1973) finds early maternal responsivity to be a major predictor of performance on the Bayley Infant Scale at 18 months. Bradley and Caldwell (1976) find maternal emotional and verbal responsivity at age 2 to be one of their best predictors of Stanford–Binet IQ at age 4. White and Watts (1973) in their study of 1- and 2-year-olds describe their most effective mothers as acting mainly in response to the overtures of their children.

With respect to our category-score results, comparison with previous studies is somewhat difficult since previous work has been based, for the most part, on categories of social interaction rather than speech acts. Nevertheless, some of our findings appear to be consistent with those of White and Watts (1973; see also Carew, Chan, & Halfar, 1976); for example, the data on interpolated responsive teaching and on fulfilling the child's desires for goods and services. Other findings appear to be consistent with previous social class comparisons by Schoggen and Schoggen (1976) and Bee et al. (1969), such as their data on prohibitions and on congruence between the goals of mother and child. Still other categories appear only in our FIS-C category system (e.g., explications, confirming the child's reports). Regarding the data on appended scores, we have already noted that the results are consistent with previous research in developmental psycholinguistics and sociolinguistics. The findings for the discourse features of baby talk are similar to those of Snow et al. (1976), and the data for DON'TS with justifications are similar to those of Olim, Hess, and Shipman (1967).

The unifying theme of support for the child's own actions, suggested by our data and consistent with previous findings, generates a cognitive–affective theory to account for the impact of the early environment on the school performance of disadvantaged children, rather than a theory of cultural deprivation or cultural differences. A strategy of support for the child's own actions amplifies his or her impact on the environment and affirms his or her role as an active explorer. This experience is likely to engender a sense of self-confidence and a feeling of mastery and power that is bound to affect the child's performance in linguistic and cognitive tasks. A self-motivated, inquisitive, self-confident child arrives at school prepared to learn and to perform effectively, at the level of his or her potential. That is, the early environment of poverty appears to have an effect on the development of educability that is indirect. It is an effect mediated by affective or motivational factors.

This cognitive–affective theory is convergent with previous formulations based on environmental studies of infants (Lewis & Goldberg, 1969; Yarrow, Rubenstein, Pederson, & Jankowski, 1972). Yarrow et al. (1972) use the term "cognitive–motivational" rather than "cognitive–affective" and point out that the "common thread in these formulations is the active, information-processing organism, initiating transactions with the environment and, in turn, being influenced by these transactions [p. 217]." Early experience may or may not support these actions of the child. When it does, it is likely to engender what White (1959) calls an "effectance" motive or a sense of mastery.

A cognitive–affective or cognitive–motivational theory is also convergent with evidence that the performance of disadvantaged children in test situations varies enormously depending on the social or emotional context of the test (Hertzig, Birch, Thomas, & Mendez, 1968; Palmer, 1970). One recent study shows discrepancies as large as 20 points for IQ tests administered in varying social situations (Seitz, Abelson, Levine, & Zigler, 1975). Based on these kinds of data, Zigler and Butterfield (1968) have suggested that motivation may be the key factor in the poor performance of disadvantaged children both on school tasks and on the tests that predict school performance. Indeed, over the years, Zigler—former director of the Office of Child Development and still the major academic representative to the governmental agencies that fund early intervention—has increasingly stressed the role of motivational factors in the cognitive performance of disadvantaged children, such factors as affectance motivation and self-image (see Zigler & Trickett, 1978). The present findings, indicating that the early home environment of the disadvantaged child may have a significant impact on these motivational factors, provide strong support for Zigler's formulation.[2]

---

[2]It is interesting to note that another motivational factor cited in Zigler and Trickett (1978), wariness of adults, has received considerable attention among difference theorists. Specifically, Labov (1970) early noted that black ghetto children are suspicious of adults, that they tend not to communicate freely in school and test situations, so that their performance in these situations does not adequately reflect their competence. However, rather than suggesting that this distrust of adults demands the attention of early intervention programs, as do Zigler and Trickett, Labov merely used his observation as evidence of linguistic relativism. That is, he argued that black children express their competence in different contexts—in the streets with their peers rather than in the adult-dominated school or test situation. Our data showing that black advantaged children communicate just as freely with adults as do white advantaged children indicate that this distrust of adults is not a matter of black culture, but a matter of educational and economic disadvantage. Moreover, consistent with Zigler and Trickett's position, our data suggest that the poor child's distrust of adults is merely one of a cluster of motivational factors that may interfere with optimum school performance among disadvantaged children, the others including a lack of self-confidence and a feeling of powerlessness.

Finally, a cognitive–affective or cognitive–motivational theory of environmental assistance is consistent with the whole-child Piagetian approach to early intervention. The underlying rationale of such intervention programs can be expressed in terms of three fundamental principles (Biber, 1977; Kamii & Devries, 1977), and our data suggest that educated mothers subscribe to all of them.

1. *Principle of active learning:* Whole-child theorists assume that learning is an active process, propelled and organized by the child. Our educated mothers seem to implicitly accept this principle as they persistently attempt to support and facilitate the child's own actions. Even when they teach specific knowledge, facts, and skills, they do so responsively.

2. *Principle of interaction between language and cognitive development on the one hand, and social and emotional development on the other:* Whole-child theorists assume that the development of language and cognition takes place in intimate interaction with social and emotional factors and developments, themselves extrinsic to questions of competence. This interaction principle is invoked in a variety of contexts (e.g., in discussing educational goals, social cognition). However, it is perhaps raised most often with regard to the emotional factors that motivate the child's active learning—such factors as self-confidence, a sense of power, and a feeling of mastery. Like the teacher in whole-child programs, our educated mothers seem persistently concerned with these emotional factors; their responsive and supportive communication style seems designed to nurture and sustain exactly this kind of motivation.

3. *Principle of developmental stages:* Whole-child theorists assume that development evolves in stages and that the most effective caregiver intervention is one that is appropriate to the developmental level of the child. With respect to cognitive development, our educated mothers seem to accept this principle implicitly, delaying the teaching of letters and numbers until the child has mastered the prior skill of speech. Our less educated mothers tended to introduce this kind of teaching prematurely.

More importantly, our educated mothers adjust their communications to the child's affective development, particularly to the early development of the ego. Since the toddler stage is the time of emerging autonomy, the time of "psychological birth [Mahler, Pine, & Bergman, 1975]," it seems essential to support the child's budding individuality. Our educated mothers tend to provide this support. Failure to do so is likely to produce problems in asserting autonomy with potentially dire consequences for the child's later school performance. The child may not acquire the confidence necessary for sustained, goal-directed activity, or may remain enmeshed in a perpetual power struggle with adult caregivers in an attempt to regain his or her psychological birthright. Evidence based on observations in inner-city classrooms (Silverstein & Krate, 1975), suggests that these problems may be the major obstacle to effective school performance among disadvantaged children. Indeed, ego theory could explain why social-class differences in cognitive performance emerge at toddler-age, as children begin to assert their power. *How can the powerless support the power strivings of their children?*

It is because of the principle of active learning that Piaget (1970) refers to his educational method as the "active method." It is because of the principle of cognitive–affective interaction that the term "whole child" has been applied to these programs, ever since their origin in the educational philosophy of Dewey. It is because of the principle of developmental stages that these programs are generally referred to as "child development" programs. Because of all of these principles, Biber, Shapiro, and Wickens (1972) have recently suggested the name "developmental-interaction." Whatever we choose to call such programs, our findings suggest that educated mothers subscribe to their basic principles. Educated mothers are Deweyites or Piagetians.

The present findings not only support the whole-child Piagetian approach to early education, they also help to define the role of the caregiver in these programs. Our data on group variations in everyday speech seem to identify two major roles for the caregiver in enhancing the educational potential of the child. To the extent that learning is a matter of acquiring the established wisdom of the culture—its existing conventions, facts, and skills—the caregiver assumes the role of socialization agent. She talks **to** the child conveying the DO's and DON'TS of control talk and transmitting the knowledge of teaching talk. To the extent that learning is an active process of self-discovery and invention, the caregiver's role is different but no less essential. Nor is it limited to providing materials for the child's spontaneous exploration; she plays a crucial social role as well. She talks responsively **with** the child, supporting and facilitating his or her goal-directed activity, providing consensual validation for the child's own observations and experiences, boosting the child's ego and modulating her own prohibitions, thereby ensuring that the child is sufficiently self-confident to maintain the often challenging, often difficult process of self-discovery. In this way, the caregiver serves as an agent of the child's individuality, enhancing the power of the child's self, rather than as a socializing agent, reinforcing the power of culture, subculture, or community.[3]

Summary

We have seen that, until recently, psychology has been concerned mainly with what adults do to children, with the role of the caregiver as socialization agent. Our disadvantaged mothers generally adopt this traditional role. It is a teacher model consonant with the didactic approach, a model as old as the *McGuffey Reader*. Research indicating that the development of language and thought is largely an active process, as well as recent evidence demonstrating that early caregiver–child interaction is in large part responsive, has prompted this reexamination of the role of the caregiver as teacher. The findings point up the importance of the teacher's role as agent of the child's individuality rather than as agent of socialization. This is the role our educated mothers generally adopt, perhaps not surprisingly in view of their ready access to current child development information. As we have pointed out, it is a model consonant with whole-child Piagetian programs.

How are we to communicate this whole-child Piagetian model to less educated mothers? As we pointed out in our introductory chapter, the problem of transmitting the whole-child approach is by no means limited to low-education, low-income caregivers. Whereas the caregiver's role in didactic programs has been highly structured in terms of specific techniques or strategies, her role in whole-child programs has remained relatively unstructured. To add structure to this role was a major aim of the present study.

The everyday speech act scores of the FIS-C, together with the naturalistic data of this microanalytic study, provide us with a new vocabulary that can help bring structure to the caregiver's role in whole-child Piagetian programs. The scores help us identify a set of verbal techniques or communication strategies that represent our best guess as to what may be productive ways of talking **with**—not **to**— young children.

---

[3]Note that in discussing the distinctive features of baby talk (see Chapter 10), a third caregiver role was described, that of alter ego, where the caregiver seems to talk **for** the child. It is too early to tell which, if any, of the features of baby talk contribute to individual or group differences in later school performance. Since baby talk appears to be a universal code (Snow & Ferguson, 1977), some features may assist in the acquisition of linguistic universals, others may contribute to variations between or with groups. Further study is needed.

To facilitate dissemination of this information to parents and teachers we conclude by presenting a curriculum illustrating how our findings might be applied to enhance communication awareness among caregivers. The curriculum is called A Whole-Child Piagetian Approach to Caregiver Communication: Talking with Young Children (TAWC) and is described in the following chapter.

Chapter 13

A Whole-Child Piagetian Approach to Caregiver Communication: Talking with Young Children

Talking with Young Children (TAWC) is a curriculum designed to supplement caregiver education programs that adopt a whole-child Piagetian approach. It is designed to foster the motivation for active learning in children, to enhance their self-confidence, their sense of power, and their feeling of mastery over the environment. Consistent with the principles of whole-child programs, TAWC also encourages active learning in the caregiver, attempting to increase their communication awareness, rather than to provide training in language or communication skills. With rare exception, the communication strategies we recommend for caregivers are already in their repertoire. The objective is to make the caregiver aware of how her everyday communication may help encourage active learning in the child. TAWC is an exercise in consciousness raising.

The curriculum can be applied in both home-based and center-based programs. In either setting, it can and should be adapted to the individual needs of each caregiver–student, as well as to the unique requirements of each program. Whole-child programs cover child–child interaction and child–material interaction as well as adult–child interaction, and TAWC is addressed only to the last of these.

Since the toddler period may be critical for engendering the motivation for self-directed learning, TAWC is especially recommended for caregivers of toddlers, both parents and teachers. We will describe it as it was developed and applied in a pilot study of a home-based program for mothers and toddlers. The pilot sample consisted of 10 low-education, low-income black mothers recruited in collaboration with Harlem Hospital. The curriculum was presented in six weekly sessions followed by biweekly review sessions covering a period of 6 to 7 months.

Application of TAWC in a Home-Based Program[1]

During all home visits, mother and child are encouraged to interact in their usual everyday fashion and a home-educator, drawing examples from the flow of ongoing activity, points out and demonstrates ways of talking with toddlers that may help them become active learners. Each session, except for the first, is divided into three 20- to 30-minute segments during which one communication strategy is presented. Only two strategies are covered in the first session because of the time needed to introduce the curriculum and establish rapport. As will be noted, the communication strategies we recommend reflect the findings of the present study. Talking with Young Children is an effort to facilitate dissemination of our research findings.

Each strategy is explained both orally and through pictorial material, the latter in the form of a stick-figure drawing which the home-educator produces as she describes the strategy orally. Drawings are used as an adjunct because some mothers have limited reading skills. The illustrations for each of the six sessions are drawn on a single page. As the sessions proceed, the pages are compiled into a booklet which the home-educator leaves with the mother in a colorful folder. We will present each strategy together with the stick-figure drawings that illustrate the six sessions.

Session I: Responsive versus Spontaneous Caregiver Talk

Since many mothers have no education in the whole-child Piagetian approach, we begin by introducing the three basic principles on which it

---

[1]We have recently begun to use the TAWC curriculum in training student-teachers at the Barnard College Toddler Center. The material is presented in weekly supervisory sessions supplemented by reading materials from this volume, especially Chapters 4, 10, 12, and 13.

is based: the principles of active learning, of interaction between cognitive and affective development, and of developmental stages. We first present the principle of active learning, pointing out that many educators now feel that helping young children to become active learners, who are eager to explore the world and figure things out for themselves, is just as important as teaching them specific facts and skills. We next present the principle of interaction between cognitive and affective development. Here we emphasize that many educators consider such motivational factors as self-confidence, a sense of power, and a feeling of mastery to be crucial in helping children become active, curious, enthusiastic learners. Finally, we explain the principle of developmental stages. In this connection, we note that the toddler period may be critical for the development of self-confidence, since children of this age are just beginning to assert their autonomy and to sense their own impact on the environment.

STRATEGY 1

We spell out the distinction between spontaneous caregiver talk and talk that is responsive to the child's communications, stressing the importance of responsive talk. Mothers are told that children probably gain confidence in their abilities when the communications they offer elicit a response, when they are not ignored. Multiple responses are also encouraged and illustrated (*That green one? Okay.*). (See Figure 13.1, Strategy 1.)

STRATEGY 2

To help augment the mother's responsive talk, we note how difficult it often is to understand both the verbal and nonverbal communications of toddlers, so that one may not always be sure how to respond. We suggest explication as a general responsive strategy for dealing with this problem, i.e., we advise the mother to venture a guess as to the meaning of the child's message, put the message into her own words, and check to see if that is what the child meant (*You want some water? You're making it wet?*). We explain that some linguists believe that such explications, by example, may help the toddler communicate more clearly the next time. We add that, in any case, the explicating response is likely to make children feel that their actions are having an impact on others, thereby enhancing their sense of power and self-confidence. (See Figure 13.1, Strategy 2.)

Strategy 1 is based on the results for the total-talk score TOTAL RESPONSIVE TALK (Chapter 6); Strategy 2, on findings for the combined subcategory ALL EXPLICATIONS (Chapter 7).

1 TALKS RESPONSIVELY

2   EXPLICATES

FIGURE 13.1.   *Stick figures illustrating Strategies 1 and 2 of Session I.*

Session II: Responses to the Child's Desire Communications

In Sessions II and III, we suggest specific responsive strategies based on our findings about the ways children communicate and the ways mothers respond to their messages. Mothers are taught that the toddler's spontaneous communications fall into three main classes: desire requests (*Up.*), reports (*See my choo-choo go.*), and learning communications (*What's that? That's a B.*). They are informed that desire requests account for about 30% of the toddler's spontaneous communications, reports account for another 30%, and learning talk accounts for about 15%. We then explain that because so much of the child's communication consists of desire requests and reports, Session II is devoted to the ways mothers respond to the former, Session III to the latter.

STRATEGY 1

We suggest that explications are often useful when the mother is responding to the child's desires as they help her make sure that she has understood the child's request. We explain that helping young children achieve the goals they set for themselves is likely to give them the self-confidence they need to pursue goal-directed activity on their own—to figure things out for themselves, even when difficult problems arise. (See Figure 13.2, Strategy 1.) This strategy represents an elaboration of Strategy 2, Session I.

1   EXPLICATES DESIRE

2   REFUSES DESIRE AND OFFERS SUBSTITUTE

3   FULFILLS DESIRE

FIGURE 13.2.   *Stick figures illustrating Strategies 1, 2, and 3 of Session II.*

We hasten to reassure the mother that many of the child's desires cannot be fulfilled for one reason or another; obviously, refusals are often necessary (e.g., the banana the child wants may be one too many; the knife may be too dangerous). When refusals are called for, we recommend offering the child a substitute gratification or distraction (some juice instead of a banana, scissors instead of a knife). This strategy validates the child's own ideas and actions, even if only partially, so that it should help to build self-confidence. (See Figure 13.2, Strategy 2.)

Giving full recognition to the frequent need for a refusal, we encourage the mother to fulfill the child's desires whenever possible (*Here's some more. I'll reach it.*). We explain that this strategy is important for affirming the toddler's budding individuality. We also express sympathy for the mother's situation, pointing out that, since toddlers are just beginning to feel their own power and want to touch, push, and pull everything in sight, it is most understandable that adults should often find their many demands exhausting or annoying. Nevertheless, appealing to the developmental principle, we encourage the mother to indulge her toddler far more than she would an older child. (See Figure 13.2, Strategy 3.)

Strategy 1 of this session is based on the results for the subcategory EXPLICATES DESIRE; Strategy 2, on the findings for subscore REFUSALS with SUBSTITUTE GRATIFICATION; and Strategy 3, the subcategory ACCOMMODATES: FULFILLS DESIRE (Chapter 7).

Session III: Responses to the Child's Reports

Mothers are taught that reports of the child can be about the self (*I'm playing doctor.*), about others (*Daddy bye-bye.*), or about things (*Look, fire truck* [looking out of window].), and that toddlers' reports are mainly about their own actions. We explain that young children seem constantly eager to share their experiences and observations with their caregivers (i.e., the collective monologue). We suggest that, as with desire requests, explications are usually helpful to make sure that the mother has understood the child's report. (See Figure 13.3, Strategy 1.) This strategy is an elaboration of Strategy 2 of Session I.

1 EXPLICATES REPORT

2 DISAPPROVES REPORT AND OFFERS SUBSTITUTE OR EXPLANATION

3 CONFIRMS REPORT

FIGURE 13.3. *Stick figures illustrating Strategies 1, 2, and 3 of Session III.*

STRATEGY 2

We point out that children sometimes report on an action that they should not be doing (e.g., pouring out the shampoo), which the caregiver must put a stop to. Here, as with desire requests, we suggest that offering a substitute or distraction (*Not the shampoo. Here's some bubbly water.*) is often helpful for maintaining and encouraging the child's confidence in continuing his or her self-propelled exploration of the world.

We also suggest that using simply worded justifications when admonishing children (*Hot, Dirty, Boo-boo*) can help them feel better about continuing their self-motivated exploration and discovery. We explain that these justifying explanations may well prevent forbidden actions, because they are likely to help children learn the consequences of their actions. In this way, justifications could serve to enhance the child's sense of power by reducing the necessity of repeated prohibitions and admonitions that impose the adult's power on the child. We also point out the great power differential that exists betwen adult and child and the feeling of powerlessness children are likely to experience when adults use their considerable power in an unqualified way. (See Figure 13.3, Strategy 2.)

STRATEGY 3

We suggest that once it is established that the child's report is understood and that there is no need for admonishment, confirmations of the report by the caregiver are very helpful in affirming the child's role as an active explorer and initiator (*Right, you're the doctor. Yeah, Daddy's at work. Yes, lots of fire trucks.*). (See Figure 13.3, Strategy 3.)

Strategy 1 of this session is based on the results for the subcategory EXPLICATES REPORT; Strategy 2 on the findings for the subscores DON'TS with SUBSTITUTE GRATIFICATION and DON'TS with JUSTIFYING EXPLANATIONS; and Strategy 3 the subcategory CONFIRMS REPORT (Chapter 7).

Session IV: Control Talk

STRATEGY 1

Mothers are taught that much caregiver talk to young children consists of directing or controlling the child. We reassure the mothers that all children need direction from adults. We illustrate the major kinds of control talk, DO's (*Let's wash up.*), DON'TS (*It'll break.*), and REFUSALS (*Not now.*). We point out that from the viewpoint of supporting the child's role as an active learner and explorer, DON'TS and REFUSALS are the main concern. This is because they are likely to discourage children's actions and diminish their sense of power. We hasten to reassure the mother that DON'TS are an essential part of child rearing. However, we also point out that DON'TS can vary in number and that they have been found to average from 1 in 4 caregiver statements to 1 in 10 or less. To encourage the child's explorations, we recommend minimizing DON'TS by arranging the home environment so that fragile or dangerous objects are out of reach and out of sight, and by establishing areas where messy play can take place. (See Figure 13.4, Strategy 1.)

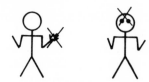

1   REDUCES DON'TS:
PUTS THINGS OUT OF REACH AND OUT OF SIGHT

2   OFFERS SUBSTITUTE OR EXPLANATION WITH DON'TS

3   OFFERS SUBSTITUTE WITH REFUSALS

FIGURE 13.4.   *Stick figures illustrating Strategies 1, 2, and 3 of Session IV.*

STRATEGY 2

We point out that the child's self-motivated exploration and active learning are less likely to be inhibited if DON'TS are accompanied by explanations of the consequences of a forbidden activity or by suggestions for substitutes. (See Figure 13.4, Strategy 2.) This strategy is an extension of Strategy 2 of Session III.

STRATEGY 3

We suggest that REFUSALS, which also inhibit the child's explorations, are likely to be less discouraging when substitutes are offered by the caregiver. (See Figure 13.4, Strategy 3.) This strategy is an extension of Strategy 2 of Session II.

Strategy 1 of this session is based on the results for the subcategory DON'TS; Strategy 2, on the findings for the subscore DON'TS with JUSTIFYING EXPLANATIONS and DON'TS with SUBSTITUTE GRATIFICATION; and Strategy 3, on the subscore REFUSALS with SUBSTITUTE GRATIFICATION (Chapter 7).

Session V: Teaching Talk

STRATEGY 1

We present the distinction between teaching responsively and teaching spontaneously. Responsive teaching, we explain, entails interpolating a teaching comment into a series of responses to the child's communication. For example, if the child asks for some juice and the caregiver responds to the desire request with an explication (*You want some juice?*), followed by a statement fulfilling the desire (*Here's some.*), the caregiver can also add a teaching comment (*See, this is a yellow cup.*). We note that this last interpolated statement constitutes responsive teaching. In contrast, if the caregiver initiates a conversation about colors, numbers, etc., she is engaging in spontaneous teaching. Responsive teaching is encouraged because children are probably more likely to make active use of it, since it occurs in the context of their own expressed interests and concerns. (See Figure 13.5, Strategy 1). This strategy is an elaboration of Strategy 1, Session I.

STRATEGY 2

We point out that interpolated teaching can take two forms. First, there is the kind we have just described, when a teaching comment is inserted into a series of responses to the child's communications. In the second kind, the caregiver inserts some teaching content into a statement of almost any type. For example, in confirming a child's report about a toy he or she is playing with, one can say, 'Right, it's a cement truck,' or 'Right, it's a red truck,' enriching the response with the teaching of vocabulary. Both kinds of interpolated teaching are encouraged because children are more likely to show interest in what is being taught when their attention and motivation are already engaged in conversational interaction. (See Figure 13.5, Strategy 2.)

STRATEGY 3

We present the distinction between age-appropriate teaching content for toddlers as against content more suited to older children. We suggest

1   TEACHES   RESPONSIVELY

2   TEACHES   AS   SECONDARY   FUNCTION

3   TEACHES   AGE-APPROPRIATE   CONTENT

FIGURE 13.5.   *Stick figures illustrating Strategies 1, 2, and 3 of Session V.*

that teaching letters and numbers may be too advanced for children who do not yet know how to talk and are busy learning how. We cite age-appropriate content for toddlers when teaching facts and skills (e.g., word-labeling such as names of objects or attributes), or sensorimotor skills (e.g., stringing beads, dressing). (See Figure 13.5, Strategy 3.)

This session is based on the findings for the category score TEACHES (Chapter 7).

Session VI: Repetitions of the Child
and Praise or Approval

STRATEGY 1

Repetitions of the child's talk are encouraged. We point out that care-giver repetitions consist mainly of explicating the child's desire requests or reports and confirming the child's reports or learning talk. In earlier lessons we have taught the importance of explications in fostering active learning, how it is likely to give children a sense of self-confidence if the caregiver responds to their messages by trying to understand them. Now we add that, in confirming the child's messages, the caregiver is also likely to build the child's self-confidence because confirmation seems to validate the child's own observations and learning experiences (*Right, the man is drilling. Yes, that's a dump truck.*). (See Figure 13.6, Strategy 1.) This strategy is a supplement to Strategy 1 of Sessions II and III and Strategy 3 of Session III.

STRATEGY 2

We point out that when caregivers repeat the toddler's one- or two-word utterances, they often put the child's message into a more correct grammatical form, adding words (e.g., *a, the, are, of*) or word endings (e.g., *ing, ed, s*) that the child has omitted (Child: *I'm bye-bye.* Caregiver: *You're going bye-bye?*). We explain that some linguists feel that these additions or expansions may help in learning grammar. We add that whether or not these expansions do, in fact, teach grammar, they are likely to give children the feeling that their own initiatives are important, thereby affirming them in their role as active learners. (See Figure 13.6, Strategy 2.)

STRATEGY 3

Finally, we discuss praise or approval, the caregiver strategy that is probably most familiar to the layperson. We describe and illustrate the three main kinds of caregiver approval that we have identified, ego-boosting (*Great! You're really something!*), confirming the validity of the child's reports (*Yup, all gone.*) and confirming the accuracy of the child's learning communications (*Right, coo-coo clock.*). We then highlight the distinction between confirming learning and the other two strategies. We point out that confirmations of learning focus attention on the acquisition of specific skills. In contrast, the pride expressed in the caregiver's ego-boosts, as well as the validation of the child's experiences expressed in the caregiver's confirmation of the child's reports, seem to signal a generalized affirmation of the child's whole being. The latter are likely to engender a feeling of self-confidence that could transcend success or

1   REPEATS   CHILD   UTTERANCE

2   EXPANDS   CHILD   UTTERANCE

3   APPROVES: THREE   WAYS

FIGURE 13.6.   *Stick figures illustrating Strategies 1, 2, and 3 of Session VI.*

failure on any particular learning task. We encourage these expressions of generalized approval.

We also point out that the ability to comprehend the meaning of ego-boosting praise probably requires some capacity for self-evaluation and that this degree of self-awareness may not develop until the toddler approaches age 3. On the other hand, toddlers seem to need frequent confirmation of both their reports and learning communications. On this basis, caregivers can expect confirmations to be far more common than ego-boosts in talk to toddlers. (See Figure 13.6, Strategy 3.)

Strategies 1 and 2 of this session are based on the results for the appended child-repetition scores (Chapter 8), and Strategy 3 is based on a comparison of the finding for the subcategories EGO-BOOSTS, CONFIRMS REPORT, and CONFIRMS LEARNING (Chapter 7).

Concluding Remarks on TAWC

What about the mothers' responses to the curriculum, either with respect to outcome or process? Since TAWC is intended to supplement existing whole-child Piagetian programs, outcome should properly be evaluated in terms of whether the curriculum contributes to the overall effectiveness of these programs. Although such outcome data are not available as yet, the mothers' reactions to our pilot program yield some promising insights into the process of caregiver education. The curriculum seems to cover three main components of caregiver–child communication: responsive talk, teaching talk, and control talk. We will discuss the mothers' reactions to each of these components.

Responsive Talk. Session I on total responsive talk, II on responding to the child's desire communications, III on responding to the child's reports, VI on repetitions of the child's utterances, as well as the strategy on responsive teaching of Session V, are all concerned with responsive talk. Together they cover the main strategies that define the responsive communication style of educated mothers. Our pilot data indicate that less educated mothers respond well to being made aware of these strategies. They begin to explicate, confirm, and repeat their children's communications more often than they have previously. Furthermore, knowledge of these strategies seems to heighten their interest in and attention to their toddlers' messages. The pilot data also suggest that as mothers increase their responsive talk, their toddlers begin to report more often, to share their experiences and observations with their mothers. These collective monologues of young children, their "thinking aloud," may play an as yet little understood role in the development of inner thought.

Teaching Talk. The data on the session for teaching talk (Session V) indicate that the strategy on interpolated responsive teaching is appealing to the mothers and is readily understood and adopted by them. However, the strategy on interpolated teaching as a secondary function of a speech act seems more difficult for them to grasp. We are still searching for ways to present this strategy more effectively.

Perhaps the most interesting maternal reaction to the session on teaching talk occurs in relation to age-appropriate content. Whether they feel pressured by didactic programs on television (many of their toddlers watch "Sesame Street") or feel anxious about their child's prospects at school, many low-education mothers seem upset that their toddlers cannot learn letters and numbers. They are greatly relieved to learn that most educators consider children of this age too young to learn these skills.

Control Talk.   The session on control talk (IV) was the one most welcomed and, for some mothers, the one most resisted. This session seems to generate more intense emotion, both positive and negative, than any of the others.

On the one hand, mothers are reassured to learn that most caregivers spend much of their time directing and controlling their children and that DON'TS are a frequent occurrence in any household with toddlers. They also seem to appreciate our suggestion about putting forbidden objects out of reach and out of sight, since this eliminates the necessity of repeated admonitions. Furthermore, they respond well to the strategy on giving simply worded explanations with DON'TS. Finding substitutes for DON'TS and REFUSALS is sometimes difficult in homes with few toys. Nevertheless, both the mother and the home-educator are often ingenious in thinking up substitutes (e.g, pushing around a box instead of the new living room table, or pouring water out of an empty lotion bottle rather than emptying a bottle with lotion in it).

On the other hand, some mothers express concern that our control strategies might tend to spoil the child. Others flatly state, *When I say no, it's no.* We sympathize fully with their legitimate concern about spoiling the child. Indeed, Coles's (1978) study suggests that spoiling may be a common problem among privileged children. Affluence can lead to overindulging these children so that their self-assertion exceeds its bounds and becomes self-indulgence.

Nevertheless, we urge the adoption of our control strategies for several compelling reasons:

1. While spoiling is a serious developmental risk for overindulged, privileged children, financial hardship makes it difficult to spoil poor children as they so often cannot get what they want. In fact, a little spoiling may be just what poorer children need to help them develop the sense of power that comes so easily to children born to privilege and power.
2. There are so many occasions for saying "no" to toddlers—mothers often say "no" more than anything else—that we need to weigh carefully how much and how to say "no" if we want to preserve the child's sense of power.

3. Toddlers are just beginning to assert themselves; they might easily be discouraged from trying. Therefore, adopting these control strategies is probably far more important for the toddler than for older children.

We might have expected these intense reactions to the session on control talk since it apparently dominates the speech of all caregivers of young children—mothers of diverse social backgrounds (see Table 7.2, page 72) as well as teachers (see Table 7.1, page 71). However, we were not prepared for the intensity of the reaction. As we considered this response to our curriculum in relation to the theoretical consideration discussed in Chapter 12, we came to view it not as an obstacle to implementing the curriculum but, quite the opposite, as the most important finding of our pilot study.

The finding suggests that basic to the problem of defining the caregiver's role as teacher is an inevitable and perpetual conflict between her two major roles; her role as agent of the child's individuality enhancing the power of the child's self, and her role as socializing agent imposing the power of adult society on the child. If we are to take seriously the principle that language and thought are, in large part, acquired through a process of active learning and experimentation, and, furthermore, if we want to help children of all economic and cultural backgrounds to fulfill their educational potential, we can ill afford to neglect this early manifestation of the eternal conflict between self and other, between the individual and society. Indeed, we must see to it that all children acquire a sense of power that is resilient enough to sustain the challenge of self-discovery.

Sooner or later in a discussion of education, one comes to the question of goals or values. The commitment of whole-child programs to enhancing the individual's capacity to withstand the power of the collective, be it culture, subculture, or community, is perhaps nowhere more eloquently expressed than in Piaget's (1964) declaration of the goals of education:

> The principal goal of education is to create men who are capable of doing new things, not simply of repeating what other generations have done—men who are creative, inventive, and discoverers. The second goal of education is to form minds which can be critical, can verify and not accept everything they are offered [p. 5].

Appendix A
Supplementary Scoring Manual for Caregiver Speech Acts

This scoring manual is intended as a supplement to the description of the scoring scheme presented in Chapter 4. It consists of two sections. The first section provides a list of FIS-C categories that fail to exceed the 1% frequency criteria in mother talk to toddlers, so that they have not been described in the text. Although these scores occur rarely in caregiver speech, it is important to be able to identify them in order to distinguish them from categories of adequate frequency. The second section provides additional scoring instructions for all FIS-C scores.

FIS-C Categories of Inadequate Frequency

The all-inclusive set of FIS-C categories incorporates the list of categories we derived previously from samples of the preschool child's spontaneous speech, the FIS-P categories (Schachter *et al.*, 1974). Although only one of these FIS-P categories, REPORTS ON SELF, OTHERS, THINGS, reaches the 1% frequency criteria in samples of caregiver speech (Schachter *et al.*, 1976 and present sample), most of the other child categories do occur occasionally as well. They include the following:

EXPRESSIVE COMMUNICATION. The caregiver simply abreacts an emotion, positive (*Yummy!*); negative (*Oh, no!*) or mixed (*Thank heavens!*).

DESIRE COMMUNICATION. The caregiver requests goods or services from child (*Would you hand me that ashtray? Can I have some?* [of child's ice cream]).

POSSESSION RIGHTS COMMUNICATION. The caregiver asserts possession rights (*That's mine. Mommy's.*).

EGO-ENHANCING COMMUNICATION. The caregiver boasts (*Wasn't that clever of Mommy? Your mommy's a genius.*).

SELF-REFERRING, SELF-INCLUDING COMMUNICATION. Child speech acts are scored in this category of the FIS-P when the child refers another child's statement to him or herself (Other Child: *I want some water.* Child: *I want some too.* or *Me too.*), or when the child repeats the utterance of another child. These self-references and repetitions of peer statements are common among young children in group settings. They seem to serve a self-referring, self-including function, reflecting a lack of differentiation between the self and the other.[1] In contrast, caregivers almost never refer statements of the young child to themselves. Additionally, caregiver repetitions of child speech seem to serve different communication functions than do the child's repetitions of child speech. Such caregiver repetitions are used mainly in explicating and confirming the child's utterances, although there are other functions as well (see Chapter 8 and Table 8.3, pp. 98–99).[2] On this basis, these caregiver repetitions are assigned whichever FIS-C subcategory score best describes

[1]For a fuller description of the way repetitions of peer speech reflect a lack of self-differentiation, see Piaget (1926).

[2]In the literature on baby talk, the term "imitations" is generally used to denote adult repetitions of the child (Snow & Ferguson, 1977), just as it is used to denote the child's repetitions of others. Because our results indicate that the former serves different functions from the latter, we use the term "repetitions-of-child" for the adult's repetitions.

their function (e.g., EXPLICATES DESIRE, CONFIRMS REPORT) and the repetition itself is assigned an appended score to denote this formal feature.

JOINING COMMUNICATION. Child speech acts are scored in this category when the child joins in a display of spontaneous affection toward another child (*You're my friend. I like you.*). Spontaneous hugs, kisses, and protestations of affection by the caregiver are assigned this score (*Hug a mug* [hugs]. *Gimme kiss.*)

COLLABORATIVE COMMUNICATION. Caregiver initiates a collaboration in a child project, game, or discussion; in dramatic play; or in a chanting game (*Peek-a-boo. I see you.*).

LEARNING COMMUNICATION. This child category did not appear in our mother data, as might be expected. Caregivers do not ask young children for help in learning.

CALLS WHEN OUT OF SIGHT. This child category does not appear in caregiver speech, because the caregiver's call is viewed as an introduction to her subsequent speech act. Both her call and her speech act that follows are assigned the same score.

In addition to these FIS-C categories which duplicate FIS-P child categories, the following predominately responsive FIS-C categories also failed to reach the 1% frequency criterion:

RESPONDS TO CHILD POSSESSION RIGHTS COMMUNICATION. Child asserts possession rights (*Mine.*). Caregiver responsive subcategories include:

EXPLICATES POSSESSION RIGHT (*That one is yours?*)
CONFIRMS POSSESSION RIGHT (*Right, it's yours.*)

RESPONDS TO CHILD SELF-REFERRING, SELF-INCLUDING COMMUNICATION. The child refers a caregiver speech statement to him or herself (*I go too. Me too.*). The caregiver responsive subcategories include:

EXPLICATES SELF-REFERRING-INCLUDING (*You too? It is?*)
CONFIRMS SELF-REFERRING-INCLUDING (*Right, you too. Uhuh.*)

Whereas children's repetitions of peer statements are scored as spontaneous self-references, their repetitions or imitations of caregiver statements are scored as responsive, because of the power differential between adult and child. On this basis, the caregiver's responses to the child's imitations of her speech are not scored RESPONDS TO CHILD SELF-REFERRING, SELF-INCLUDING COMMUNICATION. Caregiver responses to the child's imitations generally fall into two classes. Either she confirms the child's imitation—scored CONFIRMS LEARNING—or she repeats or reformulates her original statement—scored the same way as the original statement.

RESPONDS TO CHILD JOINING COMMUNICATION. Child hugs or kisses caregiver, or says, *Hug me. Do you love me, Mommy?* Caregiver responsive subcategories include:

EXPLICATES JOINING (*Hug? Love you?*)
RECIPROCATES JOINING (*Yes, yes, yes* [hug]. *I love you, pussycat.*)

RESPONDS TO CHILD CALL WHEN OUT OF SIGHT. Child calls, typically, from another room (*Mommy*). Caregiver responds as follows:

CALL REACTION (*What? Huh? What do you want? Coming. Be right there.*)

Finally, there was one predominately spontaneous FIS-C category that failed to reach the 1% criterion in mother talk to toddlers.

ENCOURAGES PERSISTENCE. Caregiver encourages the child to persist when the child is about to abandon some task because of discouragement and frustration (*You almost finished. Take it easy.*)

Supplementary Scoring Instructions

Supplementary scoring instructions cover the following topics: (*a*) rules for scoring speech acts in the sequence of discourse; (*b*) detailed scoring distinctions for each set of FIS-C scores, total-talk, category, routine, and appended; and (*c*) a list of common words and phrases that are scored in a variety of ways depending on their context.

Scoring Speech Acts in the Sequence of Discourse

Recent research on child discourse has revealed sequential structures underlying sets of interrelated speech acts. Garvey's (1975) analysis of the domain of the request in conversation among preschoolers provides a useful framework for scoring sequences in caregiver discourse. Garvey describes five possible sequential units—preparation + adjunct + request + clarification + acknowledgment. As in the following illustration, the preparation usually sets the stage for the request; the adjunct usually provides justification for the request; clarifications occur in response to the listener's questions about the request; and acknowledgments follow the listener's accommodations to the request.

LISTENER	SPEAKER
	Have you got a scissor? [preparation]
Yeah.	
	My yarn is too long. [adjunct]
	Can I use it? [request]
This one?	
	No, the big one. [clarification]
[gives]	
	Thanks. [acknowledgment]

Garvey's model identifies a key unit expressing the main function of the sequence, the request, together with a set of auxiliary units (i.e., preparation, adjunct, clarification and acknowledgment) which serve as an aid in communicating the main function. Applying the model to samples of caregiver speech, we found it useful in assigning FIS-C scores to sequences of discourse. Specifically, the rule we adopted was to assign to the auxiliary units the same category score and total-talk score assigned to the key unit.

Before illustrating this scoring procedure, it should be noted that most caregiver talk to young children does not entail auxiliary units. Sequences are usually quite simple in structure, often involving speech acts and their repetition. Nor are all auxiliary units expressed in all sequences or in the same order as in the illustration. Furthermore, there can be multiple occurrences of both auxiliary and key units within the same sequence. Finally, although auxiliary units are assigned the same FIS-C category score as the key unit, subcategory scores and subscores can differ from that of the key unit.

These procedures for scoring discourse apply most often in the case of the caregiver's commands (DO's and DON'TS) and her responses in the category RESPONDS TO CHILD DESIRE COMMUNICATION. Both cases will be illustrated.

The sequential structure of the mother's commands was found to be identical to that of Garvey's model for the child's requests as shown in the following example:

CHILD	CAREGIVER
	Where's your shoe? [preparation]
	It's getting cold. [adjunct]
	Go get it. [CONTROLS: DO's]

[Brings] *That?*

                                              No, your new one. [*clarification*]

[Brings]

                                              Good girl. [*acknowledgment*]

It can be seen that the key unit (*Go get it.*) is scored DO's. On this basis, all auxiliary units would also be scored DO's. The adjunct explanation (*It's getting cold.*) would also warrant the subscores SELF NORMS, ANY NORMATIVE EXPLANATION, and JUSTIFYING EXPLANATIONS, and the acknowledgement unit (*Good girl.*) would warrant the subscore ACKNOWLEDGING SUBMISSION. All units would be assigned the total-talk score TOTAL SPONTANEOUS TALK, since the auxiliary units merely serve as an aid in expressing a spontaneous command.

Garvey's model also proved to be applicable in scoring sequential units in the predominately responsive categories, although it required some modification. For these categories, the caregiver's explications and her requests for further elaboration of the child's communication are viewed as auxiliary preparation units, attempts to clarify the child's meaning preparatory to confirming or accommodating to the child's communication. Confirmations and accommodations are viewed as the key units in the sequence, since they often occur without the preparatory attempts to clarify the child's communication. In the following example the first two units (*You want some juice? Apple juice or orange juice?*)—scored EXPLICATES DESIRE and SEEKS FURTHER ELABORATION OF DESIRE, respectively—are preparatory to the final accommodating unit (*Here's your juice.*)—scored ACCOMMODATES: FULFILLS DESIRE.

CHILD	CAREGIVER
Juice, Mommy.	
	You want some juice? [*preparation*]
	Apple juice or orange juice? [*preparation*]
Apple juice.	
	[Gets juice bottle from refrigerator]
	Hand me that cup, Honey. [*adjunct*]
[Gives]	
	[Pours juice]
	Here's [ACCOMMODATES: FULFILLS DESIRE]
	your juice. [Gives cup]

In addition to these preparation units, there are also adjunct units in caregiver responsive sequences, adjuncts auxiliary to accommodations as the key unit. In conjunction with accommodations, caregivers often issue commands directing the child to act in such a way as to facilitate the caregiver's effort to accommodate the child. In the example given, the caregiver asks the child to hand her a cup so that she can fulfill the desire for juice. These types of commands, which facilitate an accommodation, are viewed as adjuncts to a responsive sequence and are scored the same way as the accommodation unit. In our example, the score ACCOMMODATES: FULFILLS DESIRE would be assigned.

It can be seen that conforming to our rule for scoring sequences of discourse, all units in this example are scored in the same category, RESPONDS TO CHILD DESIRE COMMUNICATION, although they vary in their subcategory scores. Also conforming to our rule, all units in the example are assigned the same total-talk score, TOTAL Ch:S → C:R RESPONSIVE TALK, because the entire sequence, auxiliary units as well as the key unit, is instigated by the child's spontaneous desire request for juice.

Having illustrated the procedure for applying Garvey's model to FIS-C category and total-talk scores, we can now consider the procedure for applying the model to subcategory scores. All auxiliary units are assigned the same subcategory score as the key unit, except for categories where the FIS-C provides distinctive subcategory scores for preparatory units. Such distinctive scores are provided for the predominately responsive categories in the subcategories for explications and requests for further elaboration, as in the previous illustration. Among the predominately spontaneous categories, TEACHES and REPORTS ON CHILD provide subcategories for preparation units. In teaching, the caregiver often elicits knowledge rhetorically (*What do you call that?*) merely in preparation for the key unit presenting knowledge (*A choo-choo train.*), so that the subcategory ELICITS KNOWLEDGE is assigned to the preparation unit and the subcategory PRESENTS KNOWLEDGE is assigned to the key unit. Similarly, a rhetorical question, scored ELICITS REPORT (*You like that, don't you?*), can be a preparation unit for the key unit, PRESENTS REPORT (*You sure do.*). Note that for the category CONTROLS there are no subcategories that can be identified as preparation units, so that the subcategory score for the key unit is assigned DO'S, DON'TS or REFUSALS.

In identifying and scoring Garvey's auxiliary units in the stream of discourse, also note the following:

Preparation Unit. Preparation units in a sequence of control talk often bear a surface resemblance to elicitations of reports on the child—ELICITS REPORT. The distinction is based on the place of the utterance in the sequence of discourse. For example, *Where did you find that?* followed by

Put it back is scored DON'TS, as a preparation for the prohibition, but *Where did you find that?* followed by *In the carriage?* is scored ELICITS REPORT.

Adjunct Units. Adjuncts in the caregiver's spontaneous sequences are generally JUSTIFYING EXPLANATIONS. They occur mainly in sequences of control talk. In responsive sequences, the adjunct commands that facilitate the caregiver's accommodations generally occur in conjunction with the score ACCOMMODATES: FULFILLS DESIRE (*Open your mouth* [gives pineapple]), although they also occur with ACCOMMODATES: COMFORTS DISTRESS (*Hold still* [applying Band-Aid]) and ACCOMMODATES: SUPPLIES LEARNING (*Turn it over.* [shows how to do puzzle]).

Clarification Units. A good deal of caregiver–toddler communication consists of mutual clarification. Caregiver clarifications in response to the child's queries include reformulations, repetitions, and elaborations of her original key unit and they are assigned the same scores as the key unit. Caregiver queries for clarification of the child's communications are assigned the scores ALL EXPLICATIONS, or ALL REQUESTS FOR FURTHER ELABORATION. The child's clarification in response to these caregiver queries is scored as responsive. However, the caregiver's responses to the child's clarifications are scored as instigated by the original child's communication that is being clarified, as it is this original child communication that evoked the entire sequence of caregiver responses. Thus, when the child's original communication is spontaneous, the entire sequence of caregiver responses is scored Ch:S → C:R.

Acknowledgment Units. Auxiliary acknowledgment units occur, almost exclusively, at the termination of a sequence of control talk. After the child conforms to her command, the caregiver may acknowledge this by saying *That's a good girl, Thank you,* etc. The latter speech acts are assigned the subscore ACKNOWLEDGING SUBMISSION. On the rare occasions when the caregiver requests goods and services of the young child and the child conforms to the request, the caregiver may similarly acknowledge the deed by saying *Good girl, Thanks,* etc. The latter acknowledgement would be assigned the same score as the key unit in this sequence, DESIRE COMMUNICATION (duplicate of FIS-P child category). It should be noted that the FIS-C distinguishes between acknowledgments that terminate sequences of caregiver control talk or desire requests and those that confirm the child's expressive, report, and learning communications—scored CONFIRMS EXPRESSIVE, CONFIRMS REPORT, and CONFIRMS LEARNING, respectively. These confirmations are viewed not as auxiliary terminal units, but as key units.

Total-Talk Scores

In scoring communications as spontaneous or responsive in order to derive total-talk scores, we need to consider both the simple case where the speaker initiates a single communication, and the listener responds with a single communication, and the complex cases entailing sequences of discourse. In simple cases, the speaker is scored spontaneous, the listener, responsive. In complex cases, Garvey's (1975) concept of key and auxiliary units is applied as a general framework in scoring.

We have already described the procedure for scoring speech acts as spontaneous or responsive in sequences containing both key units and auxiliary units. There are also sequences with multiple key units. For example, the caregiver can instigate a series of commands or teaching instructions, and the child may respond to one or more in turn. In these cases, the multiple key units of the caregiver are scored as spontaneous throughout the sequence insofar as the caregiver maintains the initiative. Similarly, the child may instigate a series of desire requests, reports, or learning questions, with the caregiver responding to each (or some) in turn. In such cases, the multiple key units of the child are scored as spontaneous throughout the sequence insofar as the child maintains the initiative.

There are times when the speakers instigating sequences yield the initiative to the listeners, adjusting their responses to the responses of the listeners. In caregiver talk, these adjusted responses are scored as Ch:R → C:R responses. Common examples of sequences that begin with caregiver spontaneous initiatives and then shift to Ch:R → C:R responses include: First, the caregiver begins with a series of spontaneous commands; the child actively resists and the caregiver shifts to Ch:R → C:R responses to overcome the resistance. Second, the caregiver begins with a series of teaching statements; the child learns and produces a learning response; and the caregiver shifts to Ch:R → C:R responses that confirm the child's learning. Finally, the caregiver begins with a series of spontaneous statements in any category; the child produces a responsive imitation; and the caregiver shifts to a Ch:R → C:R response that confirms the imitation. The latter is scored CONFIRMS LEARNING.

There are also instances where the instigator of a sequence loses the initiative temporarily and soon regains it. For example, in the midst of a sequence responding to the child's desire request, the mother may tell the child to wipe his or her nose, may interpolate a teaching response, or may be interrupted by a phone call, later to resume her series of responses to the child's initiative. These delayed responses to the child's desire request are scored as instigated by the original child initiative unless the child repeats the initiative after the interruption. In the latter case, the caregiver's response is scored as responsive to the child's repeated initiative.

In collaborative sequences where the caregiver initiates the collaboration, child responses are scored responsive throughout the series, and caregiver responses to child responses are also scored responsive. This is because we assume that the caregiver persists in the collaboration in response to the child's continuing interest and response. On the other hand, if the child instigates the collaboration, child speech acts are scored spontaneous throughout the series and the caregiver's responses are scored responsive, because we assume that the caregiver's continued response is maintained by the child's continued initiative. If the caregiver begins a collaboration (e.g., chant) in response to a child initiative in a child category other than the collaborative, the caregiver is scored as responsive to the child's initiative in the other category. When the child initiates the collaboration, we score caregiver responses as FIS-C Category IV, RESPONDS TO CHILD COLLABORATIVE COMMUNICATION. When the caregiver initiates the collaboration, we score the speech act in the FIS-C category derived from the child FIS-P category COLLABORATIVE COMMUNICATION.

Communication-Function Category Scores, Subcategories and Subscores

CATEGORY I: RESPONDS TO CHILD EXPRESSIVE COMMUNICATION

When the child of toddler-age or above cries in distress, this is interpreted as a communication, even if the child is in another room.

When the caregiver refuses to alleviate the child's distress or denies that he or she is in distress (*That didn't hurt.*), score REFUSALS.

CATEGORY II: RESPONDS TO CHILD DESIRE COMMUNICATION

When the child requests goods already provided or services already rendered, and the caregiver points this out (*You got it.*), score ACCOMMODATES: FULFILLS DESIRE.

When the caregiver notes the child reaching for an object and she explicates the child's desire, fulfills it, etc., before the child asks for her help, score her responses as spontaneous, unless caregiver and child are in such close proximity (e.g., sitting at the same table) that it is safe to assume that the child's reaching gestures are intended as desire requests.

ASSISTS CHILD TO FULFILL OWN DESIRE versus ACCOMMODATES: SUPPLIES LEARNING. When caregivers respond to a desire request by indicating how the children can fulfill their own desires (Child: *Bubbles, Mommy.*   Caregiver: *It's in there.*), score ASSISTS CHILD TO FULFILL OWN DESIRE. When the caregiver responds to a learning question by indicating how to perform a task (Child: *Where does this go?* [puzzle piece]   Caregiver: *In there.*), score ACCOMMODATES: SUPPLIES LEARNING.

DISINHIBITS DESIRE versus CONFIRMS REPORT. When the child hesitates, looking to the caregiver for encouragement or permission, and the latter says *Go ahead* or *That's okay*, score DISINHIBITS DESIRE. Far more often the caregiver says *Go ahead* or *Okay* after the child reports on an action already in progress (Child: *Be right back.*   Caregiver: *Okay.*). The latter is scored CONFIRMS REPORT.

EXPLICATES DESIRE versus ELICITS REPORT. When the child expresses a desire and the mother explicates, score EXPLICATES DESIRE. When the mother herself spontaneously elicits reports about the child's wishes or preferences (*What would you like for your birthday? Do you want to see Gramma today? What would you like for lunch?*), score ELICITS REPORT.

CATEGORY III: RESPONDS TO CHILD EGO-ENHANCING COMMUNICATION

EGO-BOOSTS versus CONFIRMS LEARNING. When the caregiver's approval expresses pride, score EGO-BOOSTS. Pride is usually revealed in the caregiver's facial expression which beams with pride, in an intonation of exaggerated approval, or in the choice of words like *Very good. Terrific!* or *Wow!*. When the caregiver responds to a learning communication (*It go there* [puzzle].) with matter-of-fact approval or confirmation (*Good. Right, there.*), score CONFIRMS LEARNING.

CATEGORY IV: RESPONDS TO CHILD COLLABORATIVE COMMUNICATON

ENGAGES IN COLLABORATIVE DISCOURSE. This subcategory usually applies to cooperative projects and games in talk to toddlers; there are virtually no role-differentiated discussions at this age level. Common examples of cooperative projects and games with toddlers include tickling and hand-clapping games and playing musical instruments together. When the game is accompanied by a chant, score ENGAGES IN COLLABORATIVE CHANT. When the game involves talk in fantasy role with altered intonation, as in the common hiding games (*My, where did*

Cedric go? Oh, I see you.), score ENGAGES IN COLLABORATIVE DRAMATIC PLAY.

ENGAGES IN COLLABORATIVE DRAMATIC PLAY versus RESPONDS TO CHILD REPORT. When the caregiver enters into the dramatization, enacting a role, score ENGAGES IN COLLABORATIVE DRAMATIC PLAY. When the child reports on his or her dramatic fantasy (*Dolly go to sleep in here.*) and the caregiver merely responds as the audience, explicating, confirming, etc. (*You gonna put your doll on the bed?*), score RESPONDS TO CHILD REPORT.

ENGAGES IN COLLABORATIVE DRAMATIC PLAY versus ELICITS REPORT. When the caregiver asks *Where are you?* in a hiding game, score ENGAGES IN COLLABORATIVE DRAMATIC PLAY. The same question intended to elicit a report is scored ELICITS REPORT.

CATEGORY V: RESPONDS TO CHILD REPORT

ACCOMMODATES: GIVES REPORT versus ACCOMMODATES: SUPPLIES LEARNING. When the child seeks information, usually about the location of another person or about the possessor of an object, and the caregiver supplies the information (Child: *Where's Gramma?*   Caregiver: *At Bernice's house.* or Child: *Sasha's?*   Caregiver: *Yes, that's Sasha's toy.*), score ACCOMMODATES: GIVES REPORT. When the child seeks knowledge and the caregiver supplies it (Child: *What's that?*   Caregiver: *It's for my eyes.*), score ACCOMMODATES: SUPPLIES LEARNING.

ACCOMMODATES: GIVES REPORT versus RESPONDS TO CHILD DESIRE COMMUNICATION. When the very young child seeks information about the location of objects rather than persons, this is typically intended as a bid for help in locating the object or a desire request. Caregiver responses are scored RESPONDS TO CHILD DESIRE COMMUNICATION (Child: *Where's the book?*   Caregiver: *I'll get it.*) unless the caregiver refuses to help (*I don't know.*), in which case score REFUSALS.

CATEGORY VI: RESPONDS TO CHILD LEARNING
COMMUNICATION

CORRECTS LEARNING. These corrections often occur in a pair of speech acts, one negative and the other positive (*That's not Cinderella. That's the sister.*). Score both speech acts CORRECTS LEARNING. Similarly, SUPPLIES LEARNING can occur in pairs of speech acts (*This is dry. This is wet.*). Score both SUPPLIES LEARNING. Note that the same kind of pairing occurs in spontaneous teaching, scored TEACHES.

CORRECTS LEARNING versus DO'S and DON'TS. When the caregiver corrects the child, her utterances sometimes bear a surface resemblance to DO'S and DON'TS (*No, not that way. This way.*). Score CORRECTS LEARNING.

SUPPLIES LEARNING versus REFUSALS. When the child working on a learning task (e.g., puzzle) asks the caregiver to do it (*You do it.*), and the caregiver instructs the child in how to proceed (*It goes there.*), the child speech act is scored as a desire request and the caregiver's first response is scored REFUSALS. If the caregiver proceeds with further instructions, the latter are scored SUPPLIES LEARNING.

RESPONDS TO CHILD LEARNING COMMUNICATION versus TEACHES. When the child is engaged in a learning task, the caregiver's speech acts may shift to and fro, from responding to the child's learning communications to teaching. For example, the child may ask where a puzzle piece should be placed and the caregiver may show the child—scored SUPPLIES LEARNING. The caregiver may then ask where a second piece belongs—scored ELICITS KNOWLEDGE. The child may then respond by putting the second piece in place and the caregiver may say *Good*, scored CONFIRMS LEARNING. The caregiver may then show how a third piece is to be placed, scored PRESENTS KNOWLEDGE, etc.

CORRECTS LEARNING versus ELICITS KNOWLEDGE. When the caregiver says *What's that?*, using a derogatory tone to denote that she is correcting the child, score CORRECTS LEARNING. Typically this question occurs with neutral intonation and is intended to elicit knowledge. When this is the case, the question is scored ELICITS KNOWLEDGE.

CATEGORY VII: CONTROLS, RESTRICTS–COMMANDS

When the child fails to respond to a positive command or suggestion (*Let's clean up.*) and the caregiver persists, attempting to overcome the child's apparent resistance, the latter speech acts are scored DO'S, even though they sometimes bear a surface resemblance to DON'TS (*Bad girl. I'm going to tell your Daddy.*). DON'TS apply only when the caregiver is prohibiting the child's own actions, not when she is prohibiting resistance to performing actions she herself has proposed.

DON'TS may be stated in positive terms so that they bear a surface resemblance to DO'S (*Put that down. Be quiet.*). Score DON'TS if the caregiver is prohibiting the child's own actions.

CONTROLS versus TEACHES. The long-term goal of control talk is usually teaching, since the caregiver is generally concerned with socializing the child. However, we define control talk in terms of its short-term goal, that of making the child do, or keeping the child from doing, a particular action, and we define teaching talk in terms of its usually didactic meaning, imparting knowledge about skills, words, concepts, or facts. On this basis, commands to perform some conventional act like *Wash your hands*, or *Put your toys away*, are scored DO's rather than TEACHES.

There are times when control talk is accompanied by didactic teaching. In these cases, a secondary score for teaching is assigned. For example, *Say "thank you"* and *Say "please"* are scored as DO's, with TEACHES as a secondary score. For another example, when the caregiver suggests that the child read or play with a teaching toy or puzzle, a secondary score PRESENTS KNOWLEDGE is added to the primary score DO's. This secondary score is not added when the caregiver suggests activities that are usually not considered didactic, like playing with play-dough or riding a tricycle. Nor is it added when control talk is accompanied by normative explanations; here subscores for normative explanations are assigned.

Secondary scores for didactic teaching can also be added to DO's that involve helping the caregiver with household chores. For example, the caregiver may order the child to put the egg in the batter in such a way as to teach the general procedure in baking (*Next we put the egg in.*). Here we assign a primary score of DO's for the command and a secondary score of PRESENTS KNOWLEDGE for teaching about a general procedure. At times, when caregiver and child are working on a chore, or when the caregiver has suggested some conventional activity like putting socks on, the caregiver may become involved in teaching skills and techniques, in which case the latter speech acts are assigned a primary score of teaching, rather than controlling.

In teaching fine motor or gross motor skills, the form of the speech act is often in the imperative. Sometimes there is a series of imperative (*Push it up. Now, down. Let me show you. Okay, now turn it on.*). Despite their imperative form, these speech acts are not scored as commands, but as PRESENTS KNOWLEDGE, since their main function is to teach the child a skill or technique.

DO's VERSUS ELICITS REPORT. When the child's actions signal that toileting is needed (e.g., squirming, hopping) and the caregiver elicits a report on these actions (*You need to go pee-pee?*), score ELICITS REPORT. When the caregiver asks these kinds of questions in the absence of such "action-signals" from the child, her question is a suggestion and is scored DO's.

SUBSCORES. Utterances scored APPEALS TO REWARDS and those scored POSTPONED GRATIFICATION sometimes bear a surface resemblance to each other. For example, *When you finish, you can put the record on,* spoken to a child who wants to play with the record before putting toys away, is scored POSTPONED GRATIFICATION, whereas *If you finish, I'll put your new record on,* spoken to a child who has not asked for the record, is scored APPEALS TO REWARD. In the latter case, the caregiver proposes an attractive action contingent upon the child submitting to her command. In the former case, the child's own desire gratification is postponed.

CATEGORY VIII: TEACHES, PROVIDES KNOWLEDGE

TEACHES versus CONFIRMATIONS. Introductory confirmations (*Yes, Right, Good*) are sometimes contained within the same intonation contour as a caregiver teaching response to the child's reports or learning communications (Child: *That's a yellow one.*   Caregiver: *Yes, and what color is this?*). Assign the confirmation score—CONFIRMS LEARNING or CONFIRMS REPORT—as the primary score and TEACHES as the secondary score.

SUBSCORES. FINE MOTOR is scored for activities involving eye–hand coordination, puzzles, beads, bubbles, etc. GROSS MOTOR is scored for activities involving large muscles (e.g., climbing, jumping, bicycling, throwing balls). PHYSICAL WORLD covers animals.[3]

CATEGORIES OF INADEQUATE FREQUENCY

EXPRESSIVE COMMUNICATION (duplicate of FIS-P child category). When the caregiver laughs or grins or says the child is funny or fun, score EXPRESSIVE COMMUNICATION.

DESIRE COMMUNICATION (duplicate of FIS-P child category). Most caregiver commands serve the purpose of controlling the child rather than gratifying the caregiver's personal desires, so that they are almost always scored CONTROLS. There are a few borderline instances. If the child is helping the caregiver with household chores and the caregiver assigns the child a variety of errands (e.g., fetching things), score DO'S rather than DESIRE COMMUNICATION.

RESPONDS TO CHILD CALL WHEN OUT OF SIGHT. When the caregiver responds *Wait a minute* or *Just a minute*, score REFUSALS, MOMENTARY POSTPONEMENT. When the child calls *Come here,* it is scored as a desire request and the caregiver's response, *I'm coming,* is scored ACCOMMO-DATES: FULFILLS DESIRE rather than CALL REACTION.

---

[3]Supplementary scoring instructions for FIS-C Categories IX: REPORTS ON CHILD and X: REPORTS ON SELF, OTHERS, THINGS are covered by the preceeding instructions for the other categories.

Routine Scores

WHAT? versus CALL REACTION. When the question *What?* signifies that the caregiver does not understand what the child says or means, assign the routine score WHAT?. The same question *What?* in response to the child's call is scored CALL REACTION. Both intonation and context are very different for each of these scores.

WHAT? versus ALL EXPLICATIONS. When the caregiver hears or understands only part of the child's communication, she may explicate the part she can interpret and substitute the word "what" for the part she is unable to interpret (*You want the what? The baby what? You hurt your what?*). These partial explications are scored in the same way as full explications. Similarly, the partial explications *What's the matter? What did you want?* and *What fell down?* are scored as full explications when they represent attempts at interpreting the child's communication. These partial explications account for roughly 20% of all explications.

Appended Scores for Formal Discourse Features

SELF-REPETITIONS

A single speech act may be scored both SELF-REPETITIONS and REPETITIONS-OF-CHILD
 Speech acts following a routine score can be scored as SELF-REPETITIONS in relation to the statement preceding the routine.

REPETITIONS-OF-CHILD

When the caregiver mishears the child, do not score REPETITIONS-OF-CHILD (Child: *Cup.*   Caregiver: *You want me to cut it?*), but do score explication, confirmation, etc., whichever reflects the intention of the caregiver.

JUSTIFYING EXPLANATIONS

In control talk all normative explanations are assigned the appended score JUSTIFYING EXPLANATIONS as well as the appropriate subscore, PHYSICAL NORMS, SOCIAL NORMS, or SELF NORMS. Sometimes, in justifying a refusal, the caregiver simultaneously postpones the child's gratification (*No, you hafta have your lunch first.*). Such postponements are scored as appended score JUSTIFYING EXPLANATIONS as well as subscore POSTPONED GRATIFICATION. APPEALS TO REWARDS and APPEALS TO THREATS OR PUNISHMENT are not scored JUSTIFYING EXPLANATIONS.

When the caregiver appeals to the possession rights of another (*No, it's your sister's.*), score JUSTIFYING EXPLANATIONS. When she appeals to her own possession rights (*That's mine.*), score POSSESSION RIGHTS COMMUNICATION (duplicate of FIS-P child category).

Words and Phrases with Varied Scoring

The following common words and phrases are scored in a variety of ways depending on their context.

"We" or "Us." Caregivers often use "we" or "us," meaning 'you,' to mask or neutralize DO's or DON'Ts, in which case they are scored as such (*Let's clean up.; Let's quiet down.*). "We," meaning 'you,' is also used in reporting on the child (*We like to climb, don't we?*). In these cases, score REPORTS ON CHILD. At times "we" refers to both 'you and I,' as in reports of shared experiences (*Remember when we took the train to Fire Island?*). In these cases, score REPORTS ON CHILD as the primary source and REPORTS ON SELF, OTHERS, THINGS as the secondary score.

"Wanna" or "Want." These words are used in four different contexts each calling for a different score. First, EXPLICATES DESIRE: This is the most common usage (Child: *Banana.*   Caregiver: *You want a banana?*). Second, DO's and DON'Ts: The words "wanna" and "want" can be used to mask and neutralize DO's (*You wanna draw now?*) and DON'Ts (*You wanna stop that?*). Third, ELICITS REPORT: "Wanna" or "want to" are sometimes used interchangeably with "gonna" or "going to" in eliciting reports on the child's actions. For example, as the child takes the truck off the shelf, the caregiver may ask *You wanna play with your truck?* meaning 'You gonna play with your truck?'. "Wanna" or "want" are also used in eliciting reports on the child's future desires (*Do you want to play with David today?*). Such instances are scored ELICITS REPORT. Finally, routine score, OFFERS FOOD AT UNSCHEDULED TIME: Speech acts in this class usually contain the word "want" (*Do you want a drink?*). When the caregiver persists with a variety of suggestions (*Want some juice: Milk?*), repeat the routine score OFFERS FOOD AT UNSCHEDULED TIME. When the child responds in the affirmative and the caregiver attempts to specify what it is the child wants to eat or drink, score ELICITS REPORT. If the child offers an alternative suggestion (*Chocolate milk.*), the latter is viewed as a desire request so that maternal responses are scored RESPONDS TO CHILD DESIRE COMMUNICATION.

"Slowly" or *"One at a time."* These words can be scored PRESENTS KNOWLEDGE when the caregiver is teaching a motor skill. They are also used in maintaining the child's persistence, in which case they are scored ENCOURAGES PERSISTENCE. Occasionally these words are used when the caregiver refuses to help the child and are then scored as REFUSALS.

"Thank you." These words are scored ACKNOWLEDGING SUBMISSION when they serve as the acknowledgment terminating a sequence of commands. They are scored RESPONDS GRATEFULLY TO COLLABORATIVE GIVING when the child has given the caregiver something and she responds with gratitude. They are scored CONFIRMS LEARNING if the caregiver is acknowledging the learning of some social grace.

Evaluative Words.   If positive (*Good. Right. Okay.*), evaluative words are scored as confirmations, ego-boosts, or ACKNOWLEDGING SUBMISSION, depending on intonation and context. If negative (*Bad boy. Naughty. That's stupid.*), evaluative words are scored DON'TS when the caregiver intends to stop some action of the child and DO's when she attempts to overcome resistance to her positive command.

Introductory Words   (*Yes, No, Look, Oh, name of child, etc.*). When pauses follow these words so that they are scored as speech act units separate from the unit they introduce, assign the same score to both units.

Terminal Tag Words   (*Right?, Okay?, See?, Huh?*). When pauses precede these words so that they are scored as speech act units separate from the unit they follow, assign the same score to both units.

Appendix B
Supplementary Tables

TABLE B.1
FIS-P Category Scores:
Mean Percentage of Child Communications for Groups

	Groups			
	Disadvantaged	Advantaged		
FIS-P Category scores	Black	Black	White	Both
Expressive Communication	5.3	6.9	5.8	6.4
Desire Communication	42.9	27.2*	37.9	32.5
Possession Rights Communication	.4	1.4	.1	.8
EGO-ENHANCING COMMUNICATION	.4	2.1	1.4	1.7
SELF-REFERRING, SELF-INCLUDING COMMUNICATION	.0	.0	.0	.0
JOINING COMMUNICATION	1.5	.6	.3	.5
COLLABORATIVE COMMUNICATIONS	6.4	10.0	5.2	7.6
REPORTS ON SELF, OTHERS, THINGS	20.5	33.5*	26.7	30.1*
LEARNING COMMUNICATION	13.2	14.1	19.2	16.6
CALLS WHEN OUT OF SIGHT	7.5	3.5	2.8	3.1

*$p < .05$ Scheffé comparing disadvantaged versus advantaged group(s).

TABLE B.2
Effect of MLU and Age of Toddler on Discourse Features of Baby Talk:
F-Ratios and Direction of Covariate Effects

| | Covariate Effects | | | |
| | MLU | | Age of toddler | |
Discourse features of baby talk	F	Direction	F	Direction
SELF-REPETITIONS	6.03*	−	1.00	−
EXACT SELF-REPETITIONS	8.77*	−	.76	−
EXACT COMPLETE	7.72*	−	1.17	−
EXACT PARTIAL	2.53	−	.04	+
ALTERED SELF-REPETITIONS	.72	−	.58	−
REPETITIONS-OF-CHILD	.56	+	.03	+
EXACT REPETITIONS-OF-CHILD[a]	1.34	−	2.13	−
EXACT COMPLETE	6.96*	−	4.79*	−
ALTERED REPETITIONS-OF-CHILD	2.05	+	.83	+
EXPANSIONS	10.42*	−	10.02*	−
OTHER ALTERED	7.83*	+	7.79*	+
QUESTIONS	6.43*	+	.06	+

[a] Exact Partial of inadequate frequency.
*$p < .05$.

References

Almy, M. *Young children's thinking: Studies of some aspects of Piaget's theory*. New York: Teachers College Press, 1966.

Austin, J. L. *How to do things with words*. Cambridge, Massachusetts: Harvard Univ. Press, 1962.

Baldwin, A., & Baldwin, C. The study of mother–child interaction. *American Scientist*, 1973, *61*, 714–721.

Baratz, S. S., & Baratz, J. C. Early childhood intervention: The social science base of institutional racism. *Harvard Educatioonal Review*, 1970, *40*, 29–50.

Bartlett, E. J. Selecting preschool language programs. In C. B. Cazden (Ed.), *Language in early childhood education*. Washington, D. C.: National Association for the Education of Young Children, 1972.

Bates, E. *Language and context: The acquisition of pragmatics*. New York, Academic Press, 1976.

Bayley, N. Comparisons of mental and motor test scores for ages 1-15 months by sex, birth order, race, geographical location, and education of parents. *Child Development*, 1965, *36*, 379–411.

Becker, W. C., Englemann, S., & Thomas, D. R. *Teaching: A course in applied psychology*. Chicago: Science Research Associates, 1971.

Bee, H. L., Van Egeren, L. F., Streissguth, A. P., Nyman, B. A., and Leckie, M. S. Social class differences in maternal teaching strategies and speech patterns. *Developmental Psychology*, 1969, *1*, 726–734.

Belsky, J. *Mother–infant interaction at home and in the laboratory: The effect of setting*. Paper presented at the biennial meeting of the Society for Research in Child Development, New Orleans, March 1977.

Bereiter, C., & Engelmann, S. *Teaching disadvantaged children in preschool.* Englewood Cliffs, New Jersey: Prentice-Hall, 1966.

Bernstein, B. Social class, linguistic codes, and grammatical elements. *Language and Speech,* 1962, *5,* 221–240.

Bernstein, B. A socio-linguistic approach to social learning. In J. Gould (Ed.), *Penguin survey of the social sciences, 1965.* Baltimore: Penguin, 1965.

Bernstein, B. A socio-linguistic approach to socialization: With some reference to educability. In F. Williams (Ed.), *Language and poverty.* Chicago: Markham, 1970.

Biber, B. A developmental-interaction approach: Bank Street College of Education. In M. C. Day & R. K. Parker (Eds.), *The preschool in action: Exploring early childhood programs.* Boston: Allyn & Bacon, 1977.

Biber, B., Shapiro, E., & Wickens, D. *Promoting cognitive growth from a developmental-interaction point of view.* Washington, D. C.: National Association for the Education of Young Children, 1971.

Blank, M., Rose, S., & Berlin, L. *The language of learning: The preschool language assessment instrument.* New York: Grune & Stratton, 1978.

Bloom, B. *Stability and change in human characteristics.* New York: Wiley, 1964.

Bloom, L. *Language development: Form and function in emerging grammars.* Cambridge, Massachusetts: M.I.T. Press, 1970.

Bradley, R. H., & Caldwell, B. M. The relation of infants' home environments to mental test performance at fifty-four months: A follow-up study. *Child Development,* 1976, *47,* 1172–1174.

Bronfenbrenner, U. Is early intervention effective? In U. Bronfenbrenner & M. Mahoney (Eds.), *Influences on human development* (2nd ed.). Hinsdale, Illinois: Dryden Press, 1975.

Bronfenbrenner, U. Toward an experimental ecology of human development. *American Psychologist,* 1977, *32,* 513–531.

Brown, R. *A first language: The early stages.* Cambridge, Massachusetts: Harvard Univ. Press, 1973.

Brown, R. Introduction. In C. Snow & C. Ferguson (Eds.), *Talking to children: Language input and acquisition.* Cambridge: Cambridge Univ. Press, 1977.

Brown, R., & Hanlon, C. Derivational complexity and order of acquisition in child speech. In J. R. Hayes (Ed.), *Cognition and the development of language.* New York: Wiley, 1970.

Bruner, J. The ontogenesis of speech acts. *Journal of Child Language,* 1975, *2,* 1–19.

Caldwell, B. M. A new approach to behavioral ecology. In *Minnesota Symposia on Child Psychology 2.* Minneapolis: Univ. Minnesota Press, 1968.

Carew, J. V., Chan, I., & Halfar, C. *Observing intelligence in young children.* Englewood Cliffs, New Jersey: Prentice-Hall, 1976.

Cazden, C. B. (Ed.). *Language in early childhood education.* Washington, D. C.: National Association for the Education of Young Children, 1972. (a)

Cazden, C. B. *Two paradoxes in the acquisition of language structure and function.* Paper presented at the Conference on the Development of Competence in Early Childhood, CIBA Foundation, London, 1972. (b)

Cazden, C. B., Baratz, J. C., Labov, W., & Palmer, F. H. Language development in day care programs. In E. H. Grotberg (Ed.), *Day care: Resources for decisions.* Washington, D. C.: Office of Economic Opportunity, Government Printing Office, 1971.

Cherry, L., & Lewis, M. Mothers and two-year-olds: A study of sex-differentiated verbal interactions. In N. Waterson & C. Snow (Eds.), *The development of communication: Social and pragmatic factors in language acquisition.* New York: Wiley, 1978.

Chomsky, N. *Syntactic structures.* The Hague: Mouton, 1957.

City schools in crisis. *Newsweek,* September 12, 1977, pp. 62–70.

Clarke-Stewart, K. A. Interactions between mothers and their young children: Characteristics and consequences. *Monographs of the Society for Research in Child Development,* 1973, *38* (6–7, Serial No. 153).

Cole, M., & Bruner, J. Cultural differences and inferences about psychological processes. *American Psychologist,* 1971, *26,* 868–876.

Cole, M., Gay, J., Glick, J. A., & Sharp, D. W. *The cultural context of learning and thinking: An exploration in experimental anthropology.* New York: Basic Books, 1971.

Cole, M., & Scribner, S. *Culture and thought: A psychological introduction.* New York: Wiley, 1974.

Coles, R. *Privileged ones: The well-off and the rich in America. Children of Crisis Series* (Vol. 5). Boston: Atlantic–Little, Brown, 1978.

Cronbach, L. J. Heredity, environment and educational policy. *Harvard Educational Review,* 1969, *39,* 338–347.

Cross, T. Mothers' speech adjustments: The contribution of selected child listener variables. In C. Snow & C. Ferguson (Eds.), *Talking to children: Language input and acquisition.* Cambridge: Cambridge Univ. Press, 1977.

Day, E. J. The development of language in twins: I. A comparison of twins and single children. *Child Development,* 1932, *3,* 179–199.

Dollard, J., & Auld, F., Jr. *Scoring human motives: A manual.* New Haven: Yale Univ. Press, 1959.

Dore, J. Holophrases, speech acts and language universals. *Journal of Child Language,* 1975, *2,* 21–40.

Dore, J. On them sheriff: A pragmatic analysis of children's responses. In S. Ervin-Tripp & C. Mitchell-Kernan (Eds.), *Child discourse.* New York: Academic Press, 1977.

Elkind, D. Cognition in infancy and early childhood. In I. Weiner & D. Elkind (Eds.), *Readings in child development.* New York: Wiley, 1972.

Erikson, E. *Childhood and society.* New York: Norton, 1963.

Ervin-Tripp, S. An analysis of the interaction of language, topic and listener. In J. J. Gumperz & D. Hymes (Eds.), *The ethnography of communication. American Anthropologist,* 1964, *66* (6, Pt. II), 86–102.

Ervin-Tripp, S. On sociolinguistic rules: Alternation and co-occurrence. In J. J. Gumperz & D. Hymes (Eds.), *Directions in sociolinguistics.* New York: Holt, 1972.

Ervin-Tripp, S., & Mitchell-Kernan, C. (Eds.). *Child discourse.* New York: Academic Press, 1977.

Fehr, F. S. Critique of hereditarian accounts of "intelligence" and contrary findings: A reply to Jensen. *Harvard Educational Review,* 1969, *39,* 571–580.

Flavell, J. H. *The developmental psychology of Jean Piaget.* Princeton, New Jersey: Van Nostrand, 1963.

Furth, H. G. *Deafness and learning: A psychosocial approach.* Belmont, California: Wadsworth Publishing, 1973.

Garvey, C. Requests and responses in children's speech. *Journal of Child Language,* 1975, *2,* 41–63.

Gelman, R., & Shatz, M. Appropriate speech adjustments: The operation of conversational constraints on talk to two-year-olds. In M. Lewis & L. Rosenblum (Eds.), *Interaction conversation and the development of language: The origins of behavior* (Vol. 4). New York: Wiley Interscience, 1977.

Gleason, J. B. Code switching in children's language. In T. E. Moore (Ed.), *Cognitive development and the acquisition of language.* New York: Academic Press, 1973.

Gleason, J. B. Talking to children: Some notes on feedback. In C. Snow & C. Ferguson (Eds.), *Talking to children: Language input and acquisition*. Cambridge: Cambridge Univ. Press, 1977.

Golden, M., & Birns, B. Social class and cognitive development in infancy. *Merrill-Palmer Quarterly*, 1968, *14*, 139–149.

Golden, M., Birns, B., Bridger, W., & Moss, A. Social-class differentiation in cognitive development among black preschool children. *Child Development*, 1971, *42*, 37–45.

Goodson, B. D., & Hess, R. D. *Parents as teachers of young children: An evaluative review of some contemporary concepts and programs*. Stanford, California: Stanford Univ., 1975. (ERIC Document Reproduction Service No. ED 136 967)

Greenberg, S., & Formanek, R. Social class differences in spontaneous verbal interactions. *Child Study Journal*, 1974, *4*, 145–153.

Gumperz, J. J., & Hymes, D. (Eds.). *Directions in sociolinguistics*. New York: Holt, 1972.

Hall, W. S., & Freedle, R. O. *Culture and language: The black American experience*. Washington, D. C.: Hemisphere, 1975.

Halliday, M. A. K. Functional diversity in language as seen from a consideration of modality and mood in English. *Foundations of Language*, 1970, *6*, 322–361.

Harkness, S. Aspects of social environment and first language acquisition in rural Africa. In C. Snow & C. Ferguson (Eds.), *Talking to children: Language input and acquisition*. Cambridge: Cambridge Univ. Press, 1977.

Hertzig, M. E., Birch, H. G., Thomas, A., & Mendez, O. A. Class and ethnic differences in the responsiveness of preschool children to cognitive demands. *Monographs of the Society for Research in Child Development*, 1968, *33* (1, Serial No. 117).

Hess, R. D. Parental behavior and children's school achievement: Implications for Head Start. In E. Grotberg (Ed.), *Critical issues in research related to disadvantaged children*. Princeton, New Jersey: Educational Testing Service, 1969.

Hess, R. D., & Shipman, V. C. Early experience on the socialization of cognitive modes in children. *Child Development*, 1965, *34*, 869–886.

Honig, A. S. *Parent involvement in early childhood education*. Washington, D. C.: National Association for the Education of Young Children, 1975.

Hunt, J. McV. *Intelligence and experience*. New York: Ronald Press, 1961.

Jakobson, R. Linguistics and poetics. In T. Sebeok (Ed.), *Style in language*. Cambridge, Massachusetts: M.I.T. Press, 1960.

Jensen, A. R. How much can we boost IQ and scholastic achievement? *Harvard Educational Review*, 1969, *39*, 1–123.

Kagan, J. S. Inadequate evidence and illogical conclusions. *Harvard Educational Review*, 1969, *39*, 274–277.

Kamii, C. K. Piaget's theory and specific instruction: A response to Bereiter and Kohlberg. *Interchange*, 1970, *1*, 33–39.

Kamii, C. K. An application of Piaget's theory to the conceptualization of a preschool curriculum. In R. K. Parker (Ed.), *The preschool in action: Exploring early childhood programs*. Boston: Allyn & Bacon, 1972.

Kamii, C., & De Vries, R. Piaget for early education. In M. C. Day & R. K. Parker (Eds.), *The preschool in action: Exploring early childhood programs*. Boston: Allyn & Bacon, 1977.

Kaplan, L. J. *Oneness and separateness: From infant to individual*. New York: Simon & Schuster, 1978.

Kohlberg, L., & Mayer, R. Development as the aim of education. *Harvard Educational Review*, 1972, *42*, 449–496.

Labov, W. The logic of nonstandard English. In F. Williams (Ed.), *Language and poverty*. Chicago: Markham, 1970.

Lewis, M., & Goldberg, S. Perceptual-cognitive development in infancy: A generalized expectancy model. *Merrill-Palmer Quarterly*, 1969, *15*, 81–100.

Maccoby, E. E., & Jacklin, C. N. *The psychology of sex differences*. Stanford, California: Stanford Univ. Press, 1974.

Madden, J., Levenstein, P., & Levenstein, S. Longitudinal IQ outcomes of the mother–child home program. *Child Development*, 1976, *47*, 1015–1025.

Mahler, M., Pine, F., & Bergman, A. *The psychological birth of the human infant: Symbiosis and individuation*. New York: Basic Books, 1975.

Mattick, I. The teacher's role in helping young children develop language competency. *Young Children*, 1972, *27*, 133–142.

Mayer, R. S. A comparative analysis of preschool models. In R. H. Anderson & H. B. Shane (Eds.), *As the twig is bent: Readings in early childhood education*. Boston: Houghton Mifflin, 1971.

McCarthy, D. The language development of the preschool child. *Institute of Child Welfare, Monograph Series 4*. Minneapolis: Univ. of Minnesota Press, 1930.

Minuchin, P., & Biber, B. A child development approach to language in the preschool disadvantaged child. In M. A. Brottman (Ed.), *Language remediation for the disadvantaged preschool child. Monographs of the Society for Research in Child Development*, 1968, *33*, 10–18.

Moerk, E. L. Verbal interactions between children and their mothers during the preschool years. *Developmental Psychology*, 1975, *11*, 788–794.

Nelson, K. Structure and strategy in learning to talk. *Monographs of the Society for Research in Child Development*, 1973, *38*(1–2, Serial No. 149).

Newport, E. L. Motherese: The speech of mothers to young children. In N. J. Castellan, D. B. Pisoni & G. R. Potts (Eds.), *Cognitive theory* (Vol. 2). Hillsdale, New Jersey: Lawrence Erlbaum Associates, 1976.

Newport, E. L., Gleitman, H., & Gleitman, L. Mother, I'd rather do it myself: Some effects and non-effects of maternal speech style. In C. Snow & C. Ferguson (Eds.), *Talking to children: Language input and acquisition*. Cambridge: Cambridge Univ. Press, 1977.

Olim, E. G., Hess, R. D., & Shipman, V. C. Role of mother's language styles in mediating their preschool children's cognitive development. *School Review*, 1967, *75*, 414–424.

Palmer, F. H. Socioeconomic status and intellective performance among Negro preschool boys. *Developmental Psychology*, 1970, *3*, 1–9.

Palmer, F. H. Minimal intervention at age two and three and subsequent intellective changes. In R. K. Parker (Ed.), *The preschool in action: Exploring early childhood programs*. Boston: Allyn & Bacon, 1972.

Phillips, R. Syntax and vocabulary of mothers' speech to young children: Age and sex comparisons. *Child Development*, 1973, *44*, 182–185.

Piaget, J. *The language and thought of the child* (3rd ed.). New York: Humanities Press, 1959. (Originally published, 1926.)

Piaget, J. Development and learning. In R. Ripple & V. Rockcastle (Eds.), *Piaget rediscovered*. Ithaca, New York: Cornell Univ. Press, 1964.

Piaget, J. *The science of education and the psychology of the child*. New York: Orion Press, 1970.

Piaget, J. *To understand is to invent*. New York: Grossman Publishers, 1973.

Piaget, J., & Inhelder, B. *The psychology of the child*. New York: Basic Books, 1969.

Provence, S., Naylor, A., & Patterson, J. *The challenge of daycare*. New Haven: Yale Univ. Press, 1977.

Rheingold, H. L., Gewirtz, J. L., & Ross, H. W. Social conditioning of vocalizations in the infant. *Journal of Comparative Physiological Psychology*, 1959, *51*, 68–73.

Rodgon, M. M., Jankowski, W., & Alenskas, L. A multi-functional approach to single-word usage. *Journal of Child Language,* 1977, *4,* 23–43.

Rubin, L. B. *Worlds of pain: Life in the working-class family.* New York: Basic Books, 1976.

Sachs, J., Brown, R., & Salerno, R. A. *Adults' speech to children.* Paper presented at the International Symposium on First Language Acquisition, Florence, Italy, 1972.

Schachter, F. F., Fosha, D., Stemp, S., Brotman, N., & Ganger, S. Everday caretaker talk to toddlers vs. threes and fours. *Journal of Child Language,* 1976, *3,* 221–245.

Schachter, F. F., Kirshner, K., Klips, B., Friedricks, M., & Sanders, K. Everyday preschool interpersonal speech usage: Methodological, developmental and sociolinguistic studies. *Monographs of the Society for Research in Child Development,* 1974, *39* (3, Serial No. 156).

Schachter, F. F., Shore, E., Hodapp, R., Chalfin, S., & Bundy, C. Do girls talk earlier?: MLU in toddlers. *Developmental Psychology,* 1978, *14,* 388–392.

Schaffer, R. *Mothering.* Cambridge, Massachusetts: Harvard Univ. Press, 1977.

Schoggen, M., & Schoggen, P. Environmental forces in the home lives of three-year-old children in three population subgroups. JSAS *Catalog of Selected Documents in Psychology,* 1976, *6*(1). (Ms. No. 1178).

Schoggen, P. Environmental forces in the everyday lives of children. In R. G. Barker (Ed.), *The stream of behavior.* New York: Appleton, 1963.

Searle, J. R. *Speech acts: An essay in the philosophy of language.* London: Cambridge Univ. Press, 1969.

Seitz, S., & Stewart, C. Imitations and expansions: Some developmental aspects of mother–child communication. *Developmental Psychology,* 1975, *11,* 763–768.

Séitz, V., Abelson, W. D., Levine, E., & Zigler, E. Effects of place of testing on the Peabody Picture Vocabulary Test scores of disadvantaged Head Start and non-Head Start children. *Child Development,* 1975, *46,* 481–486.

Shatz, M. *How to do things by asking: Form–function relations in mothers' questions to children.* Paper presented at the biennial meeting of the Society for Research in Child Development, New Orleans, March 1977.

Silverstein, B., & Krate, R. *Children of the dark ghetto: A developmental psychology.* New York: Praeger, 1975.

Skinner, B. F. *Verbal behavior.* New York: Appleton, 1957.

Smith, M. E. A study of some factors influencing the development of the sentence in young children. *Journal of Genetic Psychology,* 1935, *46,* 182–212.

Smith, M. E. Some light on the problem of bilingualism as found from a study of the progress in mastery of English among preschool children of non-American ancestry in Hawaii. *Genetic Psychology Monographs,* 1939, *21,* 121–284.

Smith, M. S. *Some short-term effects of Project Head Start: A preliminary report on the second year of planned variation, 1970–1971.* Cambridge, Massachusetts: Huron Institute, 1973.

Snow, C. E. Mother's speech to children learning language. *Child Development,* 1972, *43,* 549–565.

Snow, C. E. Mothers' speech research: From input to interaction. In C. Snow & C. Ferguson (Eds.), *Talking to children: Language input and acquisition.* Cambridge: Cambridge Univ. Press, 1977.

Snow, C. E., Arlman-Rupp, A., Hassing, Y., Jobse, J., Joosten, J., & Vorster, J. Mothers' speech in three social classes. *Journal of Psycholinguistic Research,* 1976, *5,* 1–19.

Snow, C. E., & Ferguson, C. *Talking to children: Language input and acquisition.* Cambridge: Cambridge Univ. Press, 1977.

Soskin, W. F., & John, V. The study of spontaneous talk. In R. G. Barker (Ed.), *The stream of behavior.* New York: Appleton, 1963.

Sowell, T. *Black education: Myths and tragedies.* New York: David McKay, 1972.

Spitz, R. A. The psychogenic diseases in infancy: An attempt at their etiologic classification. *The Psychoanalytic Study of the Child,* 1951, *6,* 255–275.

Sroufe, L. A. A methodological and philosophical critique of intervention-oriented research. *Developmental Psychology,* 1970, *2,* 140–145.

Stearns, M. S. *Report on preschool programs: The effects of preschool programs on disadvantaged children and their families.* Washington, D. C.: U. S. Department of Health, Education, and Welfare, Office of Child Development, 1971.

Stern, D. *The first relationship: Infant and mother.* Cambridge, Massachusetts: Harvard Univ. Press, 1977.

Sullivan, H. S. *The interpersonal theory of psychiatry.* New York: Norton, 1953.

Tulkin, S. R. An analysis of the concept of cultural deprivation. *Developmental Psychology,* 1972, *6,* 326–339.

Tulkin, S. R., & Kagan, T. Mother–child interaction in the first year of life. *Child Development,* 1972, *43,* 31–41.

Wachs, T., Uzgiris, I., & Hunt, J. McV. Cognitive development in infants of different age levels and from different environmental backgrounds: An exploratory investigation. *Merrill-Palmer Quarterly,* 1971, *17,* 283–317.

Weisberg, H. I. *Short-term cognitive effects of Head Start programs: A report on the third year of planned variation, 1971–1972.* Cambridge, Massachusetts: Huron Institute, 1973.

White, B. L. Fundamental early environmental influences on the development of competence. In M. E. Meyer (Ed.), *Third Western Symposium on Learning: Cognitive learning.* Bellingham, Washington: Western Washington State Univ. Press, 1972.

White, B. L., Kaban, B., Shapiro, B., & Attanucci, J. Competence and experience. In I. C. Uzgiris & F. Weizmann (Eds.), *The structuring of experience.* New York: Plenum Press, 1977.

White, B. L., & Watts, J. C. *Experience and environment.* Englewood Cliffs, New Jersey: Prentice-Hall, 1973.

White, R. W. Motivation reconsidered: The concept of competence. *Psychological Review,* 1959, *66,* 297–333.

White, S. H., Day, M. C., Freeman, P. K., Hantman, S. A., & Messenger, K. P. *Federal programs for young children: Review and recommendations* (3 vols.). Washington, D. C.: U. S. Government Printing Office, 1973.

Yarrow, L., Rubenstein, L., Pederson, F., & Jankowski, J. Dimensions of early stimulation and their differential effects on infant development. *Merrill-Palmer Quarterly,* 1972, *18,* 205–218.

Zigler, E., & Butterfield, E. C. Motivational aspects of changes in IQ test performance of culturally deprived nursery school children. *Child Development,* 1968, *39,* 1–14.

Zigler, E., & Trickett, P. K. IQ, social competence, and evaluation of early childhood intervention programs. *American Psychologist,* 1978, *33,* 789–798.

Index